Blackstone's

Employme

Handbook

C000156741

Blackstone's
Employment
Tribunals
Handbook
2014–2015

John Sprack

OXFORD
UNIVERSITY PRESS

OXFORD
UNIVERSITY PRESS

Great Clarendon Street, Oxford, OX2 6DP,
United Kingdom

Oxford University Press is a department of the University of Oxford.
It furthers the University's objective of excellence in research, scholarship,
and education by publishing worldwide. Oxford is a registered trade mark of
Oxford University Press in the UK and in certain other countries

© John Sprack 2014

The moral rights of the author have been asserted

First Edition published in 2014

Impression: 1

Published in the United States of America by Oxford University Press
198 Madison Avenue, New York, NY 10016, United States of America

British Library Cataloguing in Publication Data

Data available

ISBN 978-0-19-871942-7

Printed in Great Britain by
Ashford Colour Press Ltd, Gosport, Hampshire

Preface

This Handbook is aimed at all those who are involved in cases in the employment tribunals. Some of the readership will be legal practitioners, others will be individuals who are expecting to present their own case in the tribunal, yet others will be people who are charged with giving advice to either employers or employees, but do not have a legal qualification. It is therefore intended, at least in part, for trade union officials, HR professionals, CAB advisers, and other employment consultants. It should be equally useful for those advising, preparing a case, or representing as advocate, and should assist them whether they perform such a function for the employee or the employer. The size and format in which it is presented are chosen to aid portability and ease of reference.

It follows that the style in which the Handbook is written is intended to be as accessible as possible, avoiding 'legalese' and adopting plain English. At the same time, it aims to be accurate in its statement of the law, and to provide guidance in practical situations. It is concise rather than comprehensive, but the detail which is inevitably lacking in a portable work such as this is to be found in the leading practitioner's work in the field—*Blackstone's Employment Law Practice*, the 2014 edition of which was going to press as work reached completion on this Handbook. There are frequent references to that work in this text.

In the spirit of accessibility, the Handbook also makes substantial use of flowcharts, tables, and examples. Employment law is an area which derives largely from statute, and there are numerous statutory extracts reproduced throughout, with accompanying commentary.

I am indebted to the team at Oxford University Press who have supported the work throughout in a professional and helpful manner. My particular thanks are due to Michael Sprack, who not only performed duties as my research assistant, but was also able to provide guidance about what is needed for potential users, resulting from the work which he has done for the Free Representation Unit.

This book is dedicated, not to any individual, but to the employment tribunal system, which has taken a battering in the recent past, but can survive and be strengthened if it receives the goodwill which it deserves.

I have endeavoured to state the law as it stood on 10 June 2014.

John Sprack
Ashford, Kent
June 2014

Contents

Part A   Procedure and Practice

Part B   Substantive Law

Contents

Part C Remedies

Table of Cases

Table of Cases

Table of Cases

Table of Legislation

Table of Legislation

Table of Legislation

International Instruments

European Directives

List of Abbreviations

ACAS	Advisory, Conciliation and Arbitration Service
AML	additional maternity leave
CAB	Citizen's Advice Bureau
CJEU	Court of Justice of the European Union
CPR	Civil Procedure Rules
EAT	Employment Appeal Tribunal
ECHR	European Convention on Human Rights
EDT	effective date of termination
EqA 2010	Equality Act 2010
ERA 1996	Employment Rights Act 1996
ETA	Employment Tribunals Act 1996
ETO	economic, technical, or organizational
EWC	expected week of childbirth
FRU	Free Representation Unit
FTER 2002	Fixed-Term Employees (Prevention of Less Favourable Treatment) Regulations 2002 (SI 2002/298)
HMRC	Her Majesty's Revenue and Customs
HR	human resources
NMWA 1998	National Minimum Wage Act 1998
NMWR 1999	National Minimum Wage Regulations 1999 (SI 1999/584)
OML	ordinary maternity leave
PCP	provision, criterion, or practice
PTWR 2000	Part-Time Workers Regulations 2000 (SI 2000/1551)
SMP	statutory maternity pay
TULR(C)A 1992	Trade Union and Labour Relations (Consolidation) Act 1992
TUPE	Transfer of Undertakings (Protection of Employment) Regulations 2006 (SI 2006/246)
WTR 1998	Working Time Regulations 1998 (SI 1998/1833)

Part A
Procedure and Practice

1 Tribunal Procedure

Introduction

1.01   Most employment cases are dealt with in the employment tribunals. The tribunals were set up by, and derive their power from, statute. There are certain types of claim associated with employment that cannot be brought in the employment tribunal. For example, a claim for personal injury must be brought in the ordinary courts. When it comes to a claim for breach of contract, that can be brought within the employment tribunal in certain circumstances, subject to a limit of £25,000 (see Chapter 13 on Breach of Contract). If it is over that limit, it should be brought in the ordinary courts.

1.02   When a claim is brought within the employment tribunals, the rules which govern procedure are set out in the Employment Tribunals (Constitution and Rules of Procedure) Regulations 2013, SI 2013/1237. This statutory instrument consists of a set of Regulations, to which are attached three schedules. Schedule 1 contains the detailed rules of procedure which are applicable to the great majority of tribunal cases. In this chapter, it will be referred to as 'the rules'. Schedule 2 is relevant to national security cases. Schedule 3 is applicable to equal pay cases. The Regulations themselves lay down certain general principles, and in this chapter will be referred to as 'the Regulations'.

1.03   Some of the rules deal with the fees which have to be paid in respect of a tribunal case. Those rules are not dealt with in this chapter, but in Chapter 2 on Fees.

1.04   Detailed exposition of Tribunal Procedure is to be found in **Part A** of *Blackstone's Employment Law Practice 2014*.

The Regulations and the Rules

1.05   Regulation 1 deals with the commencement of the rules, stating that they come into force on 29 July 2013. This means that any proceedings before the tribunal on or after that date are governed by the Employment Tribunals Rules of Procedure 2013, rather than the earlier (2004) version of the rules. There is an exception to this, in respect of any counterclaim by an employer for breach of contract (see 1.59 or 13.13), to which the 2004 rules will apply if the respondent received from the tribunal a copy of the claim form before 29 July 2013 (reg 15(3)).

1.06   Regulation 11 lays down that the President has power to make practice directions. It is understood that the purpose of this provision

---

is to help ensure consistency across the employment tribunals, in relation to such matters as the award of costs, and the timetabling of cases, as well as directions in relation to particular cases and types of case.

1.07 As to the reference to 'the President', there is a President of Employment Tribunals responsible for the tribunals in England and Wales, and a President of Employment Tribunals responsible for the tribunals in Scotland. The President for England and Wales is appointed by the Lord Chancellor; the President for Scotland is appointed by the Lord President of the Court of Session.

The overriding objective

1.08 Rule 2 contains the overriding objective of the rules. As its title clearly implies, its terms must be borne in mind when the tribunal makes any procedural decision. To put it another way, all the rules need to be read subject to the overriding objective. It should also be stressed that the parties and their representatives are specifically bound to assist the tribunal in furthering the overriding objective, and by cooperating with each other and the tribunal:

> 2   The overriding objective of these Rules is to enable Employment Tribunals to deal with cases fairly and justly. Dealing with a case fairly and justly includes, so far as practicable—
> (a) ensuring that the parties are on an equal footing;
> (b) dealing with cases in ways which are proportionate to the complexity and importance of the issues;
> (c) avoiding unnecessary formality and seeking flexibility in the proceedings;
> (d) avoiding delay, so far as compatible with proper consideration of the issues; and
> (e) saving expense.
> A Tribunal shall seek to give effect to the overriding objective in interpreting, or exercising any power given to it by, these Rules. The parties and their representatives shall assist the Tribunal to further the overriding objective and in particular shall co-operate generally with each other and with the Tribunal.

Alternative dispute resolution

1.09 Encouragement is given to the parties to resolve their disputes at the earliest possible opportunity, and if possible outside the tribunal system. Rule 3 contains a specific requirement for employment judges to encourage the parties to consider such alternative means of resolving their disputes:

> 3   A Tribunal shall wherever practicable and appropriate encourage the use by the parties of the services of ACAS, judicial or other mediation, or other means of resolving their disputes by agreement.

Composition

1.10 A full employment tribunal consists of three members. One of them is an employment judge, who must have had a legal qualification for a period of five years. The employment judge may be salaried (usually full-time) or fee paid (part-time). In a full tribunal, he or she will sit together with two lay members. The judge will have conduct of the proceedings, but all three members participate fully in the decision making, and may ask questions.

1.11 All three members of a full tribunal will have been drawn from panels set up for the purpose, as described in reg 8:

> 8 (1) There shall be three panels of members for the Employment Tribunals (England and Wales) and three panels of members for the Employment Tribunals (Scotland).
>
> (2) The panels of members shall be—
>
> > (a) a panel of chairmen who satisfy the criteria set out in regulation 5(2) and are appointed by the appointing office holder (in these Regulations (including the Schedules) referred to as 'Employment Judges');
> >
> > (b) a panel of persons appointed by the Lord Chancellor after consultation with organisations or associations representative of employees; and
> >
> > (c) a panel of persons appointed by the Lord Chancellor after consultation with organisations or associations representative of employers.
>
> (3) Members of the panels shall hold and vacate office in accordance with the terms of their appointment, but may resign from office by written notice to the person who appointed them under paragraph (2), and any member who ceases to hold office shall be eligible for reappointment.
>
> (4) The President may establish further specialist panels of members referred to in paragraph (2) and may select persons from those panels to deal with proceedings in which particular specialist knowledge would be beneficial.

1.12 The majority of cases heard by the employment tribunals, however, are heard by an employment judge sitting alone. The position is this:

(a) a preliminary hearing should be heard by a judge sitting alone, other than in the circumstances described in r 55, and dealt with later at 1.135;

(b) All those proceedings described in s 4(3) of the Employment Tribunals Act 1996 (ETA 1996) should be heard by a judge sitting alone, unless, having regard to the matters set out in s 4(5), it is appropriate for the case to be heard by a full tribunal. There is a long list of such proceedings set out in s 4(3), which includes unfair dismissal, unauthorized deductions from wages, breach of contract, holiday pay, and compensation for failure to inform and consult about collective redundancies. (The full list can be found in **para 1.21** of *Blackstone's Employment Law Practice 2014*).

1.13 Section 4(5) of the ETA 1996 provides that the proceedings listed in s 4(3) should be heard by a full tribunal if the judge decides at any stage of the proceedings to do so, having regard to:

(a) whether there is a likelihood of a dispute arising on the facts which makes it desirable for the proceedings to be heard by a full tribunal;

(b) whether there is a likelihood of an issue of law arising which would make it desirable for the proceedings to be heard by a judge alone;

(c) any views of the parties as to whether or not the proceedings ought to be heard by a judge alone or by a full tribunal; and

(d) whether there are other proceedings which might be heard concurrently but which are not proceedings specified in s 4(3).

1.14 The judge has to exercise the discretion which is given under s 4(5) if so requested by one of the parties. It is also desirable for the judge to consider the matters in s 4(5) even if the issue is not raised by the parties, but it is not an error of law to fail to do so. More particularly, the judge should actively consider the discretion where one of the parties is a litigant in person who may be unaware of the possibility or merits of a differently constituted tribunal: *Sterling Developments (London) Ltd v Pagano* [2007] IRLR 471 (EAT).

1.15 It occasionally happens that a full tribunal is due to hear the case, but one of the lay members fails to attend, due perhaps to illness or travel difficulties. In such a case, it is possible for the tribunal to proceed, provided that the parties consent. If the tribunal is minded to proceed 'one short' in such circumstances, then it must inform the parties from which panel (employers' or employees') the absent member was chosen. If this information is not given, then any consent given by the parties is invalidated: *Rabahallah v BT Group plc* [2005] IRLR 184.

1.16 Where a tribunal consists only of the judge and one lay member, the judge has a casting vote, and the parties ought to be informed of that fact before being asked for their consent.

Representation

1.17 There is no requirement for a representative to have any legal qualification in order to appear in the employment tribunals. The choice of representatives is a matter for the party concerned, who has a statutory right under s 6 of the ETA 1996 to be represented by a representative of his or her choice.

1.18 Many parties represent themselves, and are referred to as 'litigants in person'. Others may be represented, for example, by a trade union official, an HR manager, an employment consultant, or a friend or relative. Despite the relative informality of tribunal proceedings, those parties who can afford it will often seek to be represented by a lawyer. There is, however, no legal aid available for representation in employment tribunals. Initial advice, sometimes extending to representation, will often be sought from the Citizens Advice Bureau or a law centre. Pro bono (free) representation may be available, for example, from the Free Representation Unit (FRU).

1.19 Most employment judges will provide some assistance, by way of explanation and guidance, to the party who is not legally represented. Of course, the judge has to avoid any intervention which gives the appearance of bias. Nevertheless, once a litigant in person has made their case clear, the judge will often be prepared to turn that case into a series of questions for cross-examination. In any event, judges are accustomed to explaining in ordinary language matters such as the issues in the case, and the procedure which will be adopted.

ACAS and early conciliation

1.20 As mentioned earlier, at 1.09, the rules make specific mention of the services of the Advisory, Conciliation and Arbitration Service (ACAS), which plays a wide role in facilitating industrial relations. In particular, it plays an important part in the settlement of disputes which would otherwise be determined in the employment tribunals. Traditionally, this role has been focused upon dealings with the parties once a claim has been submitted. From 6 April 2014, however, there has been in place a scheme for early conciliation, which takes place before the claim is presented. From 6 May 2014, the scheme was compulsory.

1.21 Early conciliation is based upon the principle that anybody wishing to bring a tribunal claim must first notify ACAS of their intention to claim. The scheme applies to the great majority of claims, with minor exceptions such as a claim for interim relief where speed is of the essence. Before presenting a claim, the claimant must contact ACAS on an early conciliation form. The main route of entry is through a web-based form, although there are alternatives for those who are unable to use the digital route. The form requires very limited information: the names and contact details of the claimant and their employer, employment dates where relevant, and any access requirements such as language difficulties or impairment. The form does not ask the potential claimant to specify the nature of the claim.

1.22 Once the early conciliation form has been received, it will be in the hands of an early conciliation support officer. That officer must contact the claimant. If the potential claimant cannot be contacted, or does not want conciliation, or decides to abandon the claim, the support officer will issue a certificate saying that the potential claimant has complied with their obligation to contact ACAS. The potential claimant may then pursue the claim if they so wish.

1.23 Assuming that the claimant wishes to continue with the claim and with conciliation, the support officer will then contact the respondent employer. Again, if the employer declines conciliation the support officer will issue a certificate to the potential claimant, who can then pursue the claim.

1.24 Similarly, if during the next month, the support officer decides that a settlement cannot be achieved, the claimant will receive a certificate and can pursue their claim. That period of a month can be extended by two weeks if the parties believe that it would be fruitful to extend.

1.25 If the process of early conciliation is successful, and agreement is reached, it will then be effected in the usual way, as set out in Chapter 3 on Settlement Agreements. The support officer will still issue a certificate in such a case, to cover the situation where the settlement fails.

1.26 The certificate which has been referred to previously will state the date upon which ACAS received the early conciliation form, and the date upon which the certificate is issued. The certificate will contain a unique reference number, which must be quoted when the claim form is completed.

1.27 In summary, then, the position is that the conciliation process will be ended if either party makes it clear that they are unwilling to conciliate. Subject to the possibility of an extension for two weeks, it will in any event end after a month.

1.28 It should be stressed that the conciliation process is not mandatory. The obligation on the prospective claimant is merely to notify ACAS of their intention to make a claim, so as to provide the opportunity for conciliation to take place. The process differs from the traditional activity which ACAS has undertaken in respect of tribunal claims in that it aims to avoid the claim being made, rather than aiming to avoid a tribunal hearing after the claim has been made.

1.29 Clearly the new system affects the calculation of the limitation period. Put simply, the clock will stop running when the early conciliation form is received by ACAS. It will start to run again once the early conciliation certificate is deemed to have been received. However, if the time limit would have expired less than a month after the receipt of the early conciliation certificate, the time limit is extended to a month after that date.

1.30 Throughout this process, and any post-claim conciliation, the parties should be aware that any information which they give to the conciliation officer will be passed on to the other side. It is also important to note that the role of ACAS is to achieve a settlement. The officer is not there to judge whether the case is likely to succeed, or to advise on whether a settlement should be accepted. There is no duty upon an ACAS officer to see that the terms of the settlement are fair to a party, or to advise on the merits of the case: *Clarke v Redcar and Cleveland Borough Council* [2006] IRLR 324 (EAT).

Presenting the claim

1.31 It is important that a claim to the employment tribunals is presented in time (see Chapter 6 on Time Limits), and that it contains the necessary information.

1.32 As far as the mechanics of presentation are concerned, these are dealt with in a Presidential Direction, which reads in part as follows:

> A completed claim form may be presented to an Employment Tribunal in England & Wales:
> Online by using the online form submission service provided by Her Majesty's Courts and Tribunals Service, accessible at www.employmenttribunals. service.gov.uk;
> By post to: Employment Tribunal Central Office (England & Wales), PO Box 10218, Leicester, LE1 8EG.
> A claim may also be presented in person to an Employment Tribunal Office listed in the schedule to this Practice Direction. If a claim is so presented, it must be so within tribunal business hours (9am to 4pm, Monday to Friday, not including public holidays or weekends).

[*The tribunal offices listed in the schedule are the regional offices in Birmingham, Huntingdon (East Anglia), Nottingham (East Midlands), Leeds, London Central, London East, Watford (London North and West), Croydon (London South), Newcastle, Manchester, Bristol, and Cardiff.*]

1.33 Rules 8, 9, and 10 deal with the presentation of the claim:

> 8　(1) A claim shall be started by presenting a completed claim form (using a prescribed form) in accordance with any practice direction made under regulation 11 which supplements this rule.
>
> (2) A claim may be presented in England and Wales if—
>
> (a) the respondent, or one of the respondents, resides or carries on business in England and Wales;
>
> (b) one or more of the acts or omissions complained of took place in England and Wales;
>
> (c) the claim relates to a contract under which the work is or has been performed partly in England and Wales; or

> (d) the Tribunal has jurisdiction to determine the claim by virtue of a connection with Great Britain and the connection in question is at least partly a connection with England and Wales.
>
> (3) A claim may be presented in Scotland if—
>
>   (a) the respondent, or one of the respondents, resides or carries on business in Scotland;
>
>   (b) one or more of the acts or omissions complained of took place in Scotland;
>
>   (c) the claim relates to a contract under which the work is or has been performed partly in Scotland; or
>
>   (d) the Tribunal has jurisdiction to determine the claim by virtue of a connection with Great Britain and the connection in question is at least partly a connection with Scotland.
>
> 9 Two or more claimants may make their claims on the same claim form if their claims are based on the same set of facts. Where two or more claimants wrongly include claims on the same claim form, this shall be treated as an irregularity falling under rule 6. [rule 6 is dealt with in 1.84.]
>
> 10 (1) The Tribunal shall reject a claim if—
>
>   (a) it is not made on a prescribed form; or
>
>   (b) it does not contain all of the following information—
>
>   (i) each claimant's name;
>
>   (ii) each claimant's address;
>
>   (iii) each respondent's name;
>
>   (iv) each respondent's address.
>
> (2) The form shall be returned to the claimant with a notice of rejection explaining why it has been rejected. The notice shall contain information about how to apply for a reconsideration of the rejection.

1.34 As will be seen from r 10(1)(b), there is certain information which is mandatory, omission of which will result in the rejection of the claim. In addition to this mandatory information, however, the claim form seeks information on a series of different matters. Those questions which are mandatory are marked * on the form.

1.35 Among the mandatory fields (questions 2.1 and 2.2) are those which require the claimant to give the name and address of the respondent. For the majority of claims, this will be the employer. For some claims, eg discrimination, an individual respondent may be named in addition to the employer. As far as the identity of the employer is concerned, see **section 2.19** of *Blackstone's Employment Law Practice 2014*.

1.36 The type and details of claim (questions 8.1 and 8.2) are also mandatory. It is important for the claimant to identify the correct basis for their claim, and to set out briefly and cogently the matters about which they are complaining. The claim form is not, however, the stage at which detailed evidence should be set out. That will come later with the production of witness statements and relevant documents.

1.37 The claimant is not, of course, confined to filling in the mandatory fields. The remainder of the claim form provides an opportunity to set out information which will be relevant to the progress of the case, including any details as to the remedy which is sought (see questions 9.1 and 9.2).

1.38 As far as the degree of detail which is necessary is concerned, the case of *Grimmer v KLM Cityhopper UK* [2006] IRLR 596 (EAT), which interpreted the provisions of the 2004 Rules, remains relevant in its statement of principle. The EAT held that the claimant had provided sufficient details of her claim relating to the employer's refusal of her request for flexible working, and that it should have been accepted. HHJ Prophet said:

> It is a very serious step to deny a claimant or for that matter the respondent the opportunity of having an employment rights matter resolved by an independent judicial body i.e. an employment tribunal.... The test for 'details of the claim' emerges as being whether it can be discerned from the claim as presented that the claimant is complaining of an alleged breach of an employment rights which falls within the jurisdiction of the employment tribunal. It follows that if that test is met, there is no scope for either the secretary or a chairman interpreting 'details of the claim' as being 'sufficient particulars of the claim'.

Rejection and reconsideration of the claim

1.39 Rules 10 and 12 deal with two different situations where the claim is rejected. The decision to reject a claim on the basis of r 10 can be taken by a member of the tribunal staff (see 1.33 for the text of r 10). Such a rejection would be upon the basis that the claim did not contain the name and address of either the claimant or the respondent.

1.40 Rule 12 operates on a different basis. It involves the referral of the claim by a member of staff to an employment judge, who must consider whether the claim form is defective, either because the tribunal has no jurisdiction to consider it, or because it is in a form 'which cannot sensibly be responded to or is otherwise an abuse of process'. Rule 12 reads as follows:

> 12 (1) The staff of the tribunal office shall refer a claim form to an Employment Judge if they consider that the claim, or part of it, may be—
>   (a) one which the Tribunal has no jurisdiction to consider; or
>   (b) in a form which cannot sensibly be responded to or is otherwise an abuse of the process.
>
> (2) The claim, or part of it, shall be rejected if the Judge considers that the claim, or part of it, is of a kind described in sub-paragraphs (a) or (b) of paragraph (1).
>
> (3) If the claim is rejected, the form shall be returned to the claimant together with a notice of rejection giving the Judge's reasons for rejecting the claim, or part of it. The notice shall contain information about how to apply for a reconsideration of the rejection.

1. Tribunal Procedure

1.41 If the claim is rejected in accordance either with r 10 or r 12, then the form is sent back to the claimant with a notice explaining why it has been rejected, and how to apply for reconsideration of that rejection.

1.42 If the claimant decides to apply for reconsideration, it must be done in writing within 14 days of the date upon which the notice of rejection was sent, explaining why the decision was wrong, or rectifying the defect. The claimant can request a hearing. If the employment judge decides to hold a hearing, only the claimant will attend.

1.43 If the claim is accepted, but the employment judge considers that the original rejection was correct and that the defect has now been rectified, that will have implications for the time limit. The position is that the claim will be treated as presented upon the date when the defect was rectified (not the date upon which the form was originally presented). The procedure for reconsideration of rejection is set out in r 13:

> 13 (1) A claimant whose claim has been rejected (in whole or in part) under rule 10 or 12 may apply for a reconsideration on the basis that either—
>   (a) the decision to reject was wrong; or
>   (b) the notified defect can be rectified.
> (2) The application shall be in writing and presented to the Tribunal within 14 days of the date that the notice of rejection was sent. It shall explain why the decision is said to have been wrong or rectify the defect and if the claimant wishes to request a hearing this shall be requested in the application.
> (3) If the claimant does not request a hearing, or an Employment Judge decides, on considering the application, that the claim shall be accepted in full, the Judge shall determine the application without a hearing. Otherwise the application shall be considered at a hearing attended only by the claimant.
> (4) If the Judge decides that the original rejection was correct but that the defect has been rectified, the claim shall be treated as presented on the date that the defect was rectified.

The response

1.44 When the claim form is received, the tribunal staff will date stamp it, and give it a case number. It will then be sent to the respondent named on the claim form, together with a blank response form and an explanatory booklet. The respondent must use that form, and it must be presented to the tribunal office within 28 days of the date that the claim form was sent by the tribunal (not within 28 days of its receipt by the respondent).

1.45 This procedure is dealt with in rr 15 and 16:

15 Unless the claim is rejected, the Tribunal shall send a copy of the claim form, together with a prescribed response form, to each respondent with a notice which includes information on—
    (a) whether any part of the claim has been rejected; and
    (b) how to submit a response to the claim, the time limit for doing so and what will happen if a response is not received by the Tribunal within that time limit.

16 (1) The response shall be on a prescribed form and presented to the tribunal office within 28 days of the date that the copy of the claim form was sent by the Tribunal.
    (2) A response form may include the response of more than one respondent if they are responding to a single claim and either they all resist the claim on the same grounds or they do not resist the claim.
    (3) A response form may include the response to more than one claim if the claims are based on the same set of facts and either the respondent resists all of the claims on the same grounds or the respondent does not resist the claims.

What should the response contain?

1.46 The information which the response must contain is set out in r 17(1):

17 (1) The Tribunal shall reject a response if—
    (a) it is not made on a prescribed form; or
    (b) it does not contain all of the following information—
        (i) the respondent's full name;
        (ii) the respondent's address;
        (iii) whether the respondent wishes to resist any part of the claim.
    (2) The form shall be returned to the respondent with a notice of rejection explaining why it has been rejected. The notice shall explain what steps may be taken by the respondent, including the need (if appropriate) to apply for an extension of time, and how to apply for a reconsideration of the rejection.

1.47 The information set out in the rule is, of course, the bare minimum. In order to defend the case effectively, the respondent will wish to set out the reasons why it contests the claim (unless it proposes not to resist). Opportunity to provide this defence is to be found in the response form, in answer to question 4.

Rejection and reconsideration of the response

1.48 A response may be rejected for one of three reasons:

(1) if it is not made on the prescribed form;
(2) if it does not contain the prescribed information;
(3) if it is received outside the time limit, taking into account any extension.

1. Tribunal Procedure

1.49 If the response is rejected for any of these reasons, it will be returned to the respondent, with the reason for rejection, and an indication of how to apply for an extension of time or for a reconsideration of the rejection. The procedure for rejection for these reasons is dealt with in r 17(2) (which is set out at 1.46) and r 18:

> 18 (1) A response shall be rejected by the Tribunal if it is received outside the time limit in rule 16 (or any extension of that limit granted within the original limit) unless an application for extension has already been made under rule 20 or the response includes or is accompanied by such an application (in which case the response shall not be rejected pending the outcome of the application).
>
> (2) The response shall be returned to the respondent together with a notice of rejection explaining that the response has been presented late. The notice shall explain how the respondent can apply for an extension of time and how to apply for a reconsideration.

1.50 If the respondent wants reconsideration of the rejection, an application in writing must be presented to the tribunal within 14 days of the date that the notice of rejection was sent (not the date it was received). Any such application should set out why the decision to reject was wrong, or it should rectify the defect. In addition, the respondent should state whether a hearing is requested. The application will then be considered by an employment judge, either on the papers or at a hearing attended only by the respondent. If the judge decides that the original response was defective, but that the defect has been rectified, that will have implications for the time limits as the response will be treated as presented on the date that the defect was rectified, subject to any extension of time. Reconsideration of the rejection of response is dealt with in r 19:

> 19 (1) A respondent whose response has been rejected under rule 17 or 18 may apply for a reconsideration on the basis that the decision to reject was wrong or, in the case of a rejection under rule 17, on the basis that the notified defect can be rectified.
>
> (2) The application shall be in writing and presented to the Tribunal within 14 days of the date that the notice of rejection was sent. It shall explain why the decision is said to have been wrong or rectify the defect and it shall state whether the respondent requests a hearing.
>
> (3) If the respondent does not request a hearing, or the Employment Judge decides, on considering the application, that the response shall be accepted in full, the Judge shall determine the application without a hearing. Otherwise the application shall be considered at a hearing attended only by the respondent.
>
> (4) If the Judge decides that the original rejection was correct but that the defect has been rectified, the response shall be treated as presented on the date that the defect was rectified (but the Judge may extend time under rule 5).

Rejection and reconsideration of the response

1.51   Since the most frequent reason for rejection of a response is that it was received late, the procedure for applying for an extension of time is of some practical importance. The procedure is dealt with in r 20:

> 20 (1) An application for an extension of time for presenting a response shall be presented in writing and copied to the claimant. It shall set out the reason why the extension is sought and shall, except where the time limit has not yet expired, be accompanied by a draft of the response which the respondent wishes to present or an explanation of why that is not possible and if the respondent wishes to request a hearing this shall be requested in the application.
> (2) The claimant may within 7 days of receipt of the application give reasons in writing explaining why the application is opposed.
> (3) An Employment Judge may determine the application without a hearing.
> (4) If the decision is to refuse an extension, any prior rejection of the response shall stand. If the decision is to allow an extension, any judgment issued under rule 21 shall be set aside.

1.52   Rule 5 deals with the power of the tribunal to extend or shorten time:

> 5   The Tribunal may, on its own initiative or on the application of a party, extend or shorten any time limit specified in these Rules or in any decision, whether or not (in the case of an extension) it has expired.

1.53   The rules make it clear that a respondent can apply for an extension of time to present a response even after the 28-day deadline has expired. The tribunal is unable to exercise this power in relation to a *claim* which is submitted late, because the time limits for the submission of claims are laid down in the various statutes, and the tribunal has no jurisdiction to consider a claim other than in accordance with the provisions of the statute in question. This means, in the usual case, that a claim must be submitted within three months, subject to a discretion to extend, either on the 'reasonably practicable' or the 'just and equitable' basis (see Chapter 6 on Time Limits).

1.54   Rule 21 deals with the consequences where the tribunal has not received or has rejected a response, or the respondent has decided not to resist the claim:

> 21 (1) Where on the expiry of the time limit in rule 16 no response has been presented, or any response received has been rejected and no application for a reconsideration is outstanding, or where the respondent has stated that no part of the claim is contested, paragraphs (2) and (3) shall apply.
> (2) An Employment Judge shall decide whether on the available material (which may include further information which the parties are required by a Judge to provide), a determination can properly be made of the

> claim, or part of it. To the extent that a determination can be made, the Judge shall issue a judgment accordingly. Otherwise, a hearing shall be fixed before a Judge alone.
>
> (3) The respondent shall be entitled to notice of any hearings and decisions of the Tribunal but, unless and until an extension of time is granted, shall only be entitled to participate in any hearing to the extent permitted by the Judge.

1.55 In effect, the position is that an employment judge will decide the case upon the information available, with a hearing if necessary. The respondent will only be entitled to participate in any hearing to the extent permitted by the judge.

1.56 Rule 22 deals with the position where the response is accepted:

> 22 Where the Tribunal accepts the response it shall send a copy of it to all other parties.

Employer's contract claim

1.57 Where an employee makes a claim for breach of contract under the Employment Tribunals Extension of Jurisdiction Order (England and Wales) Order 1994, art 5, the employer is entitled to make a counterclaim for breach of contract.

1.58 This has the official title 'employer's contract claim' and it is an alternative to a claim by the employer for breach of contract in the ordinary courts.

1.59 As a result, if one assumes that the claim by the employee is for discrimination and unfair dismissal, the employer will not be able to make a counterclaim, eg seeking repayment of a loan. Such a counterclaim would have to be pursued in the county court. If, however, the employee claimed wrongful dismissal (which is a claim for breach of contract) in addition to the claims for discrimination and unfair dismissal, the door would be open for the employer to bring a counterclaim in the tribunal. This has important tactical consequences for those bringing proceedings on behalf of the claimant, who may wish to avoid making the initial claim for breach of contract in certain circumstances (see Chapter 13 on Contractual Claims and Wrongful Dismissal).

1.60 The procedure which applies to an employer's counterclaim is set out in rr 23, 24, and 25:

> 23 Any employer's contract claim shall be made as part of the response, presented in accordance with rule 16, to a claim which includes an employee's contract claim. An employer's contract claim may be rejected on the same basis as a claimant's claim may be rejected under rule 12, in which case rule 13 shall apply.

24 When the Tribunal sends the response to the other parties in accordance with rule 22 it shall notify the claimant that the response includes an employer's contract claim and include information on how to submit a response to the claim, the time limit for doing so, and what will happen if a response is not received by the Tribunal within that time limit.

25 A claimant's response to an employer's contract claim shall be presented to the tribunal office within 28 days of the date that the response was sent to the claimant. If no response is presented within that time limit, rules 20 and 21 shall apply.

1.61   In summary, the employer's contract claim is made as part of the response, which must be presented in the normal way in accordance with r 16. It may be rejected on the grounds that the claim:

(a) is one which the tribunal has no jurisdiction to consider;

(b) is in a form which cannot sensibly be responded to; or

(c) is otherwise an abuse of process.

1.62   As it is part of the response, the same deadline applies to it as to the response as a whole, with the consequences as outlined in the preceding sections dealing with the response (1.46).

1.63   When the tribunal sends a copy of the response to the claimant, it must notify the claimant of the counterclaim, and inform him or her of the procedure for submitting a response and the time limit. The claimant then has 28 days to present a response to the counterclaim. The same principles apply to this response as to other responses.

1.64   Although a fee is payable upon the presentation of an employer's contract claim, r 11, which deals with the failure to send a fee with claims generally, does not appear to apply to employer's counterclaims. If no fee is submitted, however, no doubt the tribunal will take appropriate steps.

Preparation by the parties

1.65   The rules focus upon relations between the tribunal and the parties. However, the relations between the parties themselves are crucial in the preparation of the case. The parties should cooperate in getting the case ready to be heard, and the tribunal will expect them to liaise between themselves to ensure that this is done. As far as the rules are concerned, this dimension is dealt with by the obligation which the parties have to ensure compliance with the overriding objective (see 1.08, on the overriding objective).

1.66   As an example of the cooperation which is expected, take the case where a party believes that an opponent has not disclosed documents which are necessary for the fair disposition of the proceedings. Rather than approaching the tribunal immediately, a request should be sent by the party requiring the documents to their opponent specifying the documents referred to, and setting down a realistic deadline for their disclosure. Only once the deadline has expired should an application be made to the tribunal, stating that a request has been made for disclosure of the specified documents, and applying for the tribunal to make an order. The application should enclose a copy of the request, and any resultant order by an employment judge is likely to cross-refer to that request.

Delivery of documents

1.67 Much of the preparation involved for a tribunal case will deal with the delivery of documents. Detailed provisions for this process are set out in the rules. The most important are in rr 85 and 86, which deal with delivery to the tribunal and to the parties:

85 (1) Subject to paragraph (2), documents may be delivered to the Tribunal—
    (a) by post;
    (b) by direct delivery to the appropriate tribunal office (including delivery by a courier or messenger service); or
    (c) by electronic communication.

(2) A claim form may only be delivered in accordance with the practice direction made under regulation 11 which supplements rule 8.

(3) The Tribunal shall notify the parties following the presentation of the claim of the address of the tribunal office dealing with the case (including any fax or email or other electronic address) and all documents shall be delivered to either the postal or the electronic address so notified. The Tribunal may from time to time notify the parties of any change of address, or that a particular form of communication should or should not be used, and any documents shall be delivered in accordance with that notification.

86 (1) Documents may be delivered to a party (whether by the Tribunal or by another party)—
    (a) by post;
    (b) by direct delivery to that party's address (including delivery by a courier or messenger service);
    (c) by electronic communication; or
    (d) by being handed personally to that party, if an individual and if no representative has been named in the claim form or response; or to any individual representative named in the claim form or response; or, on the occasion of a hearing, to any person identified by the party as representing that party at that hearing.

(2) For the purposes of sub-paragraphs (a) to (c) of paragraph (1), the document shall be delivered to the address given in the claim form or response (which shall be the address of the party's representative, if one is named) or to a different address as notified in writing by the party in question.

(3) If a party has given both a postal address and one or more electronic addresses, any of them may be used unless the party has indicated in writing that a particular address should or should not be used.

1.68 In addition, r 87 deals with delivery to non-parties, r 88 with special cases, and r 89 with substituted service (where no address is known).

1.69 Rules 90, 91, and 92 set out important provisions in relation to the date of delivery, deemed delivery, and the duty to copy documents to other parties:

> 90 Where a document has been delivered in accordance with rule 85 or 86, it shall, unless the contrary is proved, be taken to have been received by the addressee—
>   (a) if sent by post, on the day on which it would be delivered in the ordinary course of post;
>   (b) if sent by means of electronic communication, on the day of transmission;
>   (c) if delivered directly or personally, on the day of delivery.
>
> 91 A Tribunal may treat any document as delivered to a person, notwithstanding any non-compliance with rules 86 to 88, if satisfied that the document in question, or its substance, has in fact come to the attention of that person.
>
> 92 Where a party sends a communication to the Tribunal (except an application under rule 32) it shall send a copy to all other parties, and state that it has done so (by use of 'cc' or otherwise). The Tribunal may order a departure from this rule where it considers it in the interests of justice to do so.

The 'sift'

1.70 Rules 26 to 28 are headed 'initial consideration of claim form and response'. They deal with a process which has been referred to as 'the sift'. It is intended to ensure that a weak case, whether relied upon by the claimant or the respondent, is weeded out at an early stage.

1.71 The employment judge will review the documents which are held on file after the response has been received. The primary aim of this examination is to determine whether there are arguable grounds for both the claim and the defence. If further information appears to be necessary from one or more of the parties, the judge may order the provision of that information. If the judge concludes that both the claim and the defence are arguable, he or she will make any necessary case management order, including the listing of a hearing.

1.72 However, if the judge concludes that the claim (or part of it) is outside the jurisdiction of the tribunal, or that it has no reasonable prospect of success, a notice will be sent to the parties stating the judge's view, with reasons, and ordering that the claim (or part of it) will be dismissed upon the specified date, unless the claimant explains in writing why it should not. If no such explanation is received, the claim will be dismissed. If representations are received before the stated deadline, the employment judge will either decide that the claim should proceed, or fix a hearing to determine whether it should or not. At that hearing, the respondent is entitled to attend and participate, but need not do so.

1. Tribunal Procedure

1.73 There are equivalent provisions in r 28 which apply to a response (or part of the response) which has no reasonable prospect of success. Again, the response will be dismissed subject to the right of the respondent to make representations, and attend a hearing if they are not accepted.

1.74 Rules 27 and 28 read as follows:

27 (1) If the Employment Judge considers either that the Tribunal has no juris-diction to consider the claim, or part of it, or that the claim, or part of it, has no reasonable prospect of success, the Tribunal shall send a notice to the parties—

    (a) setting out the Judge's view and the reasons for it; and

    (b) ordering that the claim, or the part in question, shall be dismissed on such date as is specified in the notice unless before that date the claimant has presented written representations to the Tribunal explaining why the claim (or part) should not be dismissed.

  (2) If no such representations are received, the claim shall be dismissed from the date specified without further order (although the Tribunal shall write to the parties to confirm what has occurred).

  (3) If representations are received within the specified time they shall be considered by an Employment Judge, who shall either permit the claim (or part) to proceed or fix a hearing for the purpose of deciding whether it should be permitted to do so. The respondent may, but need not, attend and participate in the hearing.

  (4) If any part of the claim is permitted to proceed the Judge shall make a case management order.

28 (1) If the Employment Judge considers that the response to the claim, or part of it, has no reasonable prospect of success the Tribunal shall send a notice to the parties—

    (a) setting out the Judge's view and the reasons for it;

    (b) ordering that the response, or the part in question, shall be dis-missed on such date as is specified in the notice unless before that date the respondent has presented written representations to the Tribunal explaining why the response (or part) should not be dismissed; and

    (c) specifying the consequences of the dismissal of the response, in accordance with paragraph (5) below.

  (2) If no such representations are received, the response shall be dismissed from the date specified without further order (although the Tribunal shall write to the parties to confirm what has occurred).

  (3) If representations are received within the specified time they shall be considered by an Employment Judge, who shall either permit the response (or part) to stand or fix a hearing for the purpose of deciding whether it should be permitted to do so. The claimant may, but need not, attend and participate in the hearing.

  (4) If any part of the response is permitted to stand the Judge shall make a case management order.

  (5) Where a response is dismissed, the effect shall be as if no response had been presented, as set out in rule 21 above.

Case management orders

1.75   The tribunal has extensive powers to make orders as to the way in which the case should proceed—usually referred to as case management orders. Presidential Guidance on General Case Management was issued in 2014, and relevant extracts are reproduced in Appendix 3. A number of case management orders are set out specifically in the rules, but the fact that no mention is made of a particular power within the rules does not mean that the tribunal cannot make such an order. That is made clear by the terms of r 29:

> 29 The Tribunal may at any stage of the proceedings, on its own initiative or on application, make a case management order. The particular powers identified in the following rules do not restrict that general power. A case management order may vary, suspend or set aside an earlier case management order where that is necessary in the interests of justice, and in particular where a party affected by the earlier order did not have a reasonable opportunity to make representations before it was made.

1.76   Case management orders are frequently made by the tribunal on its own initiative. In addition, a party may apply at any stage for such an order. Any such application should be in writing, include the case number and set out the reasons why such an order should be granted, including how it will assist the tribunal to deal with the case justly. The rules do not specify these matters, but they are worth bearing in mind in order to ensure that the order is dealt with as soon and as favourably as possible.

1.77   What the rules do specify is that any application which is made in writing should be notified to the other parties, stating that any objections should be sent to the tribunal as soon as possible. Where the application is made at a hearing, such notification is not necessary.

1.78   On receiving the application, the tribunal may deal with it, but it will frequently say that the matter should be dealt with at the hearing, particularly if the hearing is imminent. Applications are covered by r 30:

> 30 (1) An application by a party for a particular case management order may be made either at a hearing or presented in writing to the Tribunal.
> (2) Where a party applies in writing, they shall notify the other parties that any objections to the application should be sent to the Tribunal as soon as possible.
> (3) The Tribunal may deal with such an application in writing or order that it be dealt with at a preliminary or final hearing.

1.79   Further details as to case management orders can be found in **chapter 6** of *Blackstone's Employment Law Practice 2014*. The questionnaire which is used by the tribunals to get the parties to clarify matters

---

before a hearing which will deal with case management is to be found within the Presidential Guidance, extracts from which form Appendix 3 of this Handbook.

Time and extensions of time

1.80 A series of provisions relating to time appears in r 4. Rule 4(1) states that, where the rules or an order require an act to be done on or by a particular day, it must be done by midnight on that day. Of course, a tribunal order may specify a particular time by which an act should be done, eg 5 pm, in which case that is the operative time. Rule 4 also lays down the ways in which the number of days should be calculated, and a presumption with regard to the date upon which the document is sent (subject to proof to the contrary). Rule 4 reads as follows:

4 (1) Unless otherwise specified by the Tribunal, an act required by these Rules, a practice direction or an order of a Tribunal to be done on or by a particular day may be done at any time before midnight on that day. If there is an issue as to whether the act has been done by that time, the party claiming to have done it shall prove compliance.

   (2) If the time specified by these Rules, a practice direction or an order for doing any act ends on a day other than a working day, the act is done in time if it is done on the next working day. 'Working day' means any day except a Saturday or Sunday, Christmas Day, Good Friday or a bank holiday under section 1 of the Banking and Financial Dealings Act 1971.

   (3) Where any act is required to be, or may be, done within a certain number of days of or from an event, the date of that event shall not be included in the calculation. (For example, a response shall be presented within 28 days of the date on which the respondent was sent a copy of the claim: if the claim was sent on 1st October the last day for presentation of the response is 29th October.)

   (4) Where any act is required to be, or may be, done not less than a certain number of days before or after an event, the date of that event shall not be included in the calculation. (For example, if a party wishes to present representations in writing for consideration by a Tribunal at a hearing, they shall be presented not less than 7 days before the hearing: if the hearing is fixed for 8th October, the representations shall be presented no later than 1st October.)

   (5) Where the Tribunal imposes a time limit for doing any act, the last date for compliance shall, wherever practicable, be expressed as a calendar date.

   (6) Where time is specified by reference to the date when a document is sent to a person by the Tribunal, the date when the document was sent shall, unless the contrary is proved, be regarded as the date endorsed on the document as the date of sending or, if there is no such endorsement, the date shown on the letter accompanying the document.

1.81   Rule 5 deals with extensions to deadlines, as follows:

> 5   The Tribunal may, on its own initiative or on the application of a party,
> extend or shorten any time limit specified in these Rules or in any decision,
> whether or not (in the case of an extension) it has expired.

1.82   There is specific provision for the extension of time for presenting a response. This requires a degree of formality, and the respondent's reasons and any request for a hearing must be copied to the claimant. The claimant then has an opportunity to provide reasons why the application is opposed. The employment judge may (and frequently will) determine the application without a hearing, taking into account the reasons and representations which are being made. Rule 20 reads as follows:

> 20 (1) An application for an extension of time for presenting a response shall
> be presented in writing and copied to the claimant. It shall set out the
> reason why the extension is sought and shall, except where the time
> limit has not yet expired, be accompanied by a draft of the response
> which the respondent wishes to present or an explanation of why that
> is not possible and if the respondent wishes to request a hearing this
> shall be requested in the application.
> (2) The claimant may within 7 days of receipt of the application give rea-
> sons in writing explaining why the application is opposed.
> (3) An Employment Judge may determine the application without a hearing.
> (4) If the decision is to refuse an extension, any prior rejection of the
> response shall stand. If the decision is to allow an extension, any judg-
> ment issued under rule 21 shall be set aside.

Irregularities and non-compliance

1.83   What happens if a party fails to comply with the rules, or with an order of the tribunal? There are a number of different possibilities which are set out in r 6. The general principle is that non-compliance with the rules or with an order of the tribunal will not invalidate the proceedings or a step within the proceedings. The exceptions to this general rule are:

(a) submission of the claim on the prescribed form, giving the required information (r 8);

(b) submission of a response on the prescribed form, giving the required information (r 16);

(c) the equivalent actions in relation to an employer's counterclaim (rr 23 and 25).

1.84   A non-exhaustive list of the steps which a tribunal might take where the rules or an order have not been complied with is set out in r 6:

> 6   A failure to comply with any provision of these Rules (except rule 8(1),
> 16(1), 23 or 25) or any order of the Tribunal (except for an order under

rules 38 or 39) does not of itself render void the proceedings or any step taken in the proceedings. In the case of such non-compliance, the Tribunal may take such action as it considers just, which may include all or any of the following—

(a) waiving or varying the requirement;
(b) striking out the claim or the response, in whole or in part, in accordance with rule 37;
(c) barring or restricting a party's participation in the proceedings;
(d) awarding costs in accordance with rules 74 to 84.

Adding or removing a party

1.85 From time to time, it becomes necessary for the tribunal to add a party to or remove a party from the proceedings. For example, it may become apparent that the claimant's employer may be either company A or company B, depending upon whether a transfer took place in accordance with the TUPE regulations. If the claimant cited only company A on the claim form, the tribunal would need to consider whether it should add company B. If, in due course, it became apparent that the proper respondent is company B, it will then be necessary to remove company A. The power of the tribunal to add, remove, or substitute a party is set out in r 34:

34 The Tribunal may on its own initiative, or on the application of a party or any other person wishing to become a party, add any person as a party, by way of substitution or otherwise, if it appears that there are issues between that person and any of the existing parties falling within the jurisdiction of the Tribunal which it is in the interests of justice to have determined in the proceedings; and may remove any party apparently wrongly included.

1.86 Rule 35 deals with the position where a tribunal believes it is right that a person should be able to participate in proceedings, even if he or she is not a party:

35 The Tribunal may permit any person to participate in proceedings, on such terms as may be specified, in respect of any matter in which that person has a legitimate interest.

Lead cases

1.87 A number of the cases which are dealt with by the employment tribunals involve multiple claimants. Less commonly, a claim may be made against several respondents. Where the claim or claims involve common issues of fact or law, greater efficiency can be achieved by dealing with the litigation on a group basis. Employment tribunals have, in the past, dealt with group litigation by means of their general powers of case management. Since the introduction of the 2013 Rules, however, there has been a new rule which gives a clear legal structure to the handling of multiple cases, or the situation where several cases raise the same point of law. The mechanism which is employed is to nominate a lead claim.

1.88 Group litigation has been a particular feature, for example, of similar claims for equal pay, cases arising out of a transfer under the TUPE Regulations, and applications for a protective award stemming from large-scale collective redundancies. On occasion, claims in relation to the same issue are lodged in several different regions, either because they are brought against a single employer which has many different places of business, or because the same issues arise in relation to a number of different employers. In such a case, the President of Employment Tribunals may make an order that all cases are heard in one region. Parties wishing to ensure that such a course is taken can write to the President asking for such an order.

1.89 Rule 36 means that where the tribunal identifies a lead claim, the decision which is made by the tribunal in that case will automatically be binding upon related claims. This will have the effect of removing the need for additional hearings. The rule includes a provision which allows parties to ask the tribunal to have binding directions or decisions disapplied in respect of their own individual claim. Rule 36 reads as follows:

> 36 (1) Where a Tribunal considers that two or more claims give rise to common or related issues of fact or law, the Tribunal or the President may make an order specifying one or more of those claims as a lead case and staying, or in Scotland sisting, the other claims ('the related cases').
>
> (2) When the Tribunal makes a decision in respect of the common or related issues it shall send a copy of that decision to each party in each of the related cases and, subject to paragraph (3), that decision shall be binding on each of those parties.
>
> (3) Within 28 days after the date on which the Tribunal sent a copy of the decision to a party under paragraph (2), that party may apply in writing for an order that the decision does not apply to, and is not binding on the parties to, a particular related case.
>
> (4) If a lead case is withdrawn before the Tribunal makes a decision in respect of the common or related issues, it shall make an order as to—
>
> (a) whether another claim is to be specified as a lead case; and
>
> (b) whether any order affecting the related cases should be set aside or varied.

Unless orders

1.90 Sometimes the tribunal will make an order stating that it must be complied with by a certain date, and that if it is not, the claim or response or part thereof will be dismissed without further notice. Such orders are not made lightly, and usually constitute a response to serious and/or repeated failure to comply with the directions of the tribunal. They are generally known as 'unless orders'. In the past, there has been controversy as to the effect of such an order, and whether it can be regarded as absolutely final. The position is now covered by r 38, which reads:

> 38 (1) An order may specify that if it is not complied with by the date speci-
> fied the claim or response, or part of it, shall be dismissed without
> further order. If a claim or response, or part of it, is dismissed on this
> basis the Tribunal shall give written notice to the parties confirming
> what has occurred.
>
> (2) A party whose claim or response has been dismissed, in whole or in
> part, as a result of such an order may apply to the Tribunal in writing,
> within 14 days of the date that the notice was sent, to have the order
> set aside on the basis that it is in the interests of justice to do so.
> Unless the application includes a request for a hearing, the Tribunal
> may determine it on the basis of written representations.
>
> (3) Where a response is dismissed under this rule, the effect shall be as if
> no response had been presented, as set out in rule 21.

1.91 The effect of the rule, then, is that the unless order is final, subject to the right of the party whose claim or response has been dismissed to apply within 14 days for the order to be set aside. Where a response is dismissed, r 38(3) makes it clear that the effect is as set out in r 21—see 1.54.

Additional information

1.92 It is often necessary for a party to provide further details of their claim or response, eg if the allegations made are vague or ambiguous. The general powers of case management which the tribunal has (r 29) are frequently used to ensure that such additional information is provided.

1.93 Sometimes the tribunal will order the provision of such additional information on its own initiative. More often, such an order will come as a result of an application by a party. For example, in a discrimination case, where the claimant has alleged a series of acts of harassment without supplying details, the respondent is likely to seek details of the allegations, such as the alleged perpetrator, the date, and the precise nature of what was done. The claimant, on the other hand, may seek details of what the respondent relies upon when it says that it did everything reasonable to prevent acts of discrimination.

1.94 Best practice is for the party requiring the information to make a direct request first of the party holding the information, stating a realistic deadline for its provision. If the information is not provided, then a formal application can be made to the tribunal enclosing the previous request and any reply, and stating why the order is sought.

1.95 In *Byrne v Financial Times* [1991] IRLR 417 (EAT), it was stated that the tribunal should have in mind the following principles in deciding whether to grant an order for additional information:

(a) is the information necessary in the interests of justice, or to prevent an adjournment?

(b) Will refusal mean that the party denied the information will be taken by surprise?

(c) Will the grant of an order be oppressive or burdensome?

Will the information assist in identifying the issues in the case? Or is the request a disguised means of eliciting information prematurely?

Witness statements

1.96 It is usual for the employment tribunal to make provision for the evidence-in-chief of witnesses to be given in the form of witness statements. A direction will generally be given that such statements should be exchanged by the parties simultaneously on a certain date in advance of the hearing.

1.97 The direction will almost invariably state that the witness statement is to form the whole of the evidence-in-chief, and that the permission of the tribunal will be required for any additional evidence to be received. In the event that there are new developments between the exchange of witness statements and the hearing, best practice is to prepare a supplementary witness statement and seek the permission of the tribunal for it to be admitted. The position with regard to the eliciting of additional evidence through supplementary questions at the hearing itself is dealt with in Chapter 4 on Advocacy: Presenting the Case.

1.98 The witness statement should be kept separate from the trial bundle, for ease of reference during the hearing. Each party is responsible for ensuring that the requisite number of witness statements is provided for the hearing. Where this is in front of a full tribunal, six copies will be required; four copies are necessary if the case is heard by an employment judge sitting alone.

Witness orders

1.99 A party may apply to an employment tribunal for a witness order against a person in Great Britain to attend the tribunal and to produce any documents in their possession. The tribunal has a wide discretion in deciding whether to issue a witness order. Before doing so it will need to be satisfied that:

(a) the witness can give evidence relevant to the issues in dispute;

(b) it is necessary to issue a witness order to compel attendance. For example, this may be because the witness has refused to attend, or because their employer objects and it is necessary for them to be able to show that they are compelled to attend; and

(c) the correct name and address of the witness has been supplied.

1.100   Sometimes a party (frequently a litigant in person) will seek a witness order against someone who is hostile to their case. Often, such a tactic will be counter-productive. There is a prohibition against leading or cross-examining your own witness, so that if the witness gives unfavourable evidence there is nothing much which the party calling them can do about it. The party who has obtained the order may seek to have the witness declared 'hostile', but the tribunals are in practice reluctant to adopt such a course. The strict test for establishing that a witness is hostile is that they must be 'not desirous of telling the truth at the instance of the party calling them'. A more effective alternative may be to seek to persuade the tribunal to call the witness itself, so that both parties can cross-examine.

1.101   The power to grant a witness order is covered by r 32:

> 32 The Tribunal may order any person in Great Britain to attend a hearing to give evidence, produce documents, or produce information.

Disclosure of documents

1.102   It is right that the parties should know of any relevant documents in each other's possession. Provided that they are relevant to the case, the parties should be able to inspect them, and decide whether they should be in the trial bundle which is before the tribunal (see 1.108). The tribunal has power to order the disclosure of documents under r 31:

> 31 The Tribunal may order any person in Great Britain to disclose documents or information to a party (by providing copies or otherwise) or to allow a party to inspect such material as might be ordered by a county court or, in Scotland, by a sheriff.

1.103   It will be noted that this power is not confined to an order to the parties, but can relate to 'any person'. The rule does not lay down detailed provisions in relation to disclosure, but states that it is based upon the same principles as those used in the county court. In addition, the Presidential Guidance on General Case Management issued in 2014 deals with disclosure, and the relevant extract is reproduced in Appendix 3.

1.104   The tribunal will usually make an order for standard disclosure. This involves each party sending to the other(s) a list of the documents which it has in its possession. This process is followed by inspection of any of the documents in the list which the other party wishes to see. As a matter of practice, inspection is usually carried out by the supply of photocopies. In addition to such an order for standard disclosure, there may be an order for specific disclosure where the party in possession of a document or documents contests disclosure.

1.105 As the rule adopts the principles used in the county court, the relevant guidance is provided by the Civil Procedure Rules (CPR) rule 31. Standard disclosure under the CPR requires a party to disclose those documents on which he or she relies, any documents which support or adversely affect the case of a party to the proceedings, and any other documents which a party is required to disclose pursuant to a relevant practice direction.

1.106 There are certain grounds on which disclosure can be resisted:

(a) *Confidentiality.* In *Science Research Council v Nasse* [1979] IRLR 465 (HL), it was held that there was no general proposition of law that documents are protected from discovery by reason of confidentiality alone. On the other hand, their relevance, although a necessary condition, was not by itself sufficient. The true test was whether the discovery 'is necessary for fairly disposing of the proceedings'. Lord Wilberforce said:

> …the process is to consider fairly the strength and value of the interest in preserving confidentiality and the damage which may be caused by breaking it, then to consider whether the objective to dispose fairly of the case can be achieved without doing so and only in the last resort to order discovery.

Where the case is particularly sensitive, the tribunal may order redaction, ie that parts of a relevant document be covered up, eg the names and addresses of people involved.

(b) *Public interest immunity.* This may be claimed on the basis that withholding documents is necessary for the proper functioning of government. This has to be balanced in each case against the public interest in the fair administration of justice: *D v NSPCC* [1977] 1 All ER 589.

(c) *Diplomatic immunity.* An embassy is entitled to have its documents protected by absolute privilege from disclosure.

(d) *Legal professional privilege.* Communications between a party and his or her lawyer are protected from disclosure if they are confidential and made for the purpose of obtaining and giving legal advice. So are communications between a party and his or her lawyer and third parties such as expert witnesses, provided that the dominant purpose is preparation for contemplated litigation: *Waugh v British Railways Board* [1979] 2 All ER 1169. For more detail, see Chapter 5 on Evidence.

(e) *Without prejudice communications.* Communications between the parties made with a view to seeking a settlement of a pre-existing dispute are not generally admissible documents. There is nothing to prevent a party from referring to the fact of negotiations, or the fact that there was correspondence relating to them. It is the contents of the documents in question which are excluded from consideration by the tribunal, and consequently not subject to the process of disclosure. Where there are genuine negotiations any documents will be protected from disclosure, whether they are labelled 'without prejudice' or not. For more detail, see Chapter 5 on Evidence and Chapter 3 on Settlement Agreements.

(f) *Negotiations before termination of employment.* The protection in relation to without prejudice communications is confined to situations where there is a pre-existing dispute. The Enterprise and Regulatory Reform Act 2013 created a further category of protection, which does not require a pre-existing dispute.

This protection does not apply to discrimination cases, or to cases of automatically unfair dismissal. Neither does it apply to claims for breach of contract. The implications are dealt with further in Chapter 5 on Evidence.

1.107 Any communications with a conciliation officer of ACAS, whether written or oral, are not subject to disclosure unless the privilege is expressly waived by the party who communicated with the officer (s 18(7) of the Employment Tribunals Act 1996).

Trial bundle

1.108 For a hearing of any substance, the tribunal will require a bundle of documents relevant to the case. The standard direction is for the parties to prepare a joint bundle, which contains the documents which each of them intends to rely upon at the hearing. In most cases, the respondent is likely to be in possession of most of the relevant documents, and more often than not the tribunal will order that the respondent prepares this trial bundle. Sometimes the tribunal will state that the parties are to share the cost of preparing the bundle. It has become common for the tribunal to specify a maximum number of pages for the bundle, eg 100, the leave of the tribunal being necessary if it is to exceed that number.

1.109 Inclusion in the bundle does not mean that all the parties agree that the document in question is relevant or authentic. What it means is that at least one of the parties intends to make reference to it. In order to ensure that the bundle is not too bulky, it is sometimes sensible to include an extract from a long document, eg that portion of the disciplinary rules which the parties agree is the relevant part, rather than the whole staff handbook.

1.110 Standard directions will usually lay down a date for the production of the bundle prior to the date for exchange of witness statements. This will mean that the witness statements can refer to page numbers at the relevant point. The witness statements should not themselves be included in the bundle, so that it is easier to refer to the bundle while reading them. The bundle should be consecutively paginated, and numbered by page, rather than by document, to assist anyone (particularly the employment judge) in taking a note of proceedings. The party responsible for the preparation of the trial bundle will need to ensure that any other parties have a copy, that there are sufficient copies for the tribunal (one copy if the case is to be heard by a judge alone, three if by a full tribunal), and that there is a copy for the witness table.

Amending the claim

1.111 Where leave is sought to amend the claim, the tribunal has a discretion whether to grant the application. There is no rule in the 2013 Rules which specifically deals with amendments to the claim, but the principles set out in *Selkent Bus Co Ltd v Moore* [1996] IRLR 661 (EAT) apply, and are frequently quoted. In that case, the following matters were set out for the tribunal to consider when exercising its discretion whether to permit an amendment:

(a) *The nature and extent of the amendments.* Is it a simple error, or perhaps the additional substitution of a new label for facts already pleaded? If so, leave to amend is more likely to be granted. If it is a substantial alteration, however, which changes the basis of the claim, it is more likely to be refused.

(b) *A new claim.* If it is a new claim, it is crucial for the tribunal to consider whether it is out of time. If it is, then an extension of time will have to be considered under the usual statutory provisions (see Chapter 6 on Time Limits).

(c) *The timing and manner of the application.* An application should not be refused merely because there has been a delay making it. However, delay in making the application is a discretionary factor, which may make it less likely that the amendment is accepted. It is important that the tribunal consider why the application was not made earlier, and why it is now being made. The discovery of new facts, or information which appears from documents which are now disclosed will clearly be relevant in explaining and possibly excusing a delay.

1.112 In considering the factors to be taken into account in exercising its discretion, the tribunal should consider in particular 'any injustice or hardship which may be caused to any of the parties if the proposed amendment were allowed or, as the case may be, refused': *Cocking v Sandhurst (Stationers) Ltd* [1974] ICR 650.

1. Tribunal Procedure

1.113 An amendment to change the remedy which is sought, eg to include reinstatement or engagement, will usually be granted, as the statute allows the claimant to choose remedies once liability has been determined. It is sensible, however, for the intention to seek reinstatement or re-engagement to be notified as soon as possible, in order to put the respondent on notice and avoid the appointment of a permanent replacement.

1.114 Where an amendment to the claim is granted, it may be necessary for the tribunal to grant an adjournment and/or award costs to the respondent in appropriate cases.

Amending the response

1.115 A response can be amended with less difficulty than a claim, because there is no statutory time limit involved. The leave of the tribunal is nevertheless required, and the later that the application to amend is left, the less likely it is that it will be granted. The tribunal will wish to ensure that the claimant does not suffer any prejudice as a result of a late change on the part of the respondent. As with an amendment to the claim, the tribunal may decide that an adjournment and/or an award of costs is necessary to ensure that the claimant does not suffer as a result of a late amendment.

Striking out

1.116 The tribunal has power, within certain strictly defined circumstances, to strike out a claim or a response. The power is set out in r 37:

> 37 (1) At any stage of the proceedings, either on its own initiative or on the application of a party, a Tribunal may strike out all or part of a claim or response on any of the following grounds—
>   (a) that it is scandalous or vexatious or has no reasonable prospect of success;
>   (b) that the manner in which the proceedings have been conducted by or on behalf of the claimant or the respondent (as the case may be) has been scandalous, unreasonable or vexatious;
>   (c) for non-compliance with any of these Rules or with an order of the Tribunal;
>   (d) that it has not been actively pursued;
>   (e) that the Tribunal considers that it is no longer possible to have a fair hearing in respect of the claim or response (or the part to be struck out).
>   (2) A claim or response may not be struck out unless the party in question has been given a reasonable opportunity to make representations, either in writing or, if requested by the party, at a hearing.
>   (3) Where a response is struck out, the effect shall be as if no response had been presented, as set out in rule 21 above.

1.117   Dealing first with ground (a), a scandalous claim or response is one which is irrelevant and abusive to the other party. In *De Keyser Ltd v Wilson* [2001] IRLR 324, the EAT urged caution in such cases, suggesting that a strikeout is likely to be disproportionate if a fair hearing is still possible.

1.118   A vexatious claim or defence is one which is not pursued with the expectation that it will be successful, but in order to harass the other party because of some improper motive.

1.119   In determining whether a claim or response has 'no reasonable prospect of success', it is not necessary to decide whether the case is entirely hopeless, but rather whether it has a realistic, as opposed to a merely fanciful, prospect of success. In *Eszias v North Glamorgan NHS Trust* [2007] ICR 1126, the Court of Appeal stated that a claim should not be struck out on this basis where the central facts are in dispute, unless exceptional circumstances exist. Such exceptional circumstances might include a case where the contemporaneous documentation was inconsistent with crucial facts asserted by one party. It is worth noting that the formula 'no reasonable prospect of success' is slightly but significantly different from the test for whether a tribunal should make a deposit order, ie 'little reasonable prospect of success' (see 1.125).

1.120   Ground (b) specifies the manner in which proceedings have been conducted. In *Bolch v Chipman* [2004] IRLR 140, the EAT set out the following stages which a tribunal ought to consider when deciding whether to strike out on grounds of conduct:

(1) It must conclude not only that the party behaved unreasonably, but that proceedings have been conducted reasonably.
(2) If the proceedings have been conducted scandalously, unreasonably, or vexatiously, is a fair trial not still possible?
(3) What remedy does the tribunal consider appropriate and proportionate to its conclusion? It could, for example, order costs instead of striking out.

1.121   Ground (c) deals with non-compliance with the rules or the orders of the tribunal. In *Blockbuster Entertainment Ltd v James* [2006] IRLR 630, the claimant failed to comply with various procedural orders for disclosure and the exchange of witness statements. The tribunal struck out the claim on the ground that the case had been conducted unreasonably. The Court of Appeal characterized the power to strike out as 'draconic'. It stated that it should only be used if the unreasonable conduct:

(1) took the form of deliberate and persistent disregard of required procedural steps; or
(2) made a fair trial impossible.

In any event, the claim should only be struck out if it was proportionate to do so.

1. Tribunal Procedure

1.122   Ground (d) relates to active pursuit of the claim or response. Strikeout on this basis is most commonly employed where a claimant or respondent continually fails to respond to communication from the tribunal.

1.123   As to the impossibility of a fair hearing (ground (e)) this is clearly a matter which will be fact sensitive, and may well be related to the other grounds, such as any delay which has resulted from failure to comply with the rules or the orders of the tribunal.

Deposit orders

1.124   At a preliminary hearing, the tribunal may make an order that a party pay a deposit of an amount up to £1000 as a condition for advancing any allegation or argument. The power to make such an order is in r 39:

> 39 (1) Where at a preliminary hearing (under rule 53) the Tribunal considers that any specific allegation or argument in a claim or response has little reasonable prospect of success, it may make an order requiring a party ('the paying party') to pay a deposit not exceeding £1,000 as a condition of continuing to advance that allegation or argument.
>
> (2) The Tribunal shall make reasonable enquiries into the paying party's ability to pay the deposit and have regard to any such information when deciding the amount of the deposit.
>
> (3) The Tribunal's reasons for making the deposit order shall be provided with the order and the paying party must be notified about the potential consequences of the order.
>
> (4) If the paying party fails to pay the deposit by the date specified the specific allegation or argument to which the deposit order relates shall be struck out. Where a response is struck out, the consequences shall be as if no response had been presented, as set out in rule 21.
>
> (5) If the Tribunal at any stage following the making of a deposit order decides the specific allegation or argument against the paying party for substantially the reasons given in the deposit order—
>
> (a) the paying party shall be treated as having acted unreasonably in pursuing that specific allegation or argument for the purpose of rule 76, unless the contrary is shown; and
>
> (b) the deposit shall be paid to the other party (or, if there is more than one, to such other party or parties as the Tribunal orders), otherwise the deposit shall be refunded.
>
> (6) If a deposit has been paid to a party under paragraph (5)(b) and a costs or preparation time order has been made against the paying party in favour of the party who received the deposit, the amount of the deposit shall count towards the settlement of that order.

1.125   The test for making the order is that an allegation or argument in the claim or response has 'little reasonable prospect of success'. The order could require such a deposit in relation to a number of different allegations or arguments contained within the claim or response, so that the total amount payable by the party affected might be considerably more than £1000.

1.126　Before making the order, the employment judge must take reasonable steps to ascertain the ability of the party to comply with it. It is common practice in the tribunal, where a deposit order is in prospect, for the party in question to be given a form which enquires as to their means.

1.127　If a deposit order is made, the deposit must be paid within 21 days of the order for payment being sent to the party. An extension of 14 days may be allowed. Failure to pay will result in the allegation or argument to which the order relates being struck out. In many cases, the claimant or respondent will drop the allegation or argument in question, either because of lack of funds or because they conclude that the weakness in their case has been identified by an impartial adjudicator.

1.128　If the deposit is paid and the case proceeds, the order may still have consequences as far as costs are concerned. If the specific allegation or argument is decided against the party who made it and he or she was ordered to pay a deposit, then they will be treated as having acted unreasonably, unless they are able to show the contrary. The deposit is then paid to the other party, and will count against any costs or preparation time order if one is made. Otherwise, the deposit is refunded.

1.129　Applications for deposit orders have become much more frequent in recent years, partly because of the difficulty which faces a party seeking strikeout. It is common for applications to be made in the alternative: (1) for strikeout on the basis of no reasonable prospect of success, or alternatively (2) for a deposit order on the basis of little reasonable prospect of success. In that way, if the application to strike out fails, the application for a deposit order may be more successful.

Preliminary hearings

1.130　Rule 53 sets out a series of matters which could be determined by a preliminary hearing. Until the introduction of the 2013 Rules, there was a distinction between the case management discussion and the pre-hearing review. Both of these are now subsumed within the preliminary hearing. Rule 53 reads as follows:

> 53 (1) A preliminary hearing is a hearing at which the Tribunal may do one or more of the following—
> (a) conduct a preliminary consideration of the claim with the parties and make a case management order (including an order relating to the conduct of the final hearing);

> (b) determine any preliminary issue;
> (c) consider whether a claim or response, or any part, should be struck out under rule 37;
> (d) make a deposit order under rule 39;
> (e) explore the possibility of settlement or alternative dispute resolution (including judicial mediation).
> (2) There may be more than one preliminary hearing in any case.
> (3) 'Preliminary issue' means, as regards any complaint, any substantive issue which may determine liability (for example, an issue as to jurisdiction or as to whether an employee was dismissed).

1.131 The preliminary consideration of the claim referred to in (a) was formerly determined at a case management discussion. The preliminary hearing will now determine what the issues in the case are, and give directions for it to proceed, eg laying down the requirements on the parties for disclosure and inspection of documents, exchange of witness statements, preparation of the trial bundle, etc. It will also determine matters such as the length of any hearing, and may fix the dates for the hearing.

1.132 The determination of any preliminary issue, as set out in (b) means that the preliminary hearing may come to a decision on questions such as whether the tribunal has jurisdiction to hear the case in view of the time limit, whether there was a transfer under TUPE, whether the claimant was an employee, and whether the claimant was disabled at the material time. It may be that the determination of such an issue as a preliminary matter will mean that the final hearing is either unnecessary or much abbreviated. The tribunal will be careful, however, not to order a preliminary hearing to consider such an issue unless there is an isolated issue, the resolution of which has the potential to dispose of the case. The question may be posed in the form: Is there 'a succinct knockout point'?: *SCA Packaging Ltd v Boyle* [2009] IRLR 746 (HL).

1.133 In the course of the preliminary hearing, the tribunal may consider strikeout or a deposit order (see 1.116 and 1.124). In addition, it can explore the question of settlement.

1.134 The fixing of preliminary hearings is dealt with in r 54, which makes it clear that it may be directed either by the tribunal on its own initiative, or as a result of an application by one of the parties. Reasonable notice must be given, and in the case of the determination of a preliminary issue (since it has the potential for disposing of the case) such notice must be at least 14 days and it should specify the issue(s) in question. Rule 54 reads as follows:

> 54 A preliminary hearing may be directed by the Tribunal on its own initiative following its initial consideration (under rule 26) or at any time thereafter or as the result of an application by a party. The Tribunal shall give the

parties reasonable notice of the date of the hearing and in the case of a hearing involving any preliminary issues at least 14 days notice shall be given and the notice shall specify the preliminary issues that are to be, or may be, decided at the hearing.

1.135 A preliminary hearing will usually be conducted by a judge sitting alone, but where a preliminary issue or issues may be decided at the hearing, a party may make a written request for a full tribunal which a judge will decide. Rule 55 states:

55 Preliminary hearings shall be conducted by an Employment Judge alone, except that where notice has been given that any preliminary issues are to be, or may be, decided at the hearing a party may request in writing that the hearing be conducted by a full tribunal in which case an Employment Judge shall decide whether that would be desirable.

1.136 The usual rule is that a preliminary hearing is to be held in private. However, where a preliminary issue is to be determined, or strikeout is to be considered, that part of the hearing will normally be in public, and in such a case the tribunal may direct that the whole of the hearing will be in public. Rule 56 deals with these questions:

56 Preliminary hearings shall be conducted in private, except that where the hearing involves a determination under rule 53(1)(b) or (c), any part of the hearing relating to such a determination shall be in public (subject to rules 50 and 94) and the Tribunal may direct that the entirety of the hearing be in public.

1.137 Rule 48 makes it clear that a preliminary hearing may be converted into a final hearing and vice versa, in appropriate circumstances:

48 A Tribunal conducting a preliminary hearing may order that it be treated as a final hearing, or vice versa, if the Tribunal is properly constituted for the purpose and if it is satisfied that neither party shall be materially prejudiced by the change.

The hearing

1.138 The preceding section dealt with the preliminary hearing. This section is primarily concerned with the hearing which deals with liability, and is sometimes called the 'main hearing' or the 'full merits hearing'.

1.139 Sometimes all the important case management decisions relating to the hearing will have been taken in advance, either at a preliminary hearing or by directions issued by the tribunal in correspondence. There will have been an estimate for the length of the hearing. If a preliminary hearing was held, this estimate will have been reached after discussion with the parties. Where there is no preliminary hearing, however, then the tribunal will have made its own estimate as to how long the hearing would take. The parties should make immediate representations to the tribunal if they believe that this estimate is wrong. In particular, if insufficient time has been allotted, it is in everyone's interest to bring that point to the attention of the tribunal, to avoid the prospect of the case going part heard, ie the hearing being incomplete after the allotted time so that a new hearing date has to be fixed in order to hear the remainder of the case.

1.140   Central to the hearing of the case is the evidence which will be given by witnesses, and this matter is dealt with in the next section. In addition, parties or their representatives need to consider any special arrangements for the hearing. For example, if any audio or video recording is to be used in evidence, arrangements will need to be made to ensure that there are facilities for the recordings to be played. Generally, the tribunal will expect that the party introducing such evidence will make the necessary arrangements. If an interpreter is needed, the tribunal office dealing with the case should be notified. They will then be able to make arrangements for an official interpreter to be engaged.

1.141   A party may fail to attend the hearing. There may have been a last-minute problem, eg ill-health or transport problems, or there may have been a failure to receive the notice of hearing. Clearly the reason for the absence of the party will affect the way in which the tribunal deals with the matter, but it may not have the necessary information. In any event, the tribunal faces a choice between adjourning the case to give the absent party a chance to attend, or to deal with the case in the absence of the party. This situation is covered by r 47:

> 47 If a party fails to attend or to be represented at the hearing, the Tribunal may dismiss the claim or proceed with the hearing in the absence of that party. Before doing so, it shall consider any information which is available to it, after any enquiries that may be practicable, about the reasons for the party's absence.

1.142   Before making a decision whether to adjourn or proceed, the tribunal ought to attempt to ascertain the reason for the absence. If none has been notified, the tribunal should consider whether to telephone the party or the representative in order to determine the reason for absence: *Cooke v Glenrose Fish Company* [2004] IRLR 866.

1.143   The parties may submit written representations for the tribunal to consider. This is dealt with in r 42 which reads as follows:

> 42 The Tribunal shall consider any written representations from a party, including a party who does not propose to attend the hearing, if they are delivered to the Tribunal and to all other parties not less than 7 days before the hearing.

1.144 The written representations which are referred to in this rule do not include written evidence (eg witness statements) or aids to an oral submission (eg a skeleton argument, a list of issues, or a chronology). As far as witness statements are concerned, the timetable laid down in advance will usually have given directions as to when these should have been presented to the other side, and when they should be received by the tribunal. As far as written aids to an oral submission are concerned, the practice of most tribunals is to accept them on the day of the hearing, since they do not fall within the scope of the written representations referred to in r 42.

1.145 When it comes to the hearing itself, the judge has wide discretion as to how it should be conducted, as is set out in r 41:

> 41 The Tribunal may regulate its own procedure and shall conduct the hearing in the manner it considers fair, having regard to the principles contained in the overriding objective. The following rules do not restrict that general power. The Tribunal shall seek to avoid undue formality and may itself question the parties or any witnesses so far as appropriate in order to clarify the issues or elicit the evidence. The Tribunal is not bound by any rule of law relating to the admissibility of evidence in proceedings before the courts.

1.146 The procedure adopted in the tribunal, therefore, is less formal than that which is to be found in the courts. For example, witnesses remain seated whilst giving evidence, and representatives are seated throughout. The tribunal is addressed through the employment judge (who is addressed as 'Sir' or 'Madam').

1.147 The normal rule is that the party bearing the burden of proof on the main issue in the case should go first. For example, in an unfair dismissal case where dismissal is admitted, the respondent will normally go first because the employer must prove the reason for dismissal. In a constructive dismissal case, however, or any other case where unfair dismissal is alleged but the fact of dismissal is disputed, it is for the claimant to go first. In a discrimination case, the claimant will usually go first. It is worth pointing out, however, that the tribunal retains a discretion over the order of proceedings.

1.148 Whichever party gives evidence first will normally have the right to the last word in closing submissions. Where that party is professionally represented, however, and their opponent is not, the tribunal will often ask the professional representative to make his or her closing submissions first.

1.149 The tribunal will not usually have had the opportunity to read the witness statements or the trial bundle before the beginning of the hearing, unless some reading time has been set aside. It will usually have read the claim and response, and may possibly have read the main witness statement for each side.

1. Tribunal Procedure

1.150 The tribunal hearing will almost always be in public. The circumstances in which a private hearing is possible are dealt with at 1.156.

1.151 At the start of the case, the employment judge will usually state his or her view of the issues in the case, and ask the representatives whether they agree. The judge may well impose a timetable for the hearing, setting out the time to be taken for hearing evidence and in particular cross-examination of each witness, and time for closing submissions. The Presidential Guidance on General Case Management issued in 2014 deals with timetabling, and the relevant extract is reproduced in Appendix 3. Representatives would be well advised to have thought about a time estimate for each of these matters so as to assist the judge in setting out a timetable. As far as the implementation of the timetable is concerned, it may be used as a guide, or a guillotine may be imposed when a representative goes beyond the allotted time. It has become increasingly common for judges to ensure the efficient conduct of the hearing by laying down such a timetable, and express power to do so is set out in r 45:

> 45 A Tribunal may impose limits on the time that a party may take in presenting evidence, questioning witnesses or making submissions, and may prevent the party from proceeding beyond any time so allotted.

1.152 The tribunal may split a case so as to deal with different portions at different stages. In particular, it is common to deal separately with liability and remedies. The case is usually listed to give sufficient time to deal with liability, hear the tribunal decision, and then proceed to consider remedy immediately. However, there may not be sufficient time to deal with remedy once the decision on liability has been delivered, and this will mean that a separate date will have to be allocated for that purpose. If the tribunal has not been able to deliver its decision on liability, and has reserved it, then it will usually fix a provisional date for the remedy hearing.

1.153 At the outset of the main hearing, the parties should make certain which issues are to be dealt with, where the hearing is split. For example, where liability is to be heard first, it is necessary to ascertain what matters come under the heading of liability. Does it include matters of contributory conduct and any deduction under *Polkey*? (See Chapter 10 on Unfair Dismissal.)

1.154 Opening speeches are discouraged, and it will be an exceptional case where a party is allowed to make one. The tribunal will wish to move to the evidence as soon as possible, subject to any necessary reading of witness statements and the documents to which they refer. The typical order of proceedings is set out in **Table 1.1**, in a case where A bears the burden of proof.

Table 1.1 Tribunal hearing: the typical order of proceedings

A's case	
First witness for A	1. Examination-in-chief
	2. Cross-examination
	3. Tribunal questions
	4. Re-examination
Second and any further witnesses for A	Repeat 1 to 4 in respect of each witness
B's case	
Each of B's witnesses	See 1 to 4
B's closing submissions	
A's closing submissions	
Tribunal considers its judgment	
Tribunal delivers its judgment or reserves it and sends to the parties	

1.155 Further detail as to the role played by witness statements is provided at 1.166 to 1.168. The role of the representative is dealt with in Chapter 4 on Advocacy: Presenting the Case, and the rules of evidence with particular relevance to the tribunal are dealt with in Chapter 5 on Evidence.

Privacy

1.156 The general rule is that the final hearing should be in public, other than in specified limited circumstances. Those circumstances are set out in r 50, which reads as follows

> 50 (1) A Tribunal may at any stage of the proceedings, on its own initiative or on application, make an order with a view to preventing or restricting the public disclosure of any aspect of those proceedings so far as it considers necessary in the interests of justice or in order to protect the Convention rights of any person or in the circumstances identified in section 10A of the Employment Tribunals Act.
> (2) In considering whether to make an order under this rule, the Tribunal shall give full weight to the principle of open justice and to the Convention right to freedom of expression.
> (3) Such orders may include—
> (a) an order that a hearing that would otherwise be in public be conducted, in whole or in part, in private;
> (b) an order that the identities of specified parties, witnesses or other persons referred to in the proceedings should not be disclosed to the public, by the use of anonymisation or otherwise, whether in the course of any hearing or in its listing or in any documents entered on the Register or otherwise forming part of the public record;

>   (c) an order for measures preventing witnesses at a public hearing being identifiable by members of the public;
>   (d) a restricted reporting order within the terms of section 11 or 12 of the Employment Tribunals Act.
>
> (4) Any party, or other person with a legitimate interest, who has not had a reasonable opportunity to make representations before an order under this rule is made may apply to the Tribunal in writing for the order to be revoked or discharged, either on the basis of written representations or, if requested, at a hearing.
>
> (5) Where an order is made under paragraph (3)(d) above—
>   (a) it shall specify the person whose identity is protected; and may specify particular matters of which publication is prohibited as likely to lead to that person's identification;
>   (b) it shall specify the duration of the order;
>   (c) the Tribunal shall ensure that a notice of the fact that such an order has been made in relation to those proceedings is displayed on the notice board of the Tribunal with any list of the proceedings taking place before the Tribunal, and on the door of the room in which the proceedings affected by the order are taking place; and
>   (d) the Tribunal may order that it applies also to any other proceedings being heard as part of the same hearing.
>
> (6) 'Convention rights' has the meaning given to it in section 1 of the Human Rights Act 1998.

1.157   Rule 50(1) makes reference to s 10A of the ETA 1996. The relevant portion of that section states:

> 10A (1) Employment tribunal procedure regulations may enable an employment tribunal to sit in private for the purpose of hearing evidence from any person which in the opinion of the tribunal is likely to consist of—
>   (a) information which he could not disclose without contravening a prohibition imposed by or by virtue of any enactment,
>   (b) information which has been communicated to him in confidence or which he has otherwise obtained in consequence of the confidence reposed in him by another person, or
>   (c) information the disclosure of which would, for reasons other than its effect on negotiations with respect to any of the matters mentioned in section 178(2) of the Trade Union and Labour Relations (Consolidation) Act 1992, cause substantial injury to any undertaking of his or in which he works.

1.158   It will be seen from r 50(2) that the tribunal must fully take into account the principle of open justice. This was emphasized by the Court of Appeal in *Storer v British Gas plc* [2000] IRLR 495, where it was stated that 'the obligation to sit in public was fundamental to the function of an employment tribunal' (Henry LJ).

1.159   As will be seen from r 50(3)(a) the tribunal may, after weighing up the various factors referred to in the remainder of the rule, order that the hearing should be conducted in private, either in whole or in part. An alternative is to make an order prohibiting the disclosure of witnesses, parties, or other persons: see r 50(5)(b) and (c).

1.160 As far as 50(3)(d) is concerned, the effect of a restricted reporting order is to prevent publication of material likely to identify the persons who are the subject of the order. The rule makes reference to ss 11 and 12 of the EAT 1996 which deal respectively with:

(a)   cases involving allegations of sexual offences or sexual misconduct;

(b)   cases in which evidence of a personal nature is likely to be heard by the tribunal—this means 'any evidence of a medical, or other intimate, nature which might reasonably be assumed to be likely to cause significant embarrassment to the complainant if reported'.

1.161 The effect of the restricted reporting order is not to prevent the case from being reported, or to suppress the allegations. It applies only until the promulgation of the decision of the tribunal. From the point of view of anyone who is wishing to avoid an allegation or evidence being publicised, the disadvantage of a restricted reporting order is that its terms will be placed outside the tribunal. The result is that the media will be alerted to the prospect of a case containing details which they might wish to report once it becomes legal to do so, ie after the judgment is promulgated.

1.162 The position as far as preliminary hearings are concerned is set out at 1.136.

1.163 Rule 50(4) makes it clear that anyone with a legitimate interest may apply for an order restricting disclosure to be revoked. Usually, this will be a representative of the media.

1.164 Sexual misconduct means, according to s 11(6) of the ETA 1996:

> ... the commission of a sexual offence, sexual harassment, or other adverse conduct (of whatever nature) related to sex, and conduct is related to sex whether the relationship with sex lies in the character of the conduct or in its having reference to the sex or sexual orientation of the person at whom the conduct is directed.

1.165 For further details on the case law relating to private hearings and restricted reporting orders, see **sections 9.154** to **9.213** of *Blackstone's Employment Law Practice 2014*.

Witnesses and witness statements

1.166 Witness statements should be exchanged in advance, in accordance with any directions which the tribunal has given on the

---

matter. Sufficient copies must be supplied on the day of the hearing for the tribunal, any other parties, and the witness table. In addition, one copy must be provided for public inspection. As stated in r 44:

> 44 Subject to rules 50 and 94, any witness statement which stands as evidence in chief shall be available for inspection during the course of the hearing by members of the public attending the hearing unless the Tribunal decides that all or any part of the statement is not to be admitted as evidence, in which case the statement or that part shall not be available for inspection.

1.167 At the hearing, it is standard practice for the evidence in chief of a witness to be given by witness statement. This has replaced the former procedure, in which witnesses usually read out their statement. The practice now is for the tribunal to read this statement to itself, in advance of the witness giving evidence, and this is made clear in r 43:

> 43 Where a witness is called to give oral evidence, any witness statement of that person ordered by the Tribunal shall stand as that witness's evidence in chief unless the Tribunal orders otherwise. Witnesses shall be required to give their oral evidence on oath or affirmation. The Tribunal may exclude from the hearing any person who is to appear as a witness in the proceedings until such time as that person gives evidence if it considers it in the interests of justice to do so.

1.168 What if a party intends to rely upon evidence from a witness, but the witness does not attend the hearing? The position is that a statement should be submitted on behalf of the witness, accompanied by an explanation for their absence. The tribunal will usually (subject to the representations of the parties) admit the evidence, subject to reduced weight. The weight of the evidence will obviously be less than it would have been if the witness had attended and been available for cross-examination. In formal terms, the evidence of such a witness is hearsay, but the tribunal is entitled to admit hearsay evidence, taking into account its reduced weight.

Bias

1.169 It is a central principle of the employment tribunal system that a party is entitled to a fair trial. Consequently, the tribunal must conform to the principles of natural justice, including the absence of bias and the right to a fair hearing. There is no specific rule which deals with questions of bias, but reference should be made to **chapter 10** of *Blackstone's Employment Law Practice 2014*, which contains a detailed analysis and a number of examples.

1.170 The main principles can be summarized as follows:

(1) Bias can be divided into two categories: actual bias and apparent bias. Cases of actual bias on the part of the judge are rare, and difficult to prove.

(2) Where a judge is a party to proceedings, or has a financial or proprietary interest, other than one which is merely trivial ('*de minimis*'), apparent bias will be presumed and disqualification should be automatic.

(3) The circumstances, conduct, or behaviour of a judge or member may give rise to a suspicion that he or she is not impartial. This may constitute apparent bias but there is no presumption. The test is whether the relevant circumstances would lead a fair-minded and informed observer to conclude that there was a real possibility that the tribunal was biased: *Porter v Magill* [2002] 2 AC 354.

(4) The fair-minded and informed observer is a person who has knowledge of the litigation process, and of the particular case.

(5) It is proper for the judge to assist an unrepresented party to ensure that he or she brings out their case. On the other hand, the judge must act in such a way as to avoid the appearance of bias in doing so.

(6) The tribunal should refrain from the expression of a premature opinion which indicates a closed mind. The expression of a provisional view, subject to evidence and/or representations is, however, acceptable.

(7) There is nothing wrong with the tribunal encouraging the parties to settle. In order to do so, it may express a provisional view to assist the parties: *Jiminez v London Borough of Southwark* [2003] IRLR 477.

(8) The tribunal must be careful when considering matters which were not raised by the parties. It does not have jurisdiction to determine a complaint which has not been raised in the claim form. Further, even where a claim is within the tribunal's jurisdiction, notice must be given to the parties of material matters upon which the tribunal aims to rely if they did not have the opportunity to address them.

(9) If the tribunal is minded to take into account, after the hearing has finished, a new point which the parties have not addressed, it should recall them and give them the chance to make representations on the point. If the point is sufficiently fundamental, they may have to be given the opportunity to provide additional evidence.

(10) Where a tribunal feels that a legal authority is relevant and material to its decision, but the parties appear to have overlooked it, it should refer the authority to the parties and invite

their submissions before it makes its decision: *Albion Hotel (Freshwater) Ltd v Maia e Silva* [2002] IRLR 200 (EAT).

(11) Judges and members of the tribunal must raise any matter which may disqualify them from hearing a particular case where it gives rise to a real (rather than a fanciful) danger of bias. Any party then has the opportunity to ask for the judge or member concerned to be recused, ie to be disqualified from hearing the case.

(12) A party can then waive the right to call for the judge or member to be disqualified, provided that the waiver is clear and given with knowledge of all the relevant facts.

(13) If the parties do ask for the judge or member to be recused (so as not to hear the case), the tribunal must consider whether there is apparent bias on the test previously set out.

1.171 The tribunal should not accede too readily to a request for a rehearing before a differently constituted tribunal. It may well cause the parties additional costs, and there is a risk that the party objecting may try to eliminate a judge whom it does not want to hear its case, thus bringing about a process of 'forum shopping'. This is a particular danger where an application for recusal is made during the course of the hearing.

Withdrawal and dismissal

1.172 In about 30 per cent of all cases which are disposed of by the employment tribunals, the claimant withdraws the case. Prior to the introduction of the rules in 2013, this did not lead automatically to the dismissal of the claim. As a result, it would then have been open to the claimant (subject to questions of jurisdiction and time limits) to revive the case, either in the employment tribunal or the courts. The respondent could seek to have the case dismissed so that it could not be revived, but this process took up time. The position under the 2013 Rules is that in most circumstances, the claim will be considered dismissed once it has been withdrawn, without any action being taken by the respondent. The position is governed by rr 51 and 52:

51. Where a claimant informs the Tribunal, either in writing or in the course of a hearing, that a claim, or part of it, is withdrawn, the claim, or part, comes to an end, subject to any application that the respondent may make for a costs, preparation time or wasted costs order.

52. Where a claim, or part of it, has been withdrawn under rule 51, the Tribunal shall issue a judgment dismissing it (which means that the claimant may not commence a further claim against the respondent raising the same, or substantially the same, complaint) unless—

(a) the claimant has expressed at the time of withdrawal a wish to reserve the right to bring such a further claim and the Tribunal is satisfied that there would be legitimate reason for doing so; or

(b) the Tribunal believes that to issue such a judgment would not be in the interests of justice.

Decisions and judgments

1.173 The difference between a judgment and a decision is set out in r 1(3). As will be seen from that rule, a judgment is a particular type of decision which finally determines a claim (or part of one), or an issue capable of finally disposing a claim (or part of one). Case management orders constitute another species of decision, and are dealt with at 1.76:

> 1 (3) An order or other decision of the Tribunal is either—
>   (a) a 'case management order', being an order or decision of any kind in relation to the conduct of proceedings, not including the determination of any issue which would be the subject of a judgment; or
>   (b) a 'judgment', being a decision, made at any stage of the proceedings (but not including a decision under rule 13 or 19), which finally determines—
>   (i) a claim, or part of a claim, as regards liability, remedy or costs (including preparation time and wasted costs); or
>   (ii) any issue which is capable of finally disposing of any claim, or part of a claim, even if it does not necessarily do so (for example, an issue whether a claim should be struck out or a jurisdictional issue).

1.174 As far as the judgment is concerned, the tribunal will consider this at the end of the hearing. It may have a short adjournment in order to consider the matter, and then call the parties back in in order to deliver the judgment. Alternatively, where the matter is more complex or time does not allow for a decision to be made on the day, the tribunal will reserve its judgment, which will then be sent in writing to the parties.

1.175 In the case of a reserved judgment, it will include written reasons. Where the judgment is announced to the parties at the end of the hearing, however, written reasons will only be provided if they are requested at the hearing itself, or in writing within 14 days of the judgment being sent to the parties. According to the rules, the tribunal should inform the parties that they will only receive written reasons in such a case if they request them within the time limit.

1.176 These matters are dealt with in rr 60, 61, and 62:

> 60 Decisions made without a hearing shall be communicated in writing to the parties, identifying the Employment Judge who has made the decision.
> 61 (1) Where there is a hearing the Tribunal may either announce its decision in relation to any issue at the hearing or reserve it to be sent to the parties as soon as practicable in writing.
>   (2) If the decision is announced at the hearing, a written record (in the form of a judgment if appropriate) shall be provided to the parties (and, where the proceedings were referred to the Tribunal by a court, to that court) as soon as practicable. (Decisions concerned only with

the conduct of a hearing need not be identified in the record of that hearing unless a party requests that a specific decision is so recorded.)

(3) The written record shall be signed by the Employment Judge.

62 (1) The Tribunal shall give reasons for its decision on any disputed issue, whether substantive or procedural (including any decision on an application for reconsideration or for orders for costs, preparation time or wasted costs).

(2) In the case of a decision given in writing the reasons shall also be given in writing. In the case of a decision announced at a hearing the reasons may be given orally at the hearing or reserved to be given in writing later (which may, but need not, be as part of the written record of the decision). Written reasons shall be signed by the Employment Judge.

(3) Where reasons have been given orally, the Employment Judge shall announce that written reasons will not be provided unless they are asked for by any party at the hearing itself or by a written request presented by any party within 14 days of the sending of the written record of the decision. The written record of the decision shall repeat that information. If no such request is received, the Tribunal shall provide written reasons only if requested to do so by the Employment Appeal Tribunal or a court.

(4) The reasons given for any decision shall be proportionate to the significance of the issue and for decisions other than judgments may be very short.

(5) In the case of a judgment the reasons shall: identify the issues which the Tribunal has determined, state the findings of fact made in relation to those issues, concisely identify the relevant law, and state how that law has been applied to those findings in order to decide the issues. Where the judgment includes a financial award the reasons shall identify, by means of a table or otherwise, how the amount to be paid has been calculated.

1.177 Rule 62(5) is important in that it sets out the matters which must be contained within a judgment. In summary these are:

(a) the issues;
(b) the relevant findings of fact;
(c) the relevant law;
(d) the application of the law to the facts as found; and
(e) the calculations for any financial award.

Costs and preparation time orders

1.178 In the courts, costs follow the event. This means that the party who wins will normally recover their costs from the party who loses. The position in the employment tribunals is quite different. A series of rules lays down the circumstances in which costs may be awarded, and generally the tribunal has a discretion as to whether to award costs, and the amount to award. Costs are dealt with in the Presidential Guidance on General Case Management issued in 2014, and the relevant extract is reproduced as part of Appendix 3.

1.179   Rule 74 defines 'costs', 'legally represented', and 'lay represen-tative':

> 74 (1) 'Costs' means fees, charges, disbursements or expenses incurred by or on behalf of the receiving party (including expenses that witnesses incur for the purpose of, or in connection with, attendance at a Tribunal hearing). In Scotland all references to costs (except when used in the expression 'wasted costs') shall be read as references to expenses.
>
> (2) 'Legally represented' means having the assistance of a person (including where that person is the receiving party's employee) who—
>   (a) has a right of audience in relation to any class of proceedings in any part of the Senior Courts of England and Wales, or all proceedings in county courts or magistrates' courts;
>   (b) is an advocate or solicitor in Scotland; or
>   (c) is a member of the Bar of Northern Ireland or a solicitor of the Court of Judicature of Northern Ireland.
>
> (3) 'Represented by a lay representative' means having the assistance of a person who does not satisfy any of the criteria in paragraph (2) and who charges for representation in the proceedings.

1.180   Rule 75 sets out the effect of a costs order and a preparation time order, and makes clear the distinction between the two. In brief, a costs order deals with payment to a lawyer or a lay representative, reimbursement of a tribunal fee, and/or the payment of witness expenses. Preparation time order is the term to describe payment for time spent in preparation of the case by a party and advisers (other than any time spent at the final hearing):

> 75 (1) A costs order is an order that a party ('the paying party') make a payment to—
>   (a) another party ('the receiving party') in respect of the costs that the receiving party has incurred while legally represented or while represented by a lay representative;
>   (b) the receiving party in respect of a Tribunal fee paid by the receiving party; or
>   (c) another party or a witness in respect of expenses incurred, or to be incurred, for the purpose of, or in connection with, an individual's attendance as a witness at the Tribunal.
>
> (2) A preparation time order is an order that a party ('the paying party') make a payment to another party ('the receiving party') in respect of the receiving party's preparation time while not legally represented. 'Preparation time' means time spent by the receiving party (including by any employees or advisers) in working on the case, except for time spent at any final hearing.
>
> (3) A costs order under paragraph (1)(a) and a preparation time order may not both be made in favour of the same party in the same proceedings. A Tribunal may, if it wishes, decide in the course of the proceedings that a party is entitled to one order or the other but defer until a later stage in the proceedings deciding which kind of order to make.

1. Tribunal Procedure

1.181 Rule 76 sets out the different circumstances which trigger the power of the tribunal to make a costs order or a preparation time order. In virtually all cases, such a triggering event will give the tribunal a discretion. The only case where the tribunal is obliged to order a party to pay costs is where the respondent has been put on notice that the claimant seeks reinstatement or re-engagement, but the respondent fails unreasonably to adduce the evidence of job availability.

1.182 As far as the discretionary powers given to the tribunal to make an award of costs or a preparation time order are concerned, the matters to be take into account may be summarized as follows:

(1) vexatious, abusive, disruptive, or otherwise unreasonable actions by a party or their representative in bringing or conducting proceedings;

(2) the claim or response had no reasonable prospect of success;

(3) a party has been in breach of an order or practice direction;

(4) a hearing has been postponed or adjourned on the application of a party;

(5) a party has paid a tribunal fee in respect of a claim, counterclaim, or application which has been decided in their favour; or

(6) in respect of witness expenses.

1.183 Rule 76 reads as follows:

> 76 (1) A Tribunal may make a costs order or a preparation time order, and shall consider whether to do so, where it considers that—
>
> > (a) a party (or that party's representative) has acted vexatiously, abusively, disruptively or otherwise unreasonably in either the bringing of the proceedings (or part) or the way that the proceedings (or part) have been conducted; or
> >
> > (b) any claim or response had no reasonable prospect of success.
>
> (2) A Tribunal may also make such an order where a party has been in breach of any order or practice direction or where a hearing has been postponed or adjourned on the application of a party.
>
> (3) Where in proceedings for unfair dismissal a final hearing is postponed or adjourned, the Tribunal shall order the respondent to pay the costs incurred as a result of the postponement or adjournment if—
>
> > (a) the claimant has expressed a wish to be reinstated or re-engaged which has been communicated to the respondent not less than 7 days before the hearing; and
> >
> > (b) the postponement or adjournment of that hearing has been caused by the respondent's failure, without a special reason, to adduce reasonable evidence as to the availability of the job from which the claimant was dismissed or of comparable or suitable employment.
>
> (4) A Tribunal may make a costs order of the kind described in rule 75(1)(b) where a party has paid a Tribunal fee in respect of a claim, employer's contract claim or application and that claim, counterclaim or application is decided in whole, or in part, in favour of that party.

(5) A Tribunal may make a costs order of the kind described in rule 75(1)(c) on the application of a party or the witness in question, or on its own initiative, where a witness has attended or has been ordered to attend to give oral evidence at a hearing.

1.184 The procedure for an application for costs or preparation time order is set out in r 77:

77 A party may apply for a costs order or a preparation time order at any stage up to 28 days after the date on which the judgment finally determining the proceedings in respect of that party was sent to the parties. No such order may be made unless the paying party has had a reasonable opportunity to make representations (in writing or at a hearing, as the Tribunal may order) in response to the application.

1.185 The maximum amount of the costs order is set out in r 78:

78 (1) A costs order may—
    (a) order the paying party to pay the receiving party a specified amount, not exceeding £20,000, in respect of the costs of the receiving party;
    (b) order the paying party to pay the receiving party the whole or a specified part of the costs of the receiving party, with the amount to be paid being determined, in England and Wales, by way of detailed assessment carried out either by a county court in accordance with the Civil Procedure Rules 1998, or by an Employment Judge applying the same principles; or, in Scotland, by way of taxation carried out either by the auditor of court in accordance with the Act of Sederunt (Fees of Solicitors in the Sheriff Court) (Amendment and Further Provisions) 1993, or by an Employment Judge applying the same principles;
    (c) order the paying party to pay the receiving party a specified amount as reimbursement of all or part of a Tribunal fee paid by the receiving party;
    (d) order the paying party to pay another party or a witness, as appropriate, a specified amount in respect of necessary and reasonably incurred expenses (of the kind described in rule 75(1)(c)); or
    (e) if the paying party and the receiving party agree as to the amount payable, be made in that amount.
(2) Where the costs order includes an amount in respect of fees charged by a lay representative, for the purposes of the calculation of the order, the hourly rate applicable for the fees of the lay representative shall be no higher than the rate under rule 79(2).
(3) For the avoidance of doubt, the amount of a costs order under sub-paragraphs (b) to (e) of paragraph (1) may exceed £20,000.

1.186 To summarize, the limit is set at £20,000, except where a detailed assessment is carried out or the parties agree on an amount payable. Repayment of a tribunal fee or witness expenses are excluded from this limit. In calculating a costs order for fees charged by a lay representative, the hourly rate is limited to that for a preparation time order (see 1.187).

1. Tribunal Procedure

1.187   A preparation time order may be claimed in respect of time spent by the receiving party, including any employees or advisers, in working on the case, with the exception of any time actually spent as the final hearing. The hourly rate is limited to £34 from 6 April 2014, rising by £1 each year. These orders are dealt with in r 79:

> 79 (1) The Tribunal shall decide the number of hours in respect of which a preparation time order should be made, on the basis of—
>   (a) information provided by the receiving party on time spent falling within rule 75(2) above; and
>   (b) the Tribunal's own assessment of what it considers to be a reasonable and proportionate amount of time to spend on such preparatory work, with reference to such matters as the complexity of the proceedings, the number of witnesses and documentation required.
> (2) The hourly rate is £33 and increases on 6 April each year by £1.
> (3) The amount of a preparation time order shall be the product of the number of hours assessed under paragraph (1) and the rate under paragraph (2).

1.188   The tribunal may also make a wasted costs order against a representative (as compared with an order against a party). The tribunal is given power to order a representative to pay the wasted costs of any party, including the party whom he or she represents. The definition of 'wasted costs' is set out in r 80(1). A definition of 'representatives' is set out in r 80(2), so as to include both lawyers and lay representatives, but it excludes representatives who do not act for profit. The effect of a wasted costs order is set out in r 81, and the procedure to be adopted is in r 82. The relevant rules read as follows:

> 80 (1) A Tribunal may make a wasted costs order against a representative in favour of any party ('the receiving party') where that party has incurred costs—
>   (a) as a result of any improper, unreasonable or negligent act or omission on the part of the representative; or
>   (b) which, in the light of any such act or omission occurring after they were incurred, the Tribunal considers it unreasonable to expect the receiving party to pay.
>   Costs so incurred are described as 'wasted costs'.
> (2) 'Representative' means a party's legal or other representative or any employee of such representative, but it does not include a representative who is not acting in pursuit of profit with regard to the proceedings. A person acting on a contingency or conditional fee arrangement is considered to be acting in pursuit of profit.
> (3) A wasted costs order may be made in favour of a party whether or not that party is legally represented and may also be made in favour of a representative's own client. A wasted costs order may not be made against a representative where that representative is representing a party in his or her capacity as an employee of that party.

81 A wasted costs order may order the representative to pay the whole or part of any wasted costs of the receiving party, or disallow any wasted costs otherwise payable to the representative, including an order that the representative repay to its client any costs which have already been paid. The amount to be paid, disallowed or repaid must in each case be specified in the order.

82 A wasted costs order may be made by the Tribunal on its own initiative or on the application of any party. A party may apply for a wasted costs order at any stage up to 28 days after the date on which the judgment finally determining the proceedings as against that party was sent to the parties. No such order shall be made unless the representative has had a reasonable opportunity to make representations (in writing or at a hearing, as the Tribunal may order) in response to the application or proposal. The Tribunal shall inform the representative's client in writing of any proceedings under this rule and of any order made against the representative.

Time for compliance

1.189 Once the judgment has been issued, it should be complied with within 14 days of the date of the judgment, unless a different date is specified or the case has been stayed. Rule 66 states:

66 A party shall comply with a judgment or order for the payment of an amount of money within 14 days of the date of the judgment or order, unless—
  (a) the judgment, order, or any of these Rules, specifies a different date for compliance; or
  (b) the Tribunal has stayed (or in Scotland sisted) the proceedings or judgment.

Certificate of correction (the 'slip rule')

1.190 On occasion, a judgment or order will contain an accidental slip or a clerical mistake. If the mistake is not one which is substantial, then the provision contained in r 69 provides a relatively simple way to correct the matter:

69 An Employment Judge may at any time correct any clerical mistake or other accidental slip or omission in any order, judgment or other document produced by a Tribunal. If such a correction is made, any published version of the document shall also be corrected. If any document is corrected under this rule, a copy of the corrected version, signed by the Judge, shall be sent to all the parties.

Reconsideration (or review)

1.191 A party is entitled to ask the tribunal to reconsider a judgment, and the tribunal itself may choose to do so. The process was formerly known as 'review', but under the 2013 rules it is entitled 'reconsideration'. The principles involved are contained in r 70:

70 A Tribunal may, either on its own initiative (which may reflect a request from the Employment Appeal Tribunal) or on the application of a party,

> reconsider any judgment where it is necessary in the interests of justice
> to do so. On reconsideration, the decision ('the original decision') may be
> confirmed, varied or revoked. If it is revoked it may be taken again.

1.192   There is a 14-day deadline, within which an application for
reconsideration must be presented. Time begins to run on the date
when the written record of the decision was sent to the parties, unless
written reasons were sent later, in which case it begins to run on that
date. The application must contain reasons for the Tribunal to reconsider. Rule 71 lays down the procedure for making an application:

> 71   Except where it is made in the course of a hearing, an application for
> reconsideration shall be presented in writing (and copied to all the other
> parties) within 14 days of the date on which the written record, or other
> written communication, of the original decision was sent to the parties
> or within 14 days of the date that the written reasons were sent (if later)
> and shall set out why reconsideration of the original decision is necessary.

1.193   Any application will then be put before an employment
judge (where practicable this should be the employment judge who
made, or chaired the tribunal which made, the original decision). He
or she must consider whether there is a reasonable prospect of the original decision being changed. If there is not, the application is refused.
If the application has a reasonable prospect of success, a notice will be
sent to the parties asking for their views on the application itself, and
whether it can be determined without a hearing.

1.194   In such a case, where the employment judge has considered
that there is a reasonable prospect of success, there will be a hearing to
reconsider the original decision, or (if a hearing is not necessary) the
parties will be invited to make further written representations. The
process is described in r 72:

> 72 (1)   An Employment Judge shall consider any application made under rule
> 71. If the Judge considers that there is no reasonable prospect of the
> original decision being varied or revoked (including, unless there are
> special reasons, where substantially the same application has already
> been made and refused), the application shall be refused and the
> Tribunal shall inform the parties of the refusal. Otherwise the Tribunal
> shall send a notice to the parties setting a time limit for any response to
> the application by the other parties and seeking the views of the parties
> on whether the application can be determined without a hearing. The
> notice may set out the Judge's provisional views on the application.
>
> (2)   If the application has not been refused under paragraph (1), the original
> decision shall be reconsidered at a hearing unless the Employment Judge
> considers, having regard to any response to the notice provided under
> paragraph (1), that a hearing is not necessary in the interests of justice. If

> the reconsideration proceeds without a hearing the parties shall be given
> a reasonable opportunity to make further written representations.
> (3) Where practicable, the consideration under paragraph (1) shall be by
> the Employment Judge who made the original decision or, as the case
> may be, chaired the full tribunal which made it; and any reconsideration
> under paragraph (2) shall be made by the Judge or, as the case may
> be, the full tribunal which made the original decision. Where that is
> not practicable, the President, Vice President or a Regional Employment
> Judge shall appoint another Employment Judge to deal with the appli-
> cation or, in the case of a decision of a full tribunal, shall either direct
> that the reconsideration be by such members of the original Tribunal as
> remain available or reconstitute the Tribunal in whole or in part.

Appeals

1.195 A party can appeal to the Employment Appeal Tribunal (EAT). Unlike the process of reconsideration dealt with in the preceding section, an appeal will be heard not by the original decision maker, but by an independent body of status superior to the original tribunal. However, the appeal must be upon a point of law. This includes the wrong application of a principle of law, a misunderstanding of a statute, reaching a decision which no reasonable tribunal could have reached, or making a decision which was perverse because there was no evidence whatsoever to support it.

1.196 The procedure adopted by the EAT is dealt with in summary in Chapter 8 and in more detail in **chapter 18** of *Blackstone's Employment Law Practice 2014*.

1.197 There is a strict time limit for the lodging of an appeal. In the case of the judgment, the appeal must be instituted within 42 days of the date on which the written record of the judgment was sent to the parties, unless written reasons were requested, in which case the time limit is 42 days from the date when written reasons were sent to the parties. The appeal must be sent on the prescribed form, and attach certain specified documents.

1.198 The EAT has power to:

(a) dismiss the appeal;

(b) allow the appeal, substituting its own judgment for that of the employment tribunal;

(c) allow the appeal, and remit the case for rehearing, either in whole or in part, by the same employment tribunal or a different one.

1.199 In the great majority of cases the EAT will consist of a judge sitting alone. Exceptionally, its composition will mirror that of a full employment tribunal with the judge and two wing members, one with employee representative experience and the other with employer experience.

Scotland

1.200 Generally speaking, tribunal procedure in Scotland is similar to that in England and Wales. There are certain significant differences in law and practice, which are examined in **chapter 19** of *Blackstone's Employment Law Practice 2014*. For example:

(a) the common law of Scotland is not identical to that of England and Wales, so that the law of contract and delict (tort) display differences north and south of the border.

(b) Although the rules for Scotland provide for witness statements, they are still very much the exception. Unless the tribunal has given a specific order to the contrary, witness statements are neither expected nor acceptable. This means that the representative will have to ask a series of questions in order to elicit the evidence-in-chief of a witness.

(c) During the hearing, witnesses are kept out of the tribunal until they have given evidence ('sequestrated' in Scottish terminology), unless there is a special reason for their presence, eg to give instructions to the representative. This is the reverse of the position in England and Wales, where it is exceptional to exclude witnesses in this way.

(d) Closing speeches will usually follow the order in which evidence was led. This is in contrast to the position in England and Wales, where the party giving evidence first, delivers their closing speech last.

(e) The Scottish rule with regard to 'without prejudice' documents is different from that in England and Wales, and has a narrower ambit. A statement which is identified as a clear statement of fact does not attract privilege, and may be admissible in evidence, even if it was made in the course of negotiations between the parties.

2 Fees

Introduction

2.01   Fees are now payable for claims made to the employment tribunal. In some cases, the fee is reduced or removed for people who are receiving certain benefits, or whose income and capital are below a certain level. Where the fee is reduced or removed in this way, it is called 'remission', and is dealt with at 2.19 to 2.30.

2.02   If a claimant does not qualify for remission, he or she will have to pay a fee on making the claim (the issue fee). A further fee will be payable at a later stage if a hearing is necessary (the hearing fee).

2.03   The amount which the claimant has to pay will depend upon the type of claim made, and whether it is an issue fee or a hearing fee. As to the type of claim, Type A claims are, generally speaking, those which it is more straightforward for the tribunal to deal with, and the fees are therefore lower. Type B claims involve more complex matters, and the fee paid is higher. The classification of the most common types of claims is set out in **Table 2.1**.

2.04   Where a claimant is presenting more than one type of claim within a single claim form, he or she will only have to pay one fee— either Type A or Type B. The fee payable will be for the higher level of claim made, eg if the claimant is claiming unfair dismissal and an unauthorized deduction from wages, the Type B fee will be payable. The amounts payable for the issue fee and the hearing fee are set out in **Table 2.2**.

The issue fee

2.05   The issue fee is payable when the claim form is submitted online, or when it is posted to the tribunal. As stated earlier, some claimants will be able to benefit from remission of fees. In such a case, the remission application must be submitted at the same time as the claim. The details of applying for remission are set out at 2.19.

2.06   If the claim is submitted online, the issue fee must be paid by debit card or credit card. If it is sent by post, it must be paid by cheque or postal order. Where the claim is made online, it is via the following website: <http://www.employmenttribunals.service.gov.uk>.

2.07   The online system will state the correct amount to pay.

2. Fees

Table 2.1 Types of claim

Type	Claim
TYPE A	Redundancy pay
	Unauthorized deductions from wages
	Breach of contract
	Failure to provide written reasons for dismissal
	Failure to inform and consult over TUPE transfer
	Holiday pay
TYPE B	Discrimination and Equal Pay
	Part Time Workers Regulations
	Unfair dismissal
	Failure to inform and consult over redundancy

Table 2.2 Types of fee

Type of fee	Issue fee	Hearing fee
TYPE A	£160	£230
TYPE B	£250	£950

2.08 In the event that the claim is submitted by post, it should be sent to:

```
Employment Tribunals Central Office
PO Box 10218
Leicester
LE1 8EG
```

2.09 If the claim is made in Scotland, the address is:

```
Employment Tribunals Central Office Scotland
PO Box 27105
Glasgow
G2 9JR
```

2.10 The accompanying cheque should be payable to HM Courts and Tribunals Service.

2.11 Where the claim is sent by post, but the correct payment is not included, the claim will be rejected, and the form returned. In this event, any time limits still apply, and time continues to run. The claimant should therefore return the form immediately with the payment due, in order to reduce the risk that the claim will be out of time.

The hearing fee

2.12   When the tribunal fixes the date for hearing, it will notify the parties, and tell the claimant in a 'notice to pay' of the hearing fee which must be paid. The amount of the hearing fee depends upon the type of claim (see **Tables 2.1** and **2.2**). If the fee is not paid when it is due, a deadline will be set and failure to meet the deadline will mean that the claim is struck out (dismissed)—see Chapter 1 on Tribunal Procedure. If the claimant is entitled to remission, then the hearing fee may be reduced or removed (see 2.19 to 2.30). It is possible also that the claimant might be entitled to remission with respect to the hearing fee, even if they were not so entitled at the time when the issue fee was payable, and vice versa.

2.13   Details of how to pay will be included with the notice of hearing, and once again this can be done either online with a debit or credit card, or by post with a cheque or postal order.

Multiple fees

2.14   Where a number of claimants issue a claim together, the issue and hearing fees are on a sliding scale. In sum, the fees are greater than they would be for an individual claimant, but the total is less than it would be if each claim was presented separately. The sliding scale can be found in the leaflet T436 'Employment tribunal fees for groups'—to be found at <https://www.gov.uk/government/publications/employment-tribunal-fees>.

Other fees

2.15   There are other fees payable for applications to reconsider or appeal, to be paid by whichever party applies for the reconsideration or lodges the appeal. In addition, there are certain fees which will be payable by the employer.

2.16   These extra fees are set out in **Table 2.3**.

Reimbursement

2.17   The tribunal has the power to order either party to pay the fees of a successful party. If the claimant wins, he or she can apply to the tribunal to order that the respondent repays any fees paid. Similarly, if the respondent has paid any fees, they can apply to the tribunal for reimbursement by the claimant. In either event, the

2. Fees

Table 2.3 **Additional fees**

Employer's contract claim	£160
Application to set aside a default judgment	£100
Application to dismiss	£60
Application to reconsider a judgment after final hearing of Type A claim	£100
Application to reconsider a judgment after final hearing of Type B claim	£350
Fee for judicial mediation	£600
Issue fee for an appeal	£400
Hearing fee for an appeal	£1200

tribunal has discretion to order reimbursement fees from the unsuccessful to the successful party. It will normally exercise this discretion in favour of the successful party. In other words, if the claimant wins, the tribunal will normally order the respondent to pay the fee to the claimant.

2.18   Where the parties have reached a settlement, the tribunal does not play a part, and as a result there will not be an order for the payment of fees. It follows that, where the parties are negotiating a settlement, they should make sure that they discuss any fees paid as part of the agreement reached.

Remission

2.19   A claimant can apply to be exempt from paying all or part of a tribunal fee. This process is entitled remission. As far as the issue fee is concerned, any application for remission must accompany the claim if it is made by post. If the claim is made online, the claimant must tick the box on the form saying that he or she wishes to apply for remission, and then post the remission application, together with supporting evidence, to the Central Office either at the address given at 2.08 or that given at 2.09, as appropriate. As far as the hearing fee is concerned, the tribunal will have sent a date by which the fee must be paid or a remission application sent, and again the application and evidence must be submitted by that date.

2.20   Eligibility for remission is assessed on household disposable capital and household gross monthly income. If the claimant has a partner, their capital and income are taken into account. A partner is someone with whom the claimant lives, regardless of whether they are married or in a civil partnership. Their income and capital will be included in the assessment for eligibility even if they are in prison, in hospital, or working abroad. It will not be included if they are living separately.

2.21 In order to qualify for remission, the claimant must meet the disposable household capital test. There is a sliding scale setting out the amount of disposable capital which the claimant is allowed to have. The amount in question depends upon the size of the fee which the claimant is applying to have remitted.

2.22 In practice, any tribunal fee is unlikely to exceed £1000, and the applicable household capital threshold for a fee of that size is £3000. In other words, if the claimant has capital of £3000 or more, they will not be eligible for remission, regardless of household income or entitlement to benefits.

2.23 If the claimant (or their partner) is aged 61 or over, however, they will pass the disposable capital test if they have capital of less than £16,000, whatever the amount of the fee for the claim.

2.24 Detail as to the list of what constitutes disposable capital, and what is excluded from the definition can be found in paras 5 and 10 of the Schedule to the Courts and Tribunals Fee Remission Order 2013, SI 2013/2302.

2.25 Provided that the claimant passes the capital test, the next stage is to consider their gross monthly income. The gross monthly income test will be passed if:

(1) the claimant is in receipt of income-based Employment and Support Allowance, Income Support, income-based Job Seeker's Allowance, State Pension Guarantee Credit, or Universal Credit with gross annual earnings of less than £6000; or

(2) the claimant's income, together with that of their partner, is below the threshold shown in **Table 2.4**, bearing in mind that the relevant figures vary according to the number of children in the household.

2.26 If the household gross monthly income exceeds the threshold in question, the claimant will not be entitled to full remission, but may still be eligible for partial remission. For every £10 of their income that exceeds the applicable household gross monthly income threshold, they must pay £5 towards their tribunal fee, up to the full amount of the fee.

Table 2.4 **Income thresholds**

Number of children	Single	Couple
None	£1085	£1245
1	£1330	£1490
2	£1575	£1735

The thresholds set out in the table increase by £245 for each additional child.

2. Fees

2.27 Detailed evidence has to be included with the remission application, and guidance as to the necessary evidence is to be found at <http://www.justice.gov.uk/downloads/forms/hmcts-fees/ex160aeng.pdf>.

2.28 In the event of an unsuccessful application for remission, there is an appeal system. In addition, if a fee was paid at the required time, it is possible to obtain a refund if the claimant can later show that they would have been entitled to full or partial remission if they had provided the necessary evidence. An application for such a refund must be presented within three months of the date on which the fee was paid.

2.29 For more information on fees, see the HMCTS information sheet T435 'Employment tribunal fees for individuals' to be found at <https://www.gov.uk/government/publications/employment-tribunal-fees>.

2.30 For more information on fee remission, see the HMCTS form and guidance EX160 and EX160A 'Court and Tribunal fees—do I have to pay them?', at <http://www.justice.gov.uk/downloads/forms/hmcts-fees/ex160aeng.pdf>.

3 **Settlement Agreements**

Introduction

3.01 Most of the claims submitted to the tribunal settle. For both the claimant and the respondent, it is sensible to consider from time to time whether a settlement is a better outcome than a trial. The crucial question for each party is: am I more likely to achieve my aims by settling, or by going to trial? The law relating to settlements is dealt with in some detail in **chapter 5** of *Blackstone's Employment Law Practice 2014*.

3.02 In considering the question of whether to settle, each party needs to have in mind what its aims are. From the point of view of the claimant, such aims might include:

(1) reinstatement in his or her old job;
(2) re-engagement in an equivalent job with the same employer;
(3) a declaration that his or her dismissal was unfair or their treatment was unlawful in some other way;
(4) monetary compensation.

3.03 Any of those aims are within the power of the tribunal, provided of course that the claimant wins. But it is worth considering other aims which the claimant might have, eg:

(5) an apology;
(6) a helpful reference;
(7) a commitment to deal with the person who has discriminated against him or her by means of disciplinary action;
(8) a commitment to transfer him or her to another location or department;
(9) avoiding unfavourable publicity which might prejudice prospects of future employment.

3.04 As far as this latter set of objectives is concerned, the tribunal has no power to make the necessary order, although in respect of some of them an appropriate recommendation could be made in a discrimination case.

3.05 Turning now to the position of the employer, its objectives might, for example, include the following:

(a) keeping any compensation to the claimant to a minimum;
(b) ensuring that legal costs are as low as possible;

3. Settlement Agreements

(c) avoiding any indication, whether by admission or by judgment, that the company acted unlawfully;

(d) ensuring that there is as little disruption at the workplace as possible, eg due to the need for management to deal with the case, and other employees to give evidence;

(e) avoiding any unfavourable publicity for the company.

3.06 When these aims are considered, it can be seen that some of them will be better met by a settlement, whilst others might be more successfully dealt with at a trial.

3.07 Generally, in practice, for each of the parties, the factor which weighs most heavily in favour of a trial is likely to be a belief that the financial outcome will be better if that route is taken. There are other less tangible factors, however, which may drive one or other or both of the parties towards a hearing. From the point of view of the claimant, he or she may have a strong desire to have their 'day in court'. Looked at from the perspective of the employer, there may be a suspicion that word of the settlement will get out, and encourage other employees to bring claims. There is also sometimes an unwillingness on the part of the employer to look as if they are not prepared to back the manager who is in the firing line.

3.08 As far as the financial outcome is concerned, it is possible to perform a calculation which will inevitably be speculative, but which does provide some sort of guide as to the figure at which a settlement would be desirable. Each side can come to a broad figure as to what compensation is likely to be in the event that the claimant is successful. Assume for the moment that that figure is £12,000. The other crucial factor in the calculation is the prospect which the claimant has of winning. Assume that this is estimated at 50 per cent. Leaving aside the intangible matters which each party will have in mind in accordance with the previous lists, the rational outcome in purely financial terms would be a settlement at £6,000. Other matters such as tribunal fees, legal costs, and the impact of recoupment must also be taken into account.

3.09 The problem for both parties, apart from the uncertainties involved in this calculation, is that they will often be involved in a twin track process. The case must be prepared for trial, and often at the same time, negotiations have to take place for a settlement which will mean that the preparation for trial will prove to be abortive. Nevertheless, it is important that both options are kept in mind for as long as it is necessary to do so.

Mediation

3.10 The foregoing discussion has taken place upon the basis that the effective alternative to a trial was a negotiated settlement. However, one of the other means of 'alternative dispute resolution' (ADR), such as mediation, might be appropriate. Mediation is dealt with in some detail in **paras 5.23** to **5.41** of *Blackstone's Employment Law Practice 2014*. In brief, it is a process whereby an independent, neutral third party assists the claimant and respondent to reach a settlement. The mediator does not seek to impose a solution, and will not determine the rights and wrongs of the case. He or she will seek to identify the issues in the case, and focus upon constructive options which will satisfy both parties. The process is voluntary and informal. Usually, the mediator will not pronounce upon the merits of the case, but will make suggestions for the best way forward. Of course, that may involve testing whether the expectations of each of the parties are realistic.

3.11　An important advantage of mediation is that it is private. As is clear from the relevant part of Chapter 1 on Tribunal Procedure (see 1.156 to 1.165) the hearing in the tribunal will almost inevitably be in public.

3.12　Of course, the mediation may fail in the sense that no acceptable settlement emerges. In such a case, everything which has taken place within the mediation process is 'without prejudice' and cannot be referred to in the hearing.

3.13　Mediation is available on a commercial basis. In addition, the employment tribunal has a judicial mediation scheme. Generally this is available, resources permitting, for cases which are likely to last for three days or more. It is usually (although not exclusively) offered in discrimination cases which are likely to take that length of time. The parties are asked, in appropriate cases, at a preliminary hearing, whether they wish to take advantage of the judicial mediation scheme. If they do, mediation will usually last one day and will be conducted by an employment judge who is a trained mediator. That judge will not take part in any hearing if the mediation is unsuccessful.

ACAS conciliation

3.14　The Advisory, Conciliation and Arbitration Service (ACAS) has an important role to play in the settlement of claims submitted to the tribunal. This role begins before the claim is presented, and details of that process can be found in Chapter 1 on Tribunal Procedure, at 1.20 to 1.30.

3.15　That role is distinct from the role which ACAS plays after the claim has been presented. Once the tribunal receives the claim, it sends a copy to ACAS. The tribunal will also send to ACAS copies of any important correspondence which it receives thereafter. An ACAS conciliation officer will normally contact both of the parties, with a view to achieving a settlement. The contact between ACAS and the parties is almost invariably entirely by telephone. It achieves a high success rate, approaching 50 per cent of all claims presented.

3.16 The parties need to bear the following matters in mind:

(a) Any information which a party gives to the conciliation officer is likely to be passed to the other side. It follows that care should be taken as to what is said.

(b) The officer has no duty to ensure that the terms of a settlement are fair. The duty is to promote the settlement, and not to advise as to whether a claim is likely to succeed, or whether a settlement should be accepted: *Clarke v Redcar and Cleveland Borough Council* [2006] IRLR 324 (EAT).

'Without prejudice'

3.17 Where parties are negotiating with each other, they will often reveal information in an effort to ensure a successful outcome. In the process, a party may well make concessions. In a sense, the very act of negotiation is in itself a concession, which might be thought to show weakness on the part of the party who suggests it. If the negotiating parties believed that what they were saying was likely to be exposed to scrutiny in future proceedings in the tribunal or court, this would inhibit them and make a successful outcome less likely. As a result, there is a general rule of evidence that what takes place in the negotiating process should be 'without prejudice'. What that means is that it should not be mentioned in court or tribunal without the agreement of the parties involved.

3.18 This prohibition applies to correspondence, and as a result letters which deal with negotiations will frequently be headed 'without prejudice'. However, the prohibition will apply even if that label is not attached to the correspondence, or to a relevant conversation. Conversely, the fact that a 'without prejudice' label is attached to a document or precedes a discussion will not in itself provide protection. The test is rather whether the document or discussion is actually part of negotiating a pre-existing dispute. For a communication to be 'without prejudice', there must be an existing dispute between the parties, and the statement in question must be a genuine attempt to settle the dispute: *BNP Paribas v Mezzoterro* [2004] IRLR 508 (EAT).

3.19 Sometimes one party will send to another a communication which is labelled 'without prejudice save as to costs'. The effect will be that it cannot be referred to in any hearing as to liability or remedy, but if there is an application for costs then the party sending the communication will be able to refer to it in an effort to show that they made an offer which (so they say) was unreasonably refused by the other side.

3.20 Chapter 5 on Evidence gives further detail of the effect of 'without prejudice' communications, and the expanded scope of such communications so as to cover settlement offers where there is no pre-existing dispute.

The ACAS Code on Settlements

3.21 ACAS has produced a Code of Practice which sets out what constitutes improper practice by a party in attempting to conclude a settlement. This important document is included as Appendix 2. It makes general points about settlements but has a particular focus on the issues surrounding confidentiality in subsequent tribunal proceedings. In summary it states:

(a) either party may propose settlement;

(b) the reason for offering the settlement should be made clear;

(c) any offer should be in writing, and should be clear as to what is being offered, eg a sum of money and an agreed reference;

(d) no particular procedure need be followed before the offer is made;

(e) any settlement handled contrary to the Code might give rise to a breach of the implied term of trust and confidence, and allow the employee to resign and claim constructive dismissal;

(f) where the offer is refused, the employer must go through a fair process before deciding whether to terminate the relationship;

(g) employees should be given a clear and reasonable period within which to respond, and a minimum of ten days should be given as a general rule;

(h) where anything improper is done or said in the course of making or discussing the offer, the protection of confidentiality will only apply to the extent that the tribunal considers just;

(i) improper behaviour would include discriminatory conduct, or placing undue pressure on the other party to agree to settle.

When is a settlement binding?

3.22 There is a general principle that an employee cannot give up a statutory employment right. The reason is simple. If employees could sign away their rights without any limit, unscrupulous employers would include a term in the contract of employment which stated that the employee surrendered, for example, the right not to be unfairly dismissed.

3.23 It is important, on the other hand, that a party should be able to settle an employment claim without the necessity of going to a hearing, for the reasons set out at the start of this chapter. The compromise which the law has evolved is to enable a settlement to take place,

3. Settlement Agreements

but only within certain limits. Those limits are set out in each relevant statute. For example, s 203 of the Employment Rights Act 1996 (ERA 1996) states in part:

> 203 (1) Any provision in an agreement (whether a contract of employment or not) is void in so far as it purports—
> > (a) to exclude or limit the operation of any provision of this Act, or
> > (b) to preclude a person from bringing any proceedings under this Act before an employment tribunal.

3.24 Exceptions are set out in the remainder of s 203. In practice, there are only two exceptions of any importance:

(1) agreements reached under the auspices of ACAS;
(2) agreements reached after advice from a relevant independent adviser in accordance with the conditions in s 203(3) of the ERA 1996 or its equivalent in other legislation.

3.25 The conditions for a settlement to be binding where route (2) is followed are that:

(a) the agreement must be in writing;
(b) it must relate to the particular proceedings;
(c) the employee must have received advice from a relevant independent adviser as to the terms and effect of the agreement, and in particular its effect on his ability to pursue his rights before the tribunal;
(d) the adviser must be covered by a contract of insurance or indemnity provided for members of a profession in respect of any loss caused to the employee by the advice;
(e) the agreement must identify the adviser; and
(f) it must state that the conditions regulating agreements under the Act are met.

3.26 As to point (c), relevant legal advisers include those who are qualified lawyers, officials certified as competent by a trade union to advise, and certified advice centre workers.

3.27 It is worth stressing that these restrictions on contracting out of employment rights are relevant to *statutory* rights only. Any settlement of rights which are solely contractual will be valid, subject to the usual rules of contract.

> **Example**: Assume that an employee agrees to settle claims for unfair dismissal and wrongful dismissal (failure to pay contractual notice pay of three months). The agreement does not take place in accordance with either of routes (1) and (2). The agreement to settle the unfair dismissal claim will be invalid. The agreement to settle the notice pay claim will be valid, save in respect of any statutory notice which is due.

3.28   With regard to agreements in category (b), the limitation that they 'must relate to the particular proceedings' is an important one. Its effect is that it should not rule out possible future claims indiscriminately, as the proceedings to which the agreement relates must be clearly identified. As it was put in *Hinton v University of East London* [2005] IRLR 552 (CA): 'Compromise agreements should be tailored to the individual circumstances of the individual case'.

3.29   Generally the initiative for a settlement comes from the employer. In any event, it is usual for the employer to pay the cost of the legal advice necessary under s 203(3) and its equivalents. The advice is then given to the employee, who is the client of the adviser, regardless of who pays the bill. It is generally in the interests of the employer to do this, so as to ensure that the settlement is binding.

Settlement at the door of the tribunal

3.30   Frequently, the parties will agree to settle at the tribunal just before the hearing. That is the point at which their minds are concentrated upon the weaknesses in their case and the benefits of walking away. Although the tribunal will wonder why the parties had not been able to settle before, it will usually welcome the fact that they have now agreed, although it may wish to be assured that the claimant, in particular, understands the terms of settlement.

3.31   The question arises as to whether the parties, in such a situation, have to seek the offices of ACAS, or fulfil the requirements for independent legal advice. Generally speaking, they do not need to do so. The tribunal can be asked to make a consent order.

3.32   The claimant will, in the circumstances, be anxious to avoid the possibility of recoupment. If the tribunal makes an order which reflects the terms of an agreed sum, and which does not separately identify the basic award, past loss of earnings, and future earnings, it is unlikely that the recoupment provisions will apply. Alternatively, the tribunal may be asked to dismiss the claim on withdrawal, on the basis of terms agreed between the parties and contained in a schedule to the dismissal order. This is sometimes referred to by practitioners as a 'Tomlin Order'. Alternatively, confidentiality may be assured by putting the agreement in a separate document which is referred to in the order.

3.33   If an order is made which dismisses the claim, the provisions of s 203 of the ERA 1996 or the equivalent in other legislation will not apply: *Mayo-Deman v University of Greenwich* [2005] IRLR 845 (EAT).

3.34   In order to achieve an agreement, it is necessary for the parties to be sure that its terms will be honoured. From the point of view of the claimant, he or she will be anxious to ensure that the respondent will, for example, pay over the agreed sum of money. As a result, the tribunal will frequently order that the sum should be paid within a fixed period, and that the parties have liberty to apply within a further fixed period for the proceedings to be restored. If there is no such application, the proceedings will be dismissed upon withdrawal by the claimant. From the tribunal's point of view, it will be anxious to ensure that there is some finality to proceedings. At the same time, the opportunity given by 'liberty to apply' gives the parties the opportunity to come back to the tribunal within a short fixed period if something goes wrong with the agreement.

The effect of a valid agreement

3.35   Assume that there has been a valid agreement, but the respondent employer fails to honour it. The remedy for the claimant, where the claim has been withdrawn, is to enforce the terms of the settlement through the courts (see Chapter 7 on Enforcement).

4 Advocacy: Presenting the Case

Introduction

4.01 This chapter deals with the practical points involved in preparing and presenting a case in the employment tribunal. Obviously there are matters relating to procedure, which are dealt with in Chapter 1, and Chapter 5 on Evidence is also of relevance.

4.02 This chapter is directed primarily at those with limited experience of appearing in employment tribunals. It refers to 'representatives', although many of the points which are made are equally relevant to parties who represent themselves ('litigants in person').

Case preparation

4.03 The key to successful advocacy is preparation. If the case is thoroughly prepared, then the representative will gain in confidence, and will be able to present the case more effectively.

4.04 To begin the process of preparation, the representative needs to consider what their case is. For example, is it that the claimant was unfairly dismissed? Or is it that the employer acted fairly, and is not liable? The next step is to determine what the issues are in the case. This chapter proceeds on the basis that the claim and the response forms have already been served, so that the nature of the case and the issues are likely to be relatively clear. The various chapters in this Handbook which deal with different aspects of the law will assist in ascertaining the issues. Some potential issues will not be in dispute, and there will be no need to prepare evidence or argument in respect of them.

4.05 Take, for example, an unfair dismissal claim. The potential issues might be:

(1) Was the claim in time?
(2) Is the claimant entitled to bring a claim for unfair dismissal, eg does she have two years' continuous employment?
(3) Was the claimant dismissed?
(4) What was the reason for dismissal?
(5) Was it a potentially fair reason in accordance with the statute?
(6) Did the employer act reasonably or unreasonably in deciding to dismiss?

4.06 Assume that the employer accepts that the claim was within the three-month period after the effective date of termination, that the claimant had four years' continuous employment, and that she was dismissed after a disciplinary hearing and appeal. Issues (1), (2), and (3) are therefore not in dispute and there is no need for either side to prepare evidence and argument in relation to them. However, each side will have to determine what its case is in relation to (4), (5), and (6).

The evidence

4.07 It is up to each party to decide what evidence it needs to bring in order to win the case, and how to present it. Such evidence might, for example, be produced by:

(a) witnesses who have personal knowledge about the relevant facts and events—the parties themselves may be witnesses, and it is usual for the claimant and any dismissing officer in particular to give evidence;

(b) documents such as correspondence between the parties, notes of a disciplinary hearing, copies of the employment contract, pay slips and sickness absence records (to name some random, but common, examples);

(c) a medical report or a report from an expert on health and safety, ie expert evidence.

4.08 Care must be taken to ensure that the evidence which a party intends to produce is relevant to one or more of the issues which have been identified, in accordance with the preceding section. The aim of any such evidence is to convince the tribunal on that particular issue. (In addition the parties should bear in mind the importance of 'disclosing' any relevant evidence, whether or not it is helpful or unhelpful to their own case.)

4.09 Once the evidence has been gathered, the representative should prepare by considering the statements of his or her own witnesses. In doing so, it is useful to draw up a chronology of the events which are relevant to the case. **Table 4.1** gives an example of part of a chronology—the completed article will contain more events, but the way in which they are recorded will follow the same pattern. It is important in the course of preparation to note down in the relevant column the references where evidence of the events in question can be found. Such references would usually be to paragraphs in a witness statement, or pages in the trial bundle. In **Table 4.1**, 'C' is the claimant, the trial bundle is 'R1'.

First draft of closing submissions

4.10 If the representative has followed the steps set out previously, he or she will now have a list of the issues and a chronology. Many

Table 4.1 Partial chronology of events

Date	Event	References
1.10.09	C starts employment with R	R1/15
31.1.11	C promoted to assistant manager	R1/26, C's statement, para 8
20.4.12	C given appraisal by Chris Jones	R1/32
23.8.12	Conversation between Jones and Smith criticizing C	Jones' statement, para 11 Smith's statement, para 9
29.3.13	C given warning by Smith	R1/49
3.2.14	C sent notice of disciplinary hearing	R1/68
11.2.14	Disciplinary hearing	R1/72 to 88, C's statement, para 19, Smith's statement, para 14

advocates then go on to prepare a first draft of the closing submissions which they intend to make at the close of the case. If this is done, it can be extremely useful. It will give the representative a clear idea of where they would like to be at the conclusion of evidence. It provides a road-map, assuming that the hearing goes along the lines which the representative realistically hopes that it will. Obviously what is prepared at this stage can only be a first draft, as it is impossible to predict with any certainty just what the evidence will be. Nevertheless it provides useful guidance for the situation in which the representative hopes to be. It will of course need revision (possibly drastic revision) in the course of the hearing. It does, however, fulfil the important additional role of providing a 'security blanket' so that the representative can feel that they already have the basis of a closing speech for the time when they are called on to deliver it.

On the day

[*This section is particularly directed at those with little experience of appearing in the employment tribunal, including litigants in person.*]

4.11   On the day of the hearing, the representative should ensure that they have with them all relevant documents. This will include a copy of the trial bundle, the witness statements, and any documents which are not included in the trial bundle but which may prove relevant in the hearing. Directions in relation to the trial bundle and the witness statements are dealt with in more detail in Chapter 1 on Tribunal Procedure, where it will be seen that copies have to be provided for the tribunal and the other side. The tribunal will not usually carry out photocopying, so it is important to ensure that sufficient copies are available.

4.12   In addition, the representative should take stationery and/or a laptop with them in order to keep a note of what is said during the hearing. Frequently, there arise points about what has been said in evidence, and notes will be invaluable in order to check that the tribunal and the other side have recorded any point which you regard as important.

4.13   Most employment tribunals start at 10 am, but it is worth checking to ensure that this is in fact the correct time. Whatever the start time is, it is crucial to arrive early, and arriving one hour before proceedings start will give a proper opportunity to carry out the various tasks which are necessary.

4.14   A litigant in person would be well advised to ask someone they know and trust to accompany them to the tribunal. Such a person will provide support and advice, even if they have little or no knowledge of the law. They can provide a second opinion for the litigant in person to consider, and assist in taking notes and keeping control of the papers. The tribunal will generally allow this friend or supporter to sit next to the litigant in person, but should be informed at the outset of their identity. It is also usually possible for the party to confer quietly with that friend during the course of the hearing, provided that no disturbance is caused. In any event, notes can be passed when necessary.

4.15   On arrival at the tribunal, the standard procedure is that parties, representatives, and witnesses sign in at reception. They are then told which tribunal their case is to be heard in, and directed to one of the waiting rooms: one is for claimants and those with them, and the other for respondents and those with them.

4.16   The usual procedure is that the clerk for the hearing will visit each waiting room in turn in order to take details of the people who will be attending the hearing. This provides an opportunity to seek information about the hearing, although this is really confined to the more basic points about when it is likely to start, whether the other parties have arrived, and whether there are other cases to be heard beforehand. If there is any information which a representative wishes to convey to the tribunal, this can also be done through the clerk. In addition, any documents which the tribunal ought to have can be handed to the clerk.

4.17   The representative needs to ensure that any witnesses expected to give evidence on their behalf are present, and if they have not arrived will need to make enquiries as to where they are and when they will arrive. If they will be late, the clerk should be informed.

4.18   In addition, it is necessary to speak to any other parties in the case who are expected to attend the tribunal. Usually this will be the representative of the other side, or the party himself or herself. They will be in the other waiting room, and the clerk will be able to give directions as to its whereabouts if necessary. Any documents which the other side does not have should be handed over, and copies of any additional documents which they have brought should be received. (The exception is closing submissions, which the parties normally exchange after all the evidence has been heard.)

4.19 If the other party hands over a document which has not been seen before, and it is important to the issues in the hearing and/or lengthy, it may be necessary to request time to read it before the hearing begins. If so, a request for a short delay in the start of the hearing may be conveyed through the clerk, but this should only be done if really necessary.

4.20 It is important to remember that discussions which take place between the parties about the management of the case are 'open discussions', which means that they can be referred to in the tribunal. The representative should therefore confine what they say to the task in hand, and not deal with the strengths and weaknesses of their case.

4.21 On the other hand, quite frequently a settlement can be reached at the door of the tribunal. A representative wishing to try to settle their case can raise this with the other side. Any discussion about a settlement cannot be referred to in the tribunal unless it results in an agreement. This is termed a 'without prejudice' discussion (see Chapter 5 on Evidence). If the parties are engaged in negotiations about a settlement, it is important to tell the clerk. Even after doing so, the parties may be called into tribunal, but should explain (without going into any details at all) that discussions with a view to settlement are taking place, asking the tribunal for a limited amount of time (eg 15 minutes) to bring them to a conclusion.

Useful documents

4.22 Documents which contain additional evidence upon which a party intends to rely should be handed to the other side and to the tribunal before the hearing commences.

4.23 In addition, the following documents may be of assistance in explaining the case to the tribunal, and it is worth considering whether any or all of them should be handed to the other side and the tribunal in advance:

(a) a chronology (see 'Case preparation' at 4.09 for detail);
(b) a list of the people who are relevant to the case, with their job title or function in the proceedings (a cast list);
(c) a diagram of the structure of the employer company or organization (an organogram);
(d) a glossary of any technical terms;
(e) a list of any important agreed facts;
(f) a list of any relevant disputed facts;

(g) a skeleton argument, setting out the main submissions which are being made, together with any legal authority and references to the factual evidence.

4.24   As far as the skeleton argument referred to in (g) is concerned, this will be distinct from any skeleton argument for the closing submissions referred to later. As it is being submitted at the start of the hearing, it will not be able to refer to the evidence which is given. The closing submissions will be able to do so, and to adjust the arguments to take into account any unexpected evidence which has emerged, together with the arguments anticipated from the other side.

Speaking at the hearing

[*Again, this section is particularly directed at those with little experience of appearing in the employment tribunal, including litigants in person.*]

4.25   Those who are not familiar with the law should avoid the trap of speaking in 'legalese'. The tribunal will respond better to a party or lay representative who talks in plain English and is polite. (In fact, this is probably good advice for lawyers as well!)

4.26   It is important to speak clearly and loudly. Members of the tribunal will find it frustrating if they cannot hear clearly what is being said. In particular, delivery should be considerably slower than normal speech. About half of normal speed is probably right. This makes sense once one takes into account the fact that the judge will be trying to take a detailed note of what is being said. If what is being said is important, it is also important that the judge should be given an opportunity to take it down accurately. The standard advice is to keep an eye on the judge's pen when speaking. At the end of the sentence, if the judge is still writing, wait. When the judge stops writing, start speaking again.

4.27   It will be easier for the tribunal to understand what is being said if it is clearly structured. One way of doing this is to give clear headings or 'signposts'. An argument or submission which is structured in this way might begin: 'I wish to make four points. My first point is...My second point is...' The effect of this way of speaking is to make it easier to understand the argument which is being put forward, which becomes more persuasive as a result.

Time management

4.28   The tribunal will be concerned to ensure that time is not wasted during the course of the hearing. This is important, not just for the tribunal system, but also for the parties, because if time is wasted then the case may not be completed within the allotted time, with the result that the case goes 'part heard' and has to go over to another day. If this happens, it means that the parties will have to bear the expense and inconvenience of the additional day's hearing. Further, all those concerned will then have to struggle to recall exactly what happened on the previous occasion. Because of the number of people involved in the hearing, the date on which the remainder of the case can be heard will often be some time in the future, which compounds the problem.

4.29 As a result, it is common for the employment judge to set down a timetable at the beginning of the case, or even prior to the commencement of the case at a preliminary hearing. This timetable needs to have the input of the parties in order to be realistic and fair. That means that the representatives have to calculate how long they will take for each stage of the case. A representative consequently needs to estimate how long they will take, for example, in cross-examining a particular witness. In addition, some sort of estimate will be required as to how long the closing submissions will take. It is obviously difficult for someone without experience of advocacy to make such a calculation. However, at least he or she ought to be able to say which witnesses have to be cross-examined at some length, and which witnesses can be dealt with briefly. Such an indication will assist the judge in coming to a timetable which has the input of the parties.

4.30 In accordance with the rules (see Chapter 1 on Tribunal Procedure at 1.05 and 1.145), the judge not only has power to construct a timetable, but can implement it by means of a guillotine if necessary. This means that any timetable laid down by the judge must be respected, and that an eye should be kept on the clock, eg during the course of cross-examination or the closing speech.

4.31 Even if a representative is within the constraints of the timetable, it is important that the matters which they deal with are relevant to the issues in the case. The judge can be expected to intervene if a party strays from those issues, and the party should abide by any ruling that is given in that regard.

4.32 Overall, cooperation and politeness will help to ensure a favourable impression on the part of the tribunal, and efficient disposal of the case. The aim is to be 'the tribunal's friend'.

4.33 It can also help to raise any issues which may affect the hearing at this stage, before the tribunal begins hearing evidence. For example, a party may wish to challenge the admissibility of evidence, or bring to the tribunal's attention a problem affecting case management. However, in doing so, the party raising the issue should be as brief and helpful as possible, and it is very rare that the tribunal's suggested solution should be challenged. This is simply a matter of bringing the issue to the tribunal's attention so they can plan accordingly.

Examination-in-chief

4.34 The evidence which a witness gives on behalf of the party calling them is referred to as 'examination-in-chief'. All or most of this comes in the form of a witness statement, usually given to the other side in advance and in accordance with the directions of the tribunal. The position in the employment tribunal now is that statements are generally taken as read. In other words, the witness is not required or allowed to read the statement out to the tribunal, and the members of the tribunal will either have read it in advance, or will read it to themselves immediately after the witness comes to the witness table.

4.35 As a result, shortly after being sworn or affirmed, the witness will be cross-examined by the other side. The witness should be made aware of this fact. It means that it is important to ensure that he or she reads over the statement and is happy with its contents shortly before the hearing. The representative should enquire of the witness whether the statement is accurate before going into the tribunal, and decide how to correct any errors. The witness should also be given an opportunity to become familiar with any relevant portion of the trial bundle. It is, however, inappropriate for a witness to be coached in preparation for the hearing, and any attempt to do so is likely to be exposed, with embarrassing consequences.

4.36 Although coaching is not allowed, some general advice to witnesses may be useful. When being cross-examined, the answer given should be truthful and straightforward. It will often be 'yes' or 'no'. If either of these would be a misleading answer the witness should say so, and ask for the chance to give a more complete answer. But the witness should not make a speech, or avoid answering the question. Nor should he or she argue with the questioner. Simple, factual answers are what is required. If the witness does not remember something, they should say so. That is part of the requirement to tell the truth.

4.37 Once in the tribunal, the witness will, after being sworn or affirmed, be asked to look at their statement and confirm that it is correct. If it is not, they should be given the opportunity to correct it before being asked any questions.

4.38 Witnesses are not normally permitted to refer to notes when giving evidence. A clean copy of the witness statement will be available on the witness table, and the witness will not normally be allowed to use their own marked-up copy of that statement. There is an exception, however, for a party representing themselves in the employment tribunals. It was held in *Watson–Smith v Tagol Ltd (t/a Alangate Personnel)* (EAT/611/81) that where a party represents themselves in the employment tribunal they should be allowed to refer to notes in giving evidence. After all, a professional representative would normally have a marked-up statement from a witness to assist in dealing with their evidence.

4.39 It sometimes happens that a statement is incomplete, and the party calling the witness wishes to supplement their evidence. With the permission of the tribunal, it may be possible to ask a few supplementary questions. The tribunal will need to know the reason why the matters in question were not included in the written statement, and will need to be assured that the questions are limited in number. In addition, any such questions should not be 'leading', ie suggesting the answer which the witness ought to give. The easiest way to avoid leading questions is to begin the question neutrally with an interrogative—who, what, why, when, where, how? etc. Alternatively, the witness can be asked to describe, explain, or give an account of an event.

Cross-examination

4.40 The process of questioning witnesses for the other side, or cross-examination, has the following aims:

(a) *To elicit any favourable evidence from the witness.* Often this will not be possible, as the witness will not have anything favourable to say about your case. After all, they have been called by the other side! Nevertheless, a fair-minded witness will often be prepared to give favourable evidence on some points.

(b) *To undermine any unfavourable evidence.* In cross-examining a witness, it is usual to identify and bring their attention to significant inconsistencies, inaccuracies, and points which are inherently unlikely.

(c) *Giving the witness a chance to respond to the case being put by the question.* It is important that the witness should be given an opportunity to disagree with the other side's version of events, so that they have the chance to respond. This is usually termed 'putting your case'. In an unfair dismissal case, for example, the claimant might say 'when you held the disciplinary hearing you didn't listen to what I had to say, did you?' He would then give the manager the chance to agree or disagree with that statement.

4.41 The purpose of cross-examination is to ask questions. It is not an opportunity to argue with the witness. Nor should the tribunal be told, during the course of cross-examination, what conclusion should be drawn from what the witness has just said. The questioner should just write down anything helpful which has been said, and raise it in their closing submissions. Similarly, the cross-examiner should not comment on what the witness has said. Although it is tempting to say 'no one will believe that', such a comment is improper and will annoy the tribunal. The proper place for comments, once again, is in closing submissions.

4. Advocacy: Presenting the Case

4.42 When cross-examining, leading questions are not just permitted but are actually the best way to proceed, contrary to the position when one is dealing with one's own witness. So the respondent in an unfair dismissal claim, when cross-examining the claimant, should not say:

'Did you get the chance to appeal?'

but rather should ask:

'You had the chance to appeal didn't you?'

4.43 When cross-examining, multiple questions should be avoided. For example, the respondent should not ask:

'You had a fair investigation, a fair disciplinary hearing, and the chance to appeal, didn't you?'

but should ask separate questions:

'The investigation was fair, wasn't it?'
'And the disciplinary hearing was also fair, wasn't it?'
'In any event, you had the chance to appeal didn't you?'

4.44 Those without much experience in advocacy will find it helpful to prepare a number of questions, but should ensure that their approach is flexible, and takes into account whatever answers are given to the earlier questions. Those with more experience will find it better to work in terms of a list of topics, to avoid the temptation to work through all the questions which have been prepared, regardless of whether they are relevant in view of previous answers.

4.45 An important part of cross-examination is dealing with any inconsistencies on the part of the witness. For example, there may be evidence in a document which contradicts the witness's statement. In preparing cross-examination, it is important to check documents for such inconsistencies, and to raise them with the witness. In the course of preparation, it is vital to keep a note of the page and paragraph numbers of any such important inconsistencies. The witness can then be asked which statement is true. Assume that the claimant in an unfair dismissal case is cross-examining the manager who heard the disciplinary hearing:

'Please look at page 33 of the trial bundle, the notes of the disciplinary hearing. You stated that I had been given an oral warning 18 months ago, didn't you?' *'Yes.'*

'Now look at paragraph 11 of your witness statement. You say there that I had been given an oral warning 8 months ago, don't you?' *'Yes.'*

'Which one of those was true?' *'I'm not sure.'*

4.46 During the course of cross-examination, it is important to ensure that a note is taken, as this will be invaluable when it comes to closing submissions.

Tribunal questions

4.47 Once cross-examination is over, the tribunal may ask questions of the witness. It is important for the representative to note the questions which are asked by the tribunal, and any answer which is given. The question may well give a clue to the matters which the tribunal thinks are particularly important, and this will provide some guidance for what should be included in closing submissions.

Re-examination

4.48 The party who called the witness is entitled to ask any final questions before their evidence is complete. This is the process of re-examination. Any such questions must arise from the questions which have been asked by the other side, or by the tribunal. In addition, as re-examination is conducted by the party who called the witness, it is not permissible to 'lead' the witness during the process of re-examination (see section 4.39). In other words, the question must not suggest the answer to the witness.

4.49 A party should avoid re-examining for the sake of it. Often it is best to let the evidence of the witness stand. Occasionally, some clarification may be needed, eg by referring the witness to a document and asking whether that aids their recollection, in a case where their answer in cross-examination has been incomplete or ambiguous.

Closing submissions

4.50 After all the evidence has finished, each party is given the opportunity to make its closing submissions. This is a chance to focus upon the matters which will persuade the tribunal to come to a favourable decision, at the point immediately before they begin to decide.

4.51 The party bearing the burden of proof (see Chapter 1 on Tribunal Procedure at 1.147 and 1.148) will deliver its closing submissions last, although it may well be that if only one side is professionally represented, that side will be asked to go first.

4.52 The tribunal will often find it helpful to have a written outline of submissions in front of it during the course of a closing speech. Such a written outline is sometimes referred to as a skeleton argument, although the skeleton argument may be put before the tribunal at an earlier stage as well. In any event, the skeleton argument should identify:

(a) the issues and the main relevant background facts;
(b) any law referred to, with references to the relevant authorities;
(c) the submissions of fact to be made with reference to the evidence, ie why do they support the case of the party presenting the argument?

4.53 The closing submissions presented orally to the tribunal can then be based upon the written outline, commenting and expanding upon it rather than reading it out. The tribunal can in any event be relied upon to read the written submissions which have been handed to it.

4.54 The submissions (whether oral or written) should have a clear structure. This could well be based upon the issues outlined by the tribunal at the outset of the hearing. In making the closing submissions, it is important to deal with evidence both positive and negative. If any evidence damages the case being put forward in argument, it is better to provide an explanation and a perspective on it. Where matters of fact are in dispute, the tribunal will welcome arguments as to why the evidence of a particular witness (supporting the case of the party presenting the submissions) should be preferred to that of an opposing witness.

4.55 Any legal authorities upon which a party wishes to rely should be copied, one copy being given to the other side and sufficient copies being supplied for the members of the tribunal.

4.56 It sometimes happens that there is not sufficient time for the parties to present oral submissions at the end of the evidence. In such a case, the tribunal will usually order the parties to provide written submissions according to a timetable which it lays down. This is usually regarded as preferable to asking the parties to return to the tribunal to make oral submissions. The procedure which the EAT has laid down for such cases is:

(a) written submissions should only be directed with the consent of all parties;
(b) the judge has a responsibility to ensure that the procedure adopted complies with natural justice;
(c) the tribunal and each party should be served with the written submissions of the other parties by a fixed deadline;
(d) each party should be informed that any comments upon the submissions of the other party should be sent to the tribunal within a further fixed period.

(*London Borough of Barking and Dagenham v Oguoku* [2000] IRLR 179 (EAT)).

The decision

4.57 After receiving closing submissions, the tribunal will consider its judgment. It may either do this on the same day, delivering its judgment orally, or it may reserve judgment and send it to the parties in written form (for further details see 1.174).

5 Evidence

Introduction

5.01 The tribunal has a general power to regulate its own procedure. This includes whether to admit evidence or not, subject to the general principle that the parties are entitled to a fair hearing. In particular, the tribunal is not bound by the rules of evidence which apply in the civil or criminal courts. The position is made clear in r 41:

> 41 The Tribunal may regulate its own procedure and shall conduct the hearing in the manner it considers fair, having regard to the principles contained in the overriding objective. The following rules do not restrict that general power. The Tribunal shall seek to avoid undue formality and may itself question the parties or any witnesses so far as appropriate in order to clarify the issues or elicit the evidence. The Tribunal is not bound by any rule of law relating to the admissibility of evidence in proceedings before the courts.

5.02 More detail of the practice in relation to evidence is to be found in **sections 9.100** to **9.137** of *Blackstone's Employment Law Practice 2014*.

Relevance

5.03 It is central to the functioning of the tribunal that it can exclude irrelevant evidence, and stop lines of questioning and submissions which are not related to the issues which must be decided: *Bache v Essex County Council* [2000] IRLR 251 (CA).

5.04 Evidence which is irrelevant to the issues is inadmissible, and ought not to be allowed in tribunal proceedings: *XXX v YYY* [2004] IRLR 471. In that case, the Court of Appeal upheld the decision of the tribunal not to admit certain video evidence on the grounds that it had no probative value.

5.05 More controversial is the question whether the tribunal has the power to exclude evidence which is relevant to the issues to ensure efficient case management. In *Digby v East Cambridgeshire District Council* [2007] IRLR 585, the EAT confirmed that a tribunal has a discretion to exclude evidence which is relevant, but which is, for example, unnecessarily repetitive or only marginally relevant. The decision was put on the basis that there was a power, in the interests of case management, given by the overriding objective (see 1.08) to refuse to admit such evidence. It should be emphasized that a discretion of this nature must be exercised judicially.

Hearsay evidence

5.06 Even in the civil and criminal courts, hearsay evidence is admitted subject to certain conditions. In the employment tribunal, there is no general rule against hearsay evidence, although caution must be exercised in relation to it. In *Aberdeen Steak Houses Group plc v Ibrahim* [1988] IRLR 420, the EAT stated that it must be remembered that rules of procedure and evidence had been built up over time to provide guidance for courts and tribunals on the best way of dealing with and deciding issues.

5.07 In practice, it is common for witnesses to make reference to matters which they do not know at first hand, but have been told by others or have based upon documents, and for this to be accepted with the appropriate degree of caution. In addition, it frequently happens that a witness statement from an individual who is absent is admitted, subject to reduced weight because they cannot be cross-examined.

Legal professional privilege

5.08 Communications between a party and his or her solicitor are subject to legal professional privilege if they are confidential, and made for the purpose of obtaining and/or giving legal advice. Communications between a party, their lawyer, and third parties (eg a prospective witness) are also protected by privilege, if the dominant purpose of the communication is to prepare for contemplated or pending litigation: *Waugh v British Railways Board* [1979] IRLR 364 (HL).

5.09 Quite frequently, during a tribunal hearing there arises some reference to an occasion when one of the parties sought legal advice. There is no legal bar to prevent evidence being given about the fact that there has been correspondence or a meeting between lawyer and client. What is protected by privilege is the advice given at those meetings or in correspondence.

5.10 The privilege in question is that of the client, who can waive it in appropriate circumstances. However, a reference to the fact of a meeting or correspondence with the lawyer will usually trigger a warning, either by the employment judge or a representative, that the substance of what was discussed is privileged, so that the witness is aware of the privilege, and will only waive it on an informed basis.

Without prejudice

5.11 Negotiations which are genuinely intended to settle matters in dispute between the parties are termed 'without prejudice' communications. They are privileged, and may not be put in evidence.

5.12 Usually, the matter in respect of which communications are without prejudice will have been resolved during the process of disclosure, or in preparing the bundle for hearing. Such privileged communications should not be referred to in witness statements. Nevertheless, it sometimes happens that a witness will make reference to without prejudice communications in the course of their evidence. In such a case, it is usual for the employment judge or a representative to intervene and stop the witness from giving evidence on such communications, just as is the case where legal professional privilege is involved.

5.13 The label 'without prejudice' is not conclusive. The crucial question is whether the communication forms part of a genuine attempt to settle the dispute. The label will not confer privilege on a document which does not pass this test, and conversely the fact that 'without prejudice' is not expressly stated in the document will not deprive it of privileged status if it does pass the test.

5.14 It is an essential part of establishing 'without prejudice' status that there should be a dispute between the parties in existence at the time of the communication: *BNP Paribas v Mezzotero* [2004] IRLR 508 (EAT). In *Framlington Group Ltd v Barnetson* [2007] IRLR 598 (CA), it was stated that the test was whether in the course of negotiations the parties contemplated or might reasonably have contemplated litigation if the dispute could not be resolved.

5.15 The privilege may be waived, but as it is the privilege of both parties, it must be waived by both parties. In *Brunel University v Webster* [2007] IRLR 592 (CA), the Court of Appeal held that privilege had been waived when each party referred to the without prejudice communications in the ET 1 (claim form) and the ET 3 (response).

5.16 If there is 'unambiguous impropriety', that will be an abuse of the without prejudice privilege, and the privilege will be lost: *Unilever plc v Procter and Gamble* [2000] 1 WLR 2436. Other exceptions to the without prejudice rule can be found in *Oceanbulk Shipping & Trading SA v TMT Asia Ltd* [2011] 1 AC 662.

Pre-termination negotiations

5.17 With effect from 29 July 2013, settlement offers and discussions became inadmissible as evidence to an employment tribunal in any subsequent unfair dismissal claim. This came into force when s 14 of the Enterprise and Regulatory Reform Act inserted a new s 111A into the Employment Rights Act 1996. The aim behind this provision was to enable employers to initiate discussion about a settlement agreement with an employee whom they intended to dismiss, without the prospect of that discussion being brought up in any future proceedings, eg for constructive dismissal. The new provision in the Employment Rights Act 1996 (ERA 1996) reads:

> 111A (1) Evidence of pre-termination negotiations is inadmissible in any proceedings on a complaint under section 111.
>
> This is subject to subsections (3) to (5).
>
> (2) In subsection (1) 'pre-termination negotiations' means any offer made or discussions held, before the termination of the employment in question, with a view to it being terminated on terms agreed between the employer and the employee.
>
> (3) Subsection (1) does not apply where, according to the complainant's case, the circumstances are such that a provision (whenever made) contained in, or made under, this or any other Act requires the complainant to be regarded for the purposes of this Part as unfairly dismissed.
>
> (4) In relation to anything said or done which in the tribunal's opinion was improper, or was connected with improper behaviour, subsection (1) applies only to the extent that the tribunal considers just.
>
> (5) Subsection (1) does not affect the admissibility, on any question as to costs or expenses, of evidence relating to an offer made on the basis that the right to refer to it on any such question is reserved.

5.18 The ambit of the new protection is confined to proceedings for 'ordinary' unfair dismissal and does not extend to claims for automatically unfair dismissal, wrongful dismissal, or discrimination.

5.19 Although this protection has similarities to that which attaches to 'without prejudice' privilege, the crucial distinction is that there does not need to be a pre-existing dispute to attract the protection of s 111A of the ERA 1996. In other words, the employer can approach an employee with an offer of settlement related to dismissal even if there has been no mention previously of any issue relating to the employer's intention to dismiss.

5.20 ACAS has issued a Code of Practice on Settlements (see Appendix 2), which will be of importance in deciding whether there has been 'improper behaviour' by either party. If there has been improper behaviour, the employment tribunal can override the protection which is contained in s 111A. The ACAS Code of Practice is aimed at defining what is improper behaviour. For example, it states that an employee should be given ten days to consider the offer, accompaniment should be allowed at any discussion, and there should be no intimidation or reduction of the offer during the period for consideration.

Human rights

5.21 Generally, the parties can rely upon art 6 of the European Convention on Human Rights (ECHR), which specifies the right to a fair and public hearing. On occasion, however, this right may be said to be in conflict with a competing right under the ECHR. The usual basis upon which such a conflict is alleged is art 8—the right to private life. In such a case, the tribunal would have to consider art 8(2) which permits interference with the right to private life in pursuit of certain defined legitimate interests. Among those legitimate interests is the right of another person to a fair trial.

5.22 In *Avocet Hardware plc v Morrison* (EAT/0417/02), a telephone conversation which had been recorded without permission was admitted. The employer had relied upon the conversation as evidence in deciding to dismiss the employee, and it was held that the employer could not have had a fair trial without being able to put that evidence before the tribunal.

5.23 In *Anwell View School Governors v Dogherty* [2007] IRLR 198, the claimant covertly recorded disciplinary proceedings against her. She had recorded both the open hearings and the panel's private deliberations. The EAT held that it was right to allow recordings of the open hearing in evidence, since no right to privacy arose. However, the recording of the private deliberations of the panel was inadmissible, because the public had an interest in maintaining the integrity of the private deliberations of adjudicating bodies. It was suggested that the decision might have been different in a discrimination claim where the recording showed the only incontrovertible evidence of discrimination.

6 Time Limits

Introduction

6.01 For the employment tribunal to consider a claim, it must be presented in time. The law relating to time limits is dealt with in detail in **chapter 3** of *Blackstone's Employment Law Practice 2014*. What follows is a summary of the main principles. Crucially, a claim which is out of time cannot be considered by the tribunal, because it will have no jurisdiction to do so. The principle was made clear in *Dedman v British Building & Engineering Appliances Ltd* [1973] IRLR 379 (CA). It follows that the parties cannot agree between themselves that the case should proceed even though it is outside the time limit. The tribunals have to apply the rule strictly.

Presenting the claim

6.02 In order to discover whether a claim is in time, it is crucial to determine when it was presented to the tribunal. A claim is presented when the tribunal office receives it.

Presentation by post

6.03 As far as presentation by post is concerned, the Court of Appeal dealt with the matter in *Consignia v Seeley* [2002] IRLR 624. It laid down the following rules:

(a) the claim is presented when it arrives at an office of the tribunal;

(b) presentation by post will be presumed to have taken place when the claim would be delivered in the ordinary course of post;

(c) if a letter is sent by first class post, it will be assumed that it would be delivered on the second day after it was posted, excluding Sundays and bank holidays;

(d) if the claim form is date stamped on a Monday by the tribunal office, and the time limit expired on the Saturday or Sunday, it will be open to the tribunal to conclude that it was posted by first class post not later than the Thursday, and arrived on the Saturday;

(e) if it was found to be impossible to present the claim within the time limits, eg because the tribunal office was locked at the weekend and did not have a letterbox, then the tribunal may find that it was not reasonably practicable for the complaint to be presented within the prescribed period (see 6.12 for the effect of 'not reasonably practicable');

(f) if the letter does not arrive at the time when it would be expected to arrive in the ordinary course of post, but is unexpectedly delayed, the tribunal may conclude that it was not reasonably practicable for the complaint to be presented within the prescribed period.

Presentation by email

6.04 When a claim is submitted by email, delivery can be expected within a reasonable time thereafter. In *Initial Electronic Security Systems Ltd v Avdic* [2005] IRLR 671, it was held that it would be reasonable to expect that an email would arrive within 30 to 60 minutes of transmission.

Calculating the time limit

6.05 **Table 6.1** sets out a series of time limits, eg three months, six months. The time limit is calculated in the following way. Assume that the employee was dismissed (see 'Effective date of termination',

Table 6.1 Time limits for claims

Claim	Statutory provision	Time limit	Tribunal discretion
Unfair dismissal	s 94, ERA	3 months from effective date of termination	if 'not reasonably practicable'
Breach of contract	Employment Tribunals (Extension of Jurisdiction) Order 1994	3 months from effective date of termination	if 'not reasonably practicable'
Holiday pay	reg 30, Working Time Regulations 1998	3 months from date when payment should have been made	if 'not reasonably practicable'
Unlawful deductions from wages	s 23, ERA	3 months from date when payment of the last in any series of deductions should have been made	if 'not reasonably practicable'
Discrimination	s 123, EqA	3 months from date of the act of discrimination	if 'just and equitable'
Equal pay	s 129, EqA	6 months beginning with the last day of employment	none, but note the county court can hear such a claim for up to 6 years from the last day of employment
Redundancy payment	s 135, ERA	6 months from the 'relevant date'	if 'just and equitable' for a further 6 months

at 6.06) on 15 August, the period of three months for the presentation of an unfair dismissal claim will begin on that date. It will therefore expire on 14 November. The claim must be presented within the three-month period, and this means presentation on or before 14 November and not 15 November. In addition, it is calendar months which count, despite the fact that there are different numbers of days in each month. Consequently, if an act of discrimination is said to have taken place on 30 November 2014, the last date for presentation of the claim will be 28 February 2015. No account is taken of fractions of a day. This would mean that the claim form must be presented, in this example, no later than midnight on 28 February.

Effective date of termination

6.06 From **Table 6.1** it will be seen that in a number of cases (including unfair dismissal) time begins to run with the 'effective date of termination'. This is the date upon which the claimant was dismissed. In *Gisda CYF v Lauren Barrett* [2010] IRLR 1073, the Court of Appeal held that a letter of dismissal, which had arrived by post at the claimant's address while she was away from home did not become effective until she read the letter. She was not dismissed until that date, and so time did not begin to run until that date.

6.07 The time limit for a claim of unfair dismissal is set out in s 111(2) of the Employment Rights Act 1996 (ERA 1996):

> 111 (2) Subject to the following provisions of this section, an employment tribunal shall not consider a complaint under this section unless it is presented to the tribunal—
> (a) before the end of the period of three months beginning with the effective date of termination, or
> (b) within such further period as the tribunal considers reasonable in a case where it is satisfied that it was not reasonably practicable for the complaint to be presented before the end of that period of three months.

Continuing acts in discrimination claims

6.08 For a claim of discrimination, the time limit is three months. Time begins to run from the date of the act of discrimination, but frequently the claimant relies upon the fact that an act extended over a period. In the case of such continuing acts, time will run from the date of the last event complained of. For example, where what is alleged is a number of acts of harassment over a period of a year, does time begin to run after each individual act, or should they be treated as one act, in which case time will only run from the last incident?

6.09 The situation is covered by s 123 of the Equality Act 2010 (EqA 2010), part of which reads:

> 123 (3) For the purposes of this section—
>
> (a) conduct extending over a period is to be treated as done at the end of the period;
>
> ...

6.10 In *Hendricks v Commissioner of Police for the Metropolis* [2003] IRLR 96, the Court of Appeal gave guidance for distinguishing between 'an act extending over a period' and a succession of unconnected or isolated acts. It was held that the focus of the tribunal should be on the substance of the complaints that the employer was responsible for an ongoing situation or a continuing state of affairs. If it was, then that would be 'an act extending over a period'. If it was not, then time would begin to run from the date when each specific act was committed.

6.11 In certain circumstances, eg a claim for failure to make reasonable adjustments (see Chapter 16), a claim may be based on an omission rather than an act. In such a case, time begins to run at the point when the respondent decides to make the omission, and there is no concept of a continuing omission: *Kingston Upon Hull City Council v Matuszowicz* [2009] ICR 1170.

'Not reasonably practicable'

6.12 The discretion of the tribunal depends upon this test with respect to a number of different types of claim (see **Table 6.1**). Its meaning was considered in *Walls Meat Co Ltd v Khan* [1978] IRLR 499 (CA), where Brandon LJ stated:

> The performance of an act is not reasonably practicable if there is some impediment which reasonably prevents or interferes with, or inhibits, such performance. The impediment may be physical, for instance the illness of the complainant or a postal strike; or the impediment may be mental, namely, the state of mind of the complainant in the form of ignorance of, or mistaken belief with regard to, essential matters. Such states of mind can, however, only be regarded as impediments making it not reasonably practicable to present a complaint within the period of three months, if the ignorance on the one hand or the mistaken belief on the other, is itself reasonable. Either state of mind will, further, not be reasonable if it arises from the fault of the complainant in not making such enquiries as he should reasonably in all the circumstances have made, or from the fault of his solicitors or other professional advisers.

6.13 Once a claimant is aware of the right, for example, not to be unfairly dismissed, a tribunal will almost certainly regard it as reasonable for the claimant to make enquiries about the relevant time limit.

6.14 Tribunals have to apply this general principle to a wide number of situations. Fairly detailed general guidance, in the form of a collection of important considerations, was given by the Court of Appeal in *Palmer and Saunders v Southend-on-Sea Borough Council* [1984] ICR 372, 385. Some of the more common situations are addressed in the following sections. It would be prudent to deal with these principles if making or opposing an application for an extension of the time limit for presenting a claim.

Not reasonably practicable—legal adviser

6.15 Any fault by a claimant's legal adviser with regard to the time limit is to be attributed to the claimant. He or she cannot say 'my legal adviser did not alert me to the time limits (or told me the wrong time limits) and so it was not reasonably practicable for me to put my claim in on time'. As Lord Denning MR put it in *Dedman v British Building and Engineering Appliances Ltd* [1974] ICR 53:

> If a man engages skilled advisers to act for him and they mistake the limits and presented too late—he is out. His remedy is against them.

6.16 Skilled advisers have been held to include voluntary advisers such as the Citizens Advice Bureau and the Free Representation Unit.

Not reasonably practicable—ignorance of the facts or deadline

6.17 If the claimant is ignorant of the facts upon which the case depends, it may not be reasonably practicable to expect them to bring that case until they become aware of the facts. In *Machine Tool Industry Research Association v Simpson* [1988] IRLR 212, the claimant discovered, after the deadline for claiming unfair dismissal had expired, further facts which led her to believe that she had not been dismissed for redundancy as the employer claimed. The Court of Appeal allowed her case to proceed.

6.18 In *Marks and Spencer v Williams-Ryan* [2005] EWCA Civ 470, the Court of Appeal refused to allow an appeal by a respondent against an employment tribunal's finding that it was not reasonably practicable for the claimant to bring her claim because of her mistaken belief that she should wait until her employer's internal appeal had been made. However, the Court of Appeal did consider that the tribunal had been 'generous' in its findings, and the question of whether the claimant had made reasonable enquiries will always be relevant.

Not reasonably practicable—illness

6.19 Quite frequently, the tribunal is asked to extend the time limit on the basis that the claimant was ill (either physically or mentally) during the three-month period. Such an argument is unlikely to succeed if the claimant was legally represented during the period in question, provided that he or she was able to provide instructions. In such a case, it will be assumed that the claimant could have relied upon the legal adviser to progress the claim. *Schulz v Esso Petroleum Ltd* [1999] IRLR 488 (CA) considered the position where the claimant was able to give instructions to his solicitors for the first seven weeks of the three-month period, but then became too ill to continue to do so. The Court of Appeal held that where illness is relied upon, it should not be given similar weight regardless of when in the time limit period it falls. The weeks which led up to the expiry of the period were far more critical to the question of reasonable practicability than the earlier period.

Not reasonably practicable—internal appeal

6.20 Where an employee has been dismissed, and then pursues an internal appeal, time will continue to run during the appeal process. Generally, the tribunal will not accept an argument that it was not reasonably practicable to present the claim until the appeal was determined: *Palmer v Southend Borough Council* [1984] IRLR 119 (CA). Such an argument is likely to succeed, however, if the employer has suggested that the employee should delay in making a claim, eg because of ongoing negotiations, or has otherwise been responsible for the delay.

Within such further period as is reasonable

6.21 As will be seen from the test for tribunal discretion where reasonable practicability is at stake, the claim must be presented within a further reasonable period (see 6.07). There is no particular time limit with regard to what is considered a reasonable further period. The tribunal should take into account all relevant circumstances, including any additional difficulties which the employer would face in defending the claim as a result of the delay: *Biggs v Somerset County Council* [1996] IRLR 203 (CA).

'Just and equitable'

6.22 The discretion of the tribunal with regard to discrimination claims is subject to the test of whether it would be 'just and equitable' to extend the time limit where the claimant is outside the three months in question. This is a more relaxed test than that which applies, for example, to a claim for unfair dismissal. It follows that a tribunal might well decide, where what is alleged is a discriminatory dismissal, that it was reasonably practicable for the claim to be submitted in time, but that it would be just and equitable to allow it to proceed. That would mean that it would have no jurisdiction to hear the unfair dismissal claim, but the discrimination claim could proceed.

6.23 In *British Coal Corporation v Keeble* [1997] IRLR 336, the EAT decided that the discretion of the tribunal in applying the 'just and equitable' test is wide, and comparable to the test under s 33 of the Limitation Act 1980. The tribunal should therefore consider any prejudice to the parties caused by the delay, the length of the delay, the excuse advanced for it, and also the fact that as a result of a change in the law, the claimant has a new right (if applicable). The checklist under the Limitation Act requires the court to consider the prejudice which each party would suffer as a result of the decision to be made, and also to have regard to all the circumstances, including in particular:

(a) the length of and reasons for the delay;

(b) the extent to which the cogency of the evidence is likely to be affected by the delay;

(c) the extent to which the defendant had cooperated with any requests for information;

(d) the promptness with which the claimant acted once he or she knew of the facts giving rise to the cause of action; and

(e) the steps taken by the claimant to obtain appropriate professional advice once he or she knew of the possibility of taking action.

6.24 For the respondent to a tribunal claim, the issue of specific present prejudice, eg that evidence has been destroyed, or a particular witness is no longer available, will be particularly important.

6.25 The effect of consulting a skilled legal adviser is different when considering the exercise of the 'just and equitable' discretion from its effect with regard to the 'reasonably practicable' discretion. In *Chohan v Derby Law Centre* [2004] IRLR 685, the EAT held that incorrect advice by the claimant solicitor did amount to a 'just and equitable' excuse.

Equal pay deadline

6.26 The standard rule is that a claim for breach of the equal pay provisions of the EqA 2010 can be brought in the tribunal during the existence of the contract or within six months of the employee leaving employment (s 129 of the EqA 2010). The point at which time begins to run is not the end of the job, but the end of the contract in respect of which the equality clause has been breached.

6.27 There are three types of case in which this standard six-month time limit is modified, as provided by s 129 of the EqA 2010. These are:

(a) *A case in which there has been concealment.* The relevant question is whether the employer deliberately concealed any fact relevant to the breach of the equal pay provisions of the Act. In such a case the claim must be presented within six months of the date upon which the fact was discovered, or could reasonably have been discovered.

(b) *A disability case.* Here the relevant question is whether the woman was under a disability, in the sense of being a minor or being of unsound mind, during the six months in question. The time limit would then be six months after she ceased to be under a disability.

(c) *A stable employment case.* This applies to a series of fixed-term contracts in a stable relationship. The termination of each individual contract does not start time running. The trigger point is the termination of the final contract.

Deduction from wages deadline

6.28 Where there is a claim for deduction of wages, the time limit is three months, subject to the 'reasonably practicable' discretion (see 6.07). Time begins to run from the date of payment of wages from which the deduction was made, or the date on which the payment was received by the employee. Where there has been a series of deductions, time will run from the date that the last deduction was made, and the entire series of deductions will then be recoverable: *Group 4 Nightspeed v Gilbert* [1997] IRLR 398.

Redundancy payment deadline

6.29 The deadline for claiming a redundancy payment is dealt with in s 164(1) and (2) of the ERA 1996, which read as follows:

164 (1) an employee does not have any right to a redundancy payment unless, before the end of that period of 6 months beginning with the relevant date—

    (a) the payment has been agreed and paid,

    (b) the employee has made a claim for the payment by notice in writing given to the employer,

    (c) a question as to the employee's right to, or the amount of, the payment has been referred to an employment tribunal, or

    (d) a complaint relating to his dismissal has been presented by the employee under section 111.

(2) an employee is not deprived of his rights to a redundancy payment by subsection (1) if, during the period of 6 months immediately following the period mentioned in that subsection, the employee—

    (a) makes a claim for the payment by notice in writing given to the employer,

    (b) refers to an employment tribunal a question as to his right to, or the amount of, the payment, or

    (c) presents a complaint relating to his dismissal under section 111, and it appears to the tribunal to be just and equitable that the employee should receive a redundancy payment.

6.30   The effect of this rather complicated provision is that, where an employer accepts the employee's right to a redundancy payment but disputes the amount, the employee will be protected provided that he presents a written claim for payment within six months. In addition, a claimant would be in time if he or she presents the claim for a redundancy payment, or for unfair dismissal under section 111 of the ERA 1996 within six months of the date of termination. Further, provided that the claimant refers a redundancy payment claim or an unfair dismissal claim within a further six-month period, the tribunal has a discretion to award a redundancy payment if it considers it just and equitable so to do. Once this further six-month period has expired, however, there is no further discretion available to the tribunal to hear the claim for a redundancy payment.

Checklist—making sure the deadline is met

6.31   Professional advisers usually set up a system in order to ensure that the deadlines in relation to a claim are met. The following points are likely to form part of such a system, and will be useful to anyone who is either pursuing or defending a claim:

(a)   keeping a diary in which the key dates are entered, including the expiry of any deadline;

(b)   consulting the diary each day in order to take action in advance of any deadlines;

(c)   ensuring that the claim is presented well before the deadline expires;

(d)   where the claim is presented close to the deadline, sending it by fax and keeping confirmation of the transmission upon the file;

(e)   contacting the tribunal to confirm that the claim has in fact been received.

7 Enforcement

Introduction

7.01 Enforcement is something a litigant must always hope to avoid. It means forcing the other side to do what they have agreed, or been ordered, to do. In relation to employment tribunals this means getting money out of them. The hope is always that people will pay what they have been ordered to pay, to save time and trouble, as well as to avoid paying interest. However, when money becomes overdue, it can be necessary for a party to protect its position by trying to take it from the other side through the proper legal channels. That process is set out in this chapter.

7.02 In this regard it is important to think of enforcement before bringing a claim. It is important to check that the company name of the employer or former employer is registered at Companies House (at <http://www.companieshouse.gov.uk>), and that the employer or former employer is correctly identified on the claim form. In particular, if not much is known about the company, it is sensible to try to get advice about whether it is worthwhile bringing a claim against them before paying any fee. Law firms and advice centres sometimes have access to additional online information about companies.

7.03 Except for orders for reinstatement or re-engagement (see 20.03 and 20.04), enforcement is all done through the county court system and not through the tribunals themselves. This means that court officers, or bailiffs, have the power to enforce tribunal awards or settlements in the same way as they do awards made by the county courts.

7.04 In the case of reinstatement and re-engagement orders, where the respondent does not re-employ the claimant, the claimant's remedy lies in s 117 of the Employment Rights Act 1996 (ERA 1996). Under that section, the tribunal then has to make an 'additional award' in respect of the failure to re-engage or to reinstate. This award is 'additional' to any compensatory award ordered. The additional award must be between 26 and 52 weeks' pay, subject to the statutory maximum (£464 per week with effect from 6 April 2014). For more details see Chapter 20.

7.05 The rest of this chapter relates solely to enforcement in the county courts of 'money judgments' or 'orders for payment': any order from the tribunal requiring a party to pay another party a sum of money.

The county court's powers

7.06 The county courts have at their disposal many methods for getting the money from the person who owes it ('debtor') and paying it over to the person to whom it is owed ('creditor'):

(a) *Obtaining information.* This is where a proper court officer requires the debtor to attend the court office and provide information about the assets he or she controls. In the case of a debtor company this applies to its director or directors. At the very least this will scare a debtor into cooperating and trying to escape the attentions of the creditor (don't try to do this yourself!).

(b) *Execution against goods.* This is where the county court gives to proper court officers (bailiffs) a warrant empowering them to go and take certain types of property belonging to the debtor, which they can then sell, giving the proceeds to the creditor (again, don't do this yourself!).

(c) *Third party debt orders.* This is where the court orders a third party (usually a bank) to pay to the creditor money which they control but which belongs to the debtor. This is perhaps the easiest way of getting a judgment enforced as most employers have bank accounts, and employees often even know the account details.

(d) *Attachment of earnings.* This is where the court applies a special procedure which deducts the money from the debtor's wages and pays it direct to the creditor. This is rare against employers, as employers are usually companies and do not have a wage-slip, but it could work against individual employers.

(e) *Charging orders.* This is where the court essentially 'secures' the debt which the debtor owes to the creditor against real property (ie land). For example, if you sue a debtor who owns a house and you are awarded £10,000, but the debtor has no cash, you can seek a charging order to protect your position and give you a £10,000 share in the debtor's house. Even if it does not expressly say so, such an order would then protect your position even including interest going forward (*Ezekiel v Orakpo* (1994) The Times, 8 November 1994). The share in the property increases with the interest owed.

What do you need to get started with enforcement in the county courts?

7.07 There are three things which you can enforce in the county courts, and each works differently:

(a) judgments or orders for payment;

(b) agreements reached through ACAS ('COT3' agreements);

(c) other settlement agreements.

7.08 To enforce a judgment or order for payment, you simply complete and file (at the debtor's local county court) a form N322A which is available at <http://hmctsformfinder.justice.gov.uk/courtfinder/forms/n322a-eng.pdf>. You should attach a copy of the employment tribunal's judgment or order for payment itself, and set out any interest claimed. Interest in respect of remedies other than discrimination is currently 8 per cent per year, calculated daily starting from the 14th day on which the 'judgment' or 'order for payment' is sent to the parties (for interest in discrimination claims see 21.32). The judgment or order should come with a document setting out how the interest works, so read this carefully before calculating the interest you are owed. A small fee is payable on filing application on N322A, but it should be recoverable if you are successful.

7.09 In relation to ACAS 'COT3' agreements, the procedure is generally the same (you just attach the COT3 itself instead of the order), but in certain circumstances a different procedure is required. Pursuant to s 142 of the Tribunals, Courts and Enforcement Act 2007, the circumstances where a different procedure is required are as follows:

(a) where the debtor has sought a declaration that he or she does not have to pay the money and this is either pending or has been granted (the creditor will just have to wait until it is determined);

(b) if the rules of court so provide (which broadly speaking should not apply but see r 70.5 of the Civil Procedure Rules, available online); or

(c) where the terms of the agreement require the claimant to do something other than stopping or not starting proceedings, in which case the claimant must first apply to the county court seeking an order to the effect that the respondent owes the money.

7.10 This last point deserves some further explanation. If, for example, a COT3 agreement requires a claimant to discontinue a claim and give back his work uniform, he cannot enforce the claim until he has given back his uniform in accordance with the agreement. He then has to apply to the county court for an order that the respondent has to pay him the money he is owed *before* he tries to enforce the award. This should be done on form N244, but advice should be sought before doing this as it may well be more complicated and involve proving the relevant facts to the court's satisfaction.

7.11 Finally, enforcing settlement agreements other than COT3 agreements can be the trickiest of all. The basic principle involved is that the settlement agreement is a 'contract', and that generally the party who breaches a contract has to pay the other party damages. So if a claimant agrees to withdraw their claim, and the respondent agrees to pay, for example, £5000 in exchange, then failure to pay the £5000 is a breach of contract. The claimant should be able to win the claim for the £5000.

7.12   However, the major difference is that the 'breach of contract' route is essentially bringing a new claim from scratch in the county court. In addition, the rules about contract law are extremely complex and can be very hard to apply to day-to-day situations. If you need to enforce a settlement agreement which is not a COT3 agreement, you should almost certainly consult a CAB, law centre, or solicitor's firm on how to go about it. Unlike the employment tribunals, the courts are not designed for litigants in person, and the norm is for the losing side to pay the winning side's costs. For these reasons you should be very confident that you know what you are doing and that you are likely to win before you bring your claim.

8 **EAT Procedure**

Introduction

8.01   Appeals from the employment tribunal are to the Employment Appeal Tribunal (EAT). They are governed by the Employment
Tribunals Act 1996 and the Employment Appeal Tribunal Rules
1993, SI 1993/2854 (as amended in 2001, 2004, and 2013). The
Practice Direction (Employment Appeal Tribunal—Procedure)
2013 also provides a clear and structured guide which should
be read carefully before any appeal is instituted. What follows is
only a brief summary, to be consulted before an appeal is considered. Procedure in the EAT is covered in detail in **chapter 18** of
Blackstone's Employment Law Practice 2014, which also reproduces
the Practice Direction in Appendix 5 and extracts from the Rules
in Appendix 3.

8.02   The EAT is different from the employment tribunals in a
number of important respects. Although it is a tribunal, it is also a
'court of record', presided over by circuit judges, and it has many of
the formalities of a court, such as advocates standing to speak. It has
strict rules, set out in the Practice Direction, about the preparation
and conduct of the hearing. Most importantly, it decides different
things, and focuses almost exclusively on law rather than fact.

When to appeal

8.03   In contrast to the process laid down for reconsideration by the
tribunal itself, appeals are challenges to the fundamental reasoning of
the decision. An appeal lies to the EAT only on a 'point of law'. There
are really three circumstances where an appeal can be brought (see the
EAT Practice Direction, page 3):

(1) Where the tribunal has made an error of law which is apparent
    from the written reasons alone;
(2) Where the tribunal's reasoning is not sufficiently clear ('reasons
    challenge');
(3) Where the tribunal has made a finding of fact which is
    'perverse'.

8.04   An error of law is easiest to spot, although of course the law
itself is not always simple. A crude example would be where a tribunal
decides that the claimant has succeeded in her unfair dismissal claim,
even though it also found that she did not have employee status. The
legal reasoning is internally inconsistent: to have the right not to be
unfairly dismissed, one must have employee status (see Chapter 9).

This example might be simple enough to be corrected by an application for a reconsideration by the tribunal itself, but more complex errors of law may be better suited to an appeal. An error of law can also be thought of as a wrong turn in the tribunal's reasoning: it asked itself the wrong question, regardless of the answer it gave.

8.05 A 'reasons' challenge is an appeal based on a failure by the tribunal adequately to explain why it reached the decision which it reached. For example, if the tribunal prefers one party's evidence against the other, it should give some explanation for its preference. It could say that the party's witness had changed their story, or that their story was inherently less likely, but it cannot simply give no reason. The general test can be formulated as whether a party can understand why he or she did not succeed. As it was put in *Meek v City of Birmingham District Council* [1987] IRLR 250: 'The parties are entitled to be told why they have won or lost.'

8.06 'Perversity' is rather difficult to define. The starting point is that it is hard to appeal an employment tribunal's findings of fact: the tribunal heard all the evidence which the parties brought, and then made its decision. However, where a tribunal makes a decision that simply is not supported by the evidence at all, or is so unlikely as to be absurd, a 'perversity' appeal may have some prospects of success. Sometimes a party makes the mistake of pursuing a perversity appeal in the hope that the EAT will come to a different conclusion, but it must be stressed that this is very rare.

8.07 Appeals to the EAT are hard, complicated work. It should also be borne in mind that, although the EAT has the power to make any order which the tribunal could have made, often the result of a successful appeal is that the case is sent back ('remitted') to the employment tribunal to re-decide the one issue successfully appealed. The decision to appeal should not be taken lightly, and advice should be sought as to whether there are any arguable grounds for appeal, and their prospects of success.

Bringing an appeal

8.08 A 'Notice of Appeal' form must be completed and submitted to the EAT. A fee of £400 is payable on the presentation of an appeal. In the event that the case is set down for hearing, a further fee of £1200 is payable. It is within the discretion of the EAT to order that an unsuccessful party reimburses the fee to an appellant who is successful, and this will be the usual outcome.

8.09 The decision or judgment appealed against must be included with the Notice of Appeal, along with its written reasons, any application for a review, and any other relevant document. In the event of the unavailability of any of these documents, the reasons for the unavailability should be explained.

8.10   If an application for written reasons has been refused, a party who wishes to appeal can simply include the written refusal and ask the EAT to exercise either its power to hear the appeal without the reasons, or its power to request the written reasons from the employment tribunal.

8.11   It is important for a Notice of Appeal to set out clearly and concisely what the basis of the appeal is. This need not be a long and detailed argument, but the judge who reads the Notice of Appeal must be able to understand what it is that the appellant says amounts to an error of law, 'perversity', or failure to give reasons, and an outline of why. A badly drafted notice of appeal may result in the EAT taking no action until the appellant clarifies the basis, or even in striking out the appeal. In the case of perversity appeals, an appellant must particularize the matters which support the contention that the decision was perverse.

8.12   Where a judge or the registrar decides that a Notice of Appeal discloses no reasonable grounds for appeal, he or she may decide that no further action will be taken in relation to that appeal pursuant to rr 3(7) to (10). The appellant may then request an oral hearing before a judge to seek a reconsideration (r 3(10)).

8.13   The deadline for presenting an appeal is generally 42 days from the date on which the judgment or order was sent to the parties, but in some cases time runs from the date on which written reasons were sent (for detail, see the terms of the Practice Direction).

The sift

8.14   Once a Notice of Appeal has been submitted to the EAT, the registrar copies it to the other party or parties involved in the case, each being a 'Respondent to the Appeal'. Then the case is allocated to an EAT judge for 'the sift'. That judge will read the Notice of Appeal and decide whether it has sufficient merit to proceed, and if so how it should be heard.

8.15   The judges dismiss most appeals at this stage, and allow a minority to proceed. When a case is dismissed, the appellant has the right to request an oral hearing, pursuant to r 3(10) of the EAT Rules. This effectively gives the appellant a second bite of the cherry in that he or she can supplement the Appeal Notice of Appeal with oral argument.

8.16   Where an EAT judge decides not to dismiss an appeal, and allows it to go to a full hearing, he or she will set down in an order what needs to be done by the parties and dates for compliance. This is not all that different from an employment tribunal order, except that EAT orders usually prescribe the manner of preparation for a hearing in more detail.

8.17 The order will normally provide for a time within which the respondent must present and submit a response, the preparation of papers for the hearing, a date for the exchange of skeleton arguments, and an 'authorities bundle' (ie a bundle of the decisions of the appellate courts which each party says is relevant to the case).

Preparation for the hearing: papers

8.18 There are specific requirements for exactly how to order papers for a hearing in the EAT, referred to as a 'core bundle'. Paragraph 8.2 of the EAT Practice Direction provides as follows:

> 8.2 The documents in the core bundle should be numbered by item, then paginated continuously and indexed, in the following order:
> 8.2.1 Judgment, decision or order appealed from and written reasons
> 8.2.2 Sealed Notice of Appeal
> 8.2.3 Respondent's Answer if a Full Hearing ('FH'), respondent's Submissions if a PH
> 8.2.4 ET1 claim (and any Additional Information or Written Answers)
> 8.2.5 ET3 response (and any Additional Information or Written Answers)
> 8.2.6 Questionnaire and Replies, if any (discrimination and equal pay cases)
> 8.2.7 Relevant orders, judgments and written reasons of the Employment Tribunal
> 8.2.8 Relevant orders and judgments of the EAT
> 8.2.9 Affidavits and Employment Tribunal comments (where ordered)
> 8.2.10 Any documents agreed or ordered (subject to para. 8.3 below).

Evidence

8.19 It is not usual for the parties to submit evidence to the EAT. Permission must be sought to do so, usually within 14 days of the date of the EAT's order setting the case down for a hearing. The reason why evidence is rarely allowed is that the EAT does not usually consider questions of fact.

Fresh evidence and new points of law

8.20 The general rule is that each party must set out its full case in the employment tribunal. Any attempt at the appeal stage to introduce new evidence or argument is unlikely to succeed. But there are certain limited circumstances in which a party may introduce evidence or argument for the first time at the appeal stage: see *Ladd v Marshall* [1954] WLR 1489. The Practice Direction sets this out in more detail.

Skeleton arguments and authorities

8.21 A skeleton argument should be a clear and succinct explanation of a party's case, and it is intended primarily as a foundation which can be added to by an advocate speaking to the tribunal. For this reason, a clear structure is absolutely essential. A skeleton argument should have numbered paragraphs, and deal with issues in turn. It must be clear to the judge reading the skeleton argument (a) what a party wants, (b) why they say they should get it, and (c) how the different parts of the argument fit together (eg alternative arguments). Perhaps most importantly, it should set out what each party says the law is, so that the judge can understand what he or she has to decide.

Hearings and judgments

8.22   Hearings in the EAT are before a judge rather than an employment judge, but in contrast with the position in the county court or the High Court, they are addressed as 'Sir' or 'Madam'. This is true even if, for example, the judge happens to be a peer of the realm. However, the EAT is more formal than the employment tribunal in other respects, eg in that advocates stand to address the judge.

8.23   It is important not to let this rather more formal atmosphere intimidate or distract you. As with employment tribunals, EAT hearings are public and you can contact the EAT in advance if you would like to observe proceedings, just to get a sense of what this is like.

8.24   On the day, it is worth remembering that, as with all advocacy, 90 per cent of the job is explaining why your case should succeed. If you bear this in mind, and remain calm and respectful, then you will give yourself a higher degree of influence over the proceedings, and increase the chances of a favourable outcome. The judge will bear in mind your level of experience, and you may be surprised at how freely they interact with advocates. They are particularly inquisitive in honing down what the issues are between the parties, as the focus of the EAT is on the law rather than on the facts.

8.25   Once the EAT judge has heard from both sides, he or she will either hand down a judgment on the day, or reserve judgment and make it at a later date in writing. Further appeal lies to the Court of Appeal, a process which lies outside the scope of this book. Reference should be made to *Blackstone's Employment Law Practice 2014*, chapter 21, and advice should be taken.

Part B
Substantive Law

9 Employment Status

Introduction

9.01 The employment status of an individual will determine his or her rights under employment law. In particular, it will determine the statutory rights which the individual enjoys, over and above those in the contract. It is therefore important, whenever someone lays claim to a particular employment right, to ascertain whether they have acquired the necessary status. The main rights are set out in **Table 9.1**, which shows how status determines the rights of the person concerned.

Employees

9.02 Most of the rights which are contained in the Employment Rights Act 1996 (ERA 1996) are confined to employees. For example, the right not to be unfairly dismissed, the right to maternity leave, the right to a redundancy payment and the right to written reasons for dismissal all depend upon the individual in question being an employee. Section 230 of the ERA 1996 lays down the definition of an employee as follows:

> 230(2) In this Act 'contract of employment' means a contract of service or apprenticeship, whether express or implied, and (if it is express) whether oral or in writing.

9.03 As can be seen, this definition is not helpful. In particular, it leans heavily upon the concept of a 'contract of service', which is not defined in the statute. That means that one is reliant upon the decisions of the higher courts in ascertaining whether someone is an employee or not.

9.04 In summary, the case law sets out the following conditions which must be met in order to establish a contract of employment:

(a) A contract between the 'employer' and the 'employee'.
(b) Mutuality of obligation between the parties.
(c) An obligation on the part of the 'employee' to perform the work personally.
(d) Control of the 'employee' by the employer.

9.05 These four conditions (a) to (d) are all 'musts'. Once they are satisfied, that does not conclude the matter, as one must also look at whether there are factors which are inconsistent with the existence of a contract of employment (see 9.10).

9. Employment Status

Table 9.1 Main employment rights

Statutory right	Employees	Workers	'in employment' according to Equality Act
Unfair dismissal	Yes	No	No
Maternity leave	Yes	No	No
Redundancy payment	Yes	No	No
Written reasons for dismissal	Yes	No	No
Statutory holiday pay	Yes	Yes	No
Right to claim unlawful deductions	Yes	Yes	No
National minimum wage	Yes	Yes	No
Right for part-time workers not to be treated less favourably than full-time workers	Yes	Yes	No
Right not to be dismissed or suffer a detriment for whistleblowing	Yes	Yes	No
Right to be accompanied at a disciplinary or grievance meeting	Yes	Yes	No
Right not to be discriminated against because of a characteristic protected under the Equality Act	Yes	Yes	Yes
Right to equal pay	Yes	Yes	Yes

9.06   As to (a) the contract, as the statute makes clear, it may be express or implied and, if express it may be written or oral.

9.07   As far as (b) mutuality of obligation is concerned, the 'employee' and the 'employer' must be under legal obligations to one another. Usually, these obligations are upon the employee to work, and on the employer to pay for that work: *Carmichael v National Power plc* [2000] IRLR 43 (HL).

9.08   As point (c) of the list at 9.04 indicates, the individual must be obliged to provide the services himself or herself. Freedom to subcontract (ie to get someone else to do the work) is inconsistent with an employment contract: *Express and Echo Publications v Tanton* [1999] IRLR 367 (CA).

9.09 As stated in condition (d) at 9.04, it is necessary that the employer should have control over the employee. This will cover matters such as control over the work which is done, the hours which are worked, the location, and the manner in which the work is done. It has become increasingly clear from decisions of the appellate courts that the employer need not actually tell the employee how to do the job. What is important is that the employer has the right to tell the employee how to do the job: *White v Troutbeck SA* [2013] IRLR 286 (EAT).

9.10 In addition to the four 'musts' contained in (a) to (d) set out at 9.04, one must also consider the overall context of the relationship. Taken as a whole, is the contract consistent with a contract of employment? The following factors are among those which will be taken into account:

(1) Who provides the equipment to do the job? If the 'employer' does so, it makes it more likely that it is a contract of employment.

(2) Does the 'employee' take any financial risk? If so, that will be a factor tending against an employment relationship.

(3) Does the 'employee' hire their own helpers? Again, that is a factor tending against employment.

(4) Are there any restrictions upon working for anyone else? Any such restrictions will weigh in favour of an employment relationship.

(5) What are the arrangements in relation to sickness and holidays? Do these reflect what one would normally expect in an employment relationship?

(6) Is the individual subject to a disciplinary code administered by the 'employer'? If so, this will make it more likely that what is being inspected is a contract of employment.

9.11 It should be emphasized that points (1) to (6) are factors to be weighed in the balance, and none of them is by itself conclusive. What is important is the answer to the question: taken overall, does this appear to be a contract of employment?

9.12 A court or tribunal will look at the reality of the situation, rather than the way in which the parties describe their status. It follows that a written contract which states that it is not a contract of employment will not be conclusive. Nevertheless, it will be powerful evidence as to the intention of the parties, and will probably be conclusive if the factual position is uncertain. Similarly, the tax status of the 'employee' will not be definitive, but in cases of doubt it may well weigh in the balance to conclude the matter one way or the other: *Quashie v Stringfellows Restaurants* [2013] IRLR 99 (CA).

9.13 As to the taxation position, if the individual concerned is an employee, the employer is obliged to deduct income tax and national insurance contributions from their wages at source, and make payments under PAYE regulations. An employee will be taxable under Schedule E.

Workers

9.14 The test for determining who is a worker is derived from statute. Generally, the definition is similar, no matter which statute or statutory instrument is relied upon to establish the right in question. For example, in the Working Time Regulations 1998, reg 2(1), the definition reads as follows:

> 'worker' means an individual who has entered into or works under (or, where the employment has ceased, worked under)—
> (a) a contract of employment; or
> (b) any other contract, whether express or implied and (if it is express) whether oral or in writing, whereby the individual undertakes to do or perform personally any work or services for another party to the contract whose status is not by virtue of the contract that of a client or customer of any profession or business undertaking carried on by the individual; . . .

9.15 It follows that, in order for an individual to be a worker:

(1) there must be a contract;
(2) it must be to carry out work or services personally for another party to the contract; and
(3) that other party must not be a client or customer of the worker's business or undertaking.

9.16 There has been some case law on the exception contained in (c): *Byrne Bros (Formwork) Ltd v Baird* [2002] IRLR 96 (EAT). In summary, the position is this:

(a) If the individual is genuinely self-employed then he or she will not be a worker.
(b) If the individual has an arm's-length and independent arrangement with a third party to be treated as working for themselves, then they will not be a worker.
(c) If the individual actively markets their services as an independent person to the world in general, they are unlikely to be a worker.

9.17 Factors to consider include the duration of the engagement, how exclusive it is, and whether the 'worker' is free to work for others, as well as the method of payment.

9.18 As to the statutory rights enjoyed by a worker, the most important are set out in **Table 9.1**.

9.19 As far as taxation is concerned, most (but not all) workers will be taxed under Schedule D (Schedule E treatment is possible, but not usual). The worker will usually submit an invoice and charge VAT if they pass the earnings threshold. It will be their responsibility to account to HMRC for tax and national insurance contributions. The employer has no obligation to deduct PAYE or pay national insurance.

Discrimination

9.20 In order to be protected from discrimination, an individual must satisfy the test which is set out in s 83(2) of the Equality Act 2010:

> 83 (2) 'Employment' means—
>   (a) employment under a contract of employment, a contract of apprenticeship or a contract personally to do work;
>   (b) Crown employment;
>   (c) employment as a relevant member of the House of Commons staff;
>   (d) employment as a relevant member of the House of Lords staff.

9.21 This definition is wider than that which applies to determine whether someone is an employee or a worker. Anyone who is an employee or a worker, as set out in the preceding sections, will also qualify for protection under the Equality Act. However, the definition is broader than that for a worker, because it does not exclude those who provide work for a customer or client in the course of a business or profession.

9.22 Although the conditions are easier to fulfil than those for employment or worker status, they must still be met. The individual doing the work must do so under a contract with the person for whom the work is done. In addition, the contract must have as its dominant purpose the execution of work or labour: *Mirror Group Newspapers Ltd v Gunning* [1986] IRLR 27 (CA).

Agency workers

9.23 Generally speaking, agency workers have difficulty in establishing a relationship of employment. There are two possibilities— employment by the employment agency, and employment by the hirer or end user. Usually the employment agency will not have sufficient control to establish an employment relationship. As far as the hirer is concerned, the barrier to establishing the employment relationship lies in showing the existence of a contract. The agency worker will need to show an implied contract of employment with the hirer. This means that he or she must show that it is necessary to imply such a contract in order to explain the relationship between the parties. This is inevitably difficult, as the obvious explanation for the relationship is that the agency worker carries out their work for the hirer because the employment agency has arranged for them to do so: *James v London Borough of Greenwich* [2008] IRLR 302 (CA).

9.24   Although the agency worker will not usually be able to establish employment status, he or she will be entitled to certain rights, eg those under:

(a) the Agency Workers' Regulations;

(b) the legislation on national minimum wages;

(c) legislation conferring the right to be accompanied at grievance and disciplinary meetings;

(d) the right not to suffer detriment or be dismissed because of whistleblowing;

(e) rights under the Working Time Regulations 1998 in respect of hours and the breaks to which an employee is entitled;

(f) rights under the Equality Act.

Casual workers

9.25   There is no legally defined category of 'casual workers'. However, certain issues arise in relation to those who work irregularly, eg on a seasonal basis. There are usually two separate questions where an individual has a relationship which is irregular or seasonal. First, during the time when he or she is working, is there a contract of employment? This would be determined upon the principles set out at 9.04. Even if it is determined in the individual's favour, that may not assist them if, for example, they are seeking to establish a period of continuous employment of two years in order to claim unfair dismissal. The second question therefore is whether there is a global or umbrella contract which covers the period between active working, so that the individual can acquire the requisite period of continuous employment.

9.26   The argument about an umbrella contract is frequently about the intention of the parties as to what will happen in the future. Will work be provided? Will the employee perform it? Can any inference be drawn from the conduct of the parties, eg from the pattern of work which the employee has carried out?

9.27   There are various provisions which allow periods where an individual is *not* employed to be counted as part of a period of continuous employment. These are to be found in ss 210 to 218 of the ERA 1996. Because they are mainly of relevance in computing a period of continuous employment for unfair dismissal purposes, they are dealt with in Chapter 10 on Unfair Dismissal (see 10.12 to 10.16).

10 Unfair Dismissal

Introduction

10.01 The right not to be unfairly dismissed is perhaps the most important of the statutory rights to protect employment. This chapter gives a brief outline of the law relating to unfair dismissal. For further detail, reference should be made to **chapter 24** of *Blackstone's Employment Law Practice 2014*.

10.02 The issues in an unfair dismissal claim can be summarized as follows:

(a) Does the claimant qualify for the right not to be unfairly dismissed?
(b) Was the claimant dismissed?
(c) What was the reason for dismissal?
(d) Does this fall within the potentially fair reasons laid down by statute?
(e) Did the employer act reasonably or unreasonably in deciding to dismiss?

10.03 The process of deciding whether the claim succeeds or not is set out in **Figure 10.1**.

Qualification

10.04 The first question is whether the claimant has the right not to be unfairly dismissed. This right is only available to employees, and the tests for determining whether someone has the status of employee are set out in Chapter 9 on Employment Status.

10.05 More precisely, a period of continuous employment of at least two years is currently required before an employee acquires the right not to be unfairly dismissed. For those whose employment started before 6 April 2012, the necessary period of continuous employment was one year.

10.06 In order to work out whether someone has been continuously employed for the requisite period, it is necessary to determine when their employment ended. This is their 'effective date of termination' (EDT), and is defined in s 97 of the Employment Rights Act 1996 (ERA 1996), which reads in part as follows:

> 97 (1) Subject to the following provisions of this section, in this Part 'the effective date of termination'—
>
>   (a) in relation to an employee whose contract of employment is terminated by notice, whether given by his employer or by the employee, means the date on which the notice expires,

10. Unfair Dismissal

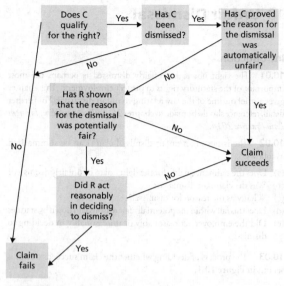

C = Claimant
R = Respondent (employer)

Figure 10.1 Unfair dismissal (ss 95, 98, 108 of the ERA 1996)

(b) in relation to an employee whose contract of employment is terminated without notice, means the date on which the termination takes effect, and

(c) in relation to an employee who is employed under a contract for a fixed term which expires without being renewed under the same contract, means the date on which the term expires

[(c) in relation to an employee who is employed under a limited-term contract which terminates by virtue of the limiting event without being renewed under the same contract, means the date on which the termination takes effect].

(2) Where—

(a) the contract of employment is terminated by the employer, and

(b) the notice required by section 86 to be given by an employer would, if duly given on the material date, expire on a date later than the effective date of termination (as defined by subsection (1)), for the purposes of sections 108(1), 119(1) and 227(3) the later date is the effective date of termination.

(3) In subsection (2)(b) 'the material date' means—

(a) the date when notice of termination was given by the employer, or

(b) where no notice was given, the date when the contract of employment was terminated by the employer.

10.07 The date of dismissal is not, therefore, the date upon which the employee is told that he or she is dismissed. It is the date upon which any notice which they are given expires. Notice runs from the day after the employee is notified.

> **Example**: The claimant was given a week's notice on Monday. Notice begins to run on Tuesday, and the last day of notice will be Monday. That will be the effective date of termination.

10.08 Where the notice given falls short of that which is required by statute, it will be extended as a result of the operation of s 97(2)—see 10.06. As to the minimum period of statutory notice, that is laid down in s 86 of the ERA 1996, the relevant portion of which reads:

> 86 (1) The notice required to be given by an employer to terminate the contract of employment of a person who has been continuously employed for one month or more—
> (a) is not less than one week's notice if his period of continuous employment is less than two years,
> (b) is not less than one week's notice for each year of continuous employment if his period of continuous employment is two years or more but less than twelve years, and
> (c) is not less than twelve weeks' notice if his period of continuous employment is twelve years or more.
> (2) The notice required to be given by an employee who has been continuously employed for one month or more to terminate his contract of employment is not less than one week.

> **Example**: The claimant began to work for his employer on 1 April 2012. He was dismissed without notice on 27 March 2014. The employer's case is that he was dismissed for poor performance. He is entitled to a week's statutory notice, which he did not receive. This must be added to his period of employment, with the result that the effective date of termination is 3 April 2014. As a result, he has two years' continuous employment and acquires the right to make a claim for unfair dismissal.

10.09 It should be stressed that this provision adding statutory notice to the period of employment does not apply when calculating time limits. More generally, of course, if a claim for unfair dismissal is presented out of time, the tribunal will not have jurisdiction to hear it, other than in the limited circumstances set out in Chapter 6 on Time Limits.

10.10 Confusion sometimes arises when an employee is dismissed with pay in lieu of notice. As far as the effective date of termination is concerned, the position is that:

(a) if the employee is dismissed with notice, the EDT is the date of expiry of the notice period, even if the employee is not required to work during that notice period ('garden leave');

(b) if payment is made in lieu of notice, and in accordance with the contract, it is taken to be compensation for immediate dismissal, and the EDT will not be extended by the period of notice.

See *Adams v GKN Sankey Ltd* [1980] IRLR 416 (EAT).

10.11 Another area which sometimes causes confusion is where the employee pursues an internal appeal. In such a case, if the original decision to dismiss is confirmed by the appeal, is the EDT the date of the original decision, or the date of its confirmation by appeal? Subject to any contractual provision to the contrary, the usual rule is that the date of the original decision constitutes the EDT: *West Midlands Co-operative Society Ltd v Tipton* [1986] IRLR 112 (HL).

How is continuous employment calculated?

10.12 There are statutory rules which set out how a period of continuous employment should be calculated. According to s 210 (5) of the ERA 1996:

> 210 (5) a person's employment during any period shall, unless the contrary is shown, be presumed to have been continuous.

10.13 Section 212 then sets out a series of provisions as to what counts towards continuous employment. It reads in part as follows:

> 212 (1) Any week during the whole or part of which an employee's relations with his employer are governed by a contract of employment counts in computing the employee's period of employment.
>
> (2) ...
>
> (3) Subject to subsection (4), any week (not within subsection (1)) during the whole or part of which an employee is—
>
>   (a) incapable of work in consequence of sickness or injury,
>
>   (b) absent from work on account of a temporary cessation of work, or
>
>   (c) absent from work in circumstances such that, by arrangement or custom, he is regarded as continuing in the employment of his employer for any purpose, ...
>
>   (d) ...
>
> counts in computing the employee's period of employment.
>
> (4) Not more than twenty-six weeks count under subsection (3)(a) ... between any periods falling under subsection (1).

10.14 To summarize, if an employee's relations with the employer are governed by a contract of employment for the whole or part of any week, that week counts in calculating continuous employment. If there is no contract of employment then the general rule will be that continuity is broken. However, even where there is no contract of employment, a week will count in calculating continuous employment if it falls within s 212(3) of the ERA 1996.

10.15 The weeks which are deemed to count towards the period of continuous employment therefore include:

(a) those in which the employee is incapable of work because of sickness or injury, up to a maximum of 26 weeks;

(b) those in which the employee is absent from work on account of a temporary cessation of work (in *Fitzgerald v Hall, Russell & Co Ltd* [1970] AC 984 (HL), it was held that the work which must cease is that of the employee rather than that of the employer);

(c) those in which the employee is absent from work in circumstances such that, by arrangement or custom, he is regarded as continuing in the employer's employment for any purpose.

10.16 In addition, s 216 of the ERA 1996 lays down certain circumstances in which a week will not count, but continuity will not be broken, eg in an industrial dispute.

Exceptions to the need for continuous employment

10.17 Some types of unfair dismissal do not require any period of continuous employment before a claim can be brought. These are sometimes referred to as Day One rights, and they are set out in s 108 of the ERA 1996. For a complete list, it is necessary to refer to that section and the sections to which it, in turn, refers. The most important categories are dismissals:

(1) for making a protected disclosure (whistleblowing);

(2) for asserting a statutory right;

(3) for trade union reasons;

(4) for certain health and safety reasons, as defined in s 100 of the ERA 1996;

(5) for pregnancy or other parental leave-related reasons;

(6) for asserting a right to the national minimum wage, or any rights under the Tax Credits Act 1999 or under the Working Time Regulations 1998;

(7) for exercising the right to accompany, or be accompanied by, a worker at a grievance or disciplinary hearing;

(8) where the employee was selected for redundancy, and the principal reason was, in reality, one of those listed in points (1) to (7).

10.18 Although the complete list in s 108 is extensive, by far the majority of claims for unfair dismissal do require a minimum of two years' continuous employment.

Territorial jurisdiction

10.19 The territorial scope of unfair dismissal legislation was considered in *Lawson v Serco* [2006] IRLR 289 (HL). In that case, the House of

Lords made it clear that those who were not employed in Great Britain were excluded from the right not to be unfairly dismissed. However, peripatetic employees based in Great Britain, or expatriate employees working for a business carried on in Great Britain may be entitled to bring an unfair dismissal claim. The courts have considered a number of marginal cases, which are referred to in **sections 1.33** to **1.42** of *Blackstone's Employment Law Practice 2014*.

Excluded categories

10.20   Members of the armed forces cannot bring a claim for unfair dismissal. Section 192 of the ERA 1996, which would give them that right, has never been brought into force.

10.21   Police officers are also excluded from the right to claim unfair dismissal, with two exceptions:

(a)   where the dismissal is within the terms of s 100 of the ERA 1996, which deals with certain dismissals related to health and safety;

(b)   dismissal for making a protected disclosure (whistleblowing).

In either of these cases, the police officer will be able to make a claim for unfair dismissal, as if he or she was an employee under a contract of employment.

Illegal contracts

10.22   An employee cannot claim unfair dismissal on the basis of a contract which is illegal. The illegality which is alleged most frequently is tax evasion. An employer may put forward the argument that the contract is illegal because the employee is claiming to be self-employed, and not paying the tax which is due to HMRC. In some such cases, the failure to pay tax is really the fault of the employer, and it would be harsh to negate the employee's rights on that basis. The crucial point is that the employee must know of the illegality: *Newland v Symons and Willer (Hairdressers) Ltd* [1981] IRLR 359 (EAT). The knowledge in question is knowledge of the facts, ignorance of the law being no excuse. In addition, the employee may be entitled to enforce the contract where he or she was subject to force or duress.

10.23   In practice, an employer will sometimes argue in the alternative as follows:

(1)   the claimant was not an employee; or

(2)   if she was an employee, she was evading tax by claiming that she was self-employed, with the consequence that her contract was illegal and cannot be used to bring a claim for unfair dismissal.

If the employer succeeds on either argument, the claim will fail.

10.24 However, the mere fact that a claimant had self-employment status with HMRC, and is in fact employed, does not in itself amount to tax evasion or lead to the contract being pronounced illegal. The claimant may have genuinely believed that they were self-employed, and paid their tax properly. See Chapter 9 on Employment Status.

10.25 If the employer raises a defence of illegality of contract, the issues which will be explored by the tribunal are likely to be those just discussed.

Dismissal

10.26 Plainly, for a claim for unfair dismissal to succeed, the claimant must have been dismissed. It is for the claimant to prove the dismissal. The statutory definition is set out in s 95 of the ERA 1996:

> 95 (1) For the purposes of this Part an employee is dismissed by his employer if (and, subject to subsection (2) . . ., only if)—
>
>   (a) the contract under which he is employed is terminated by the employer (whether with or without notice),
>
>   (b) he is employed under a limited-term contract and that contract terminates by virtue of the limiting event without being renewed under the same contract, or
>
>   (c) the employee terminates the contract under which he is employed (with or without notice) in circumstances in which he is entitled to terminate it without notice by reason of the employer's conduct.

10.27 As will be seen, the statutory definition is wider than the word 'dismissal' as used in everyday conversation would imply. It covers:

(a) dismissal by the employer;

(b) expiry of a limited-term contract without renewal;

(c) termination of the contract by the employee, where he or she is entitled to do so without notice (commonly called constructive dismissal).

Dismissal by the employer

10.28 Most dismissals are carried out directly by the employer. Occasionally there is a dispute as to whether the words and actions of the employer constitute dismissal. Sometimes the employer's words are unambiguous, eg: 'You're fired.' On other occasions, the position may be less clear, eg: 'I can't put up with your behaviour any more. You'll have to go.'

10.29 Where the words used are unambiguous, the employee is entitled to regard them as constituting dismissal: *Southern v Franks Charlesly & Co* [1981] IRLR 278 (CA). Where the words are ambiguous, however, the test to be applied is: 'How would a reasonable person have understood the words (and, if applicable, the actions) for which the employer is responsible?' If the reasonable person would regard them as constituting a dismissal, then that is what they are. Assume, on the other hand, that a reasonable person would not have regarded them as a dismissal, and the employee walked out, then it will be a resignation, and must be looked at in the light of the rules relating to constructive dismissal (see 10.32).

10.30 Sometimes, what would appear to amount to a dismissal, will not actually be a dismissal, where the employer acts in the heat of the moment and immediately withdraws the words in question: *Martin v Yeomen Aggregates Ltd* [1983] IRLR 49 (EAT).

Termination of a limited-term contract

10.31 Where a contract is for a fixed term with regard to time, or is due to expire upon the completion of a task, then it is described as 'limited term'. Where such a contract expires without being renewed, that constitutes a dismissal. The dismissal may not necessarily be unfair, and the fact that the contract was for a limited term may, in certain circumstances, constitute 'some other substantial reason' for terminating it by non-renewal (see 10.64 for 'some other substantial reason'). The question will then be: 'Did the employer act reasonably or unreasonably in not renewing the contract?'

Constructive dismissal

10.32 The situation where an employee resigns in circumstances where he or she is entitled to do so because of a fundamental breach of contract by the employer, is usually termed 'constructive dismissal', although it is not labelled as such in s 95(1)(c) of the ERA 1996 (see 10.26).

10.33 In order to show constructive dismissal, the employee must establish:

(1) a fundamental breach of contract on the part of the employer;
(2) which caused the resignation; and
(3) which took place without such delay as to constitute acceptance of the breach.

Each of these three requirements will be dealt with in turn.

Fundamental breach of contract

10.34 It is the fact that the employer has breached the contract in a fundamental way which entitles the employee to resign. The test was set out by Lord Denning MR in *Western Excavating (ECC) Ltd v Sharp* [1978] IRLR 27 (CA) as follows:

> An employee is entitled to treat himself as constructively dismissed if the employer is guilty of conduct which is a significant breach going

to the root of the contract of employment; or which shows that the employer no longer intends to be bound by one or more of the essential terms of the contract. The employee in those circumstances is entitled to leave without notice or to give notice, but the conduct in either case must be sufficiently serious to entitle him to leave at once.

10.35 The conduct which will constitute a fundamental breach of contract will vary in accordance with the facts. To give a couple of examples, the following have been held to be fundamental breaches of contract:

(a) a significant and intentional reduction in pay;

(b) an appreciable reduction in status;

(c) a material reduction in benefits.

Further examples are given in **section 24.13** of *Blackstone's Employment Law Practice 2014*.

10.36 Within each contract of employment there is an implied term of mutual trust and confidence. This states that an employer will not 'without reasonable and proper cause conduct themselves in a manner calculated or likely to destroy or seriously damage the relationship of confidence and trust between the parties': *Courtaulds Northern Textiles Ltd v Andrew* [1979] IRLR 84 (EAT). There are many ways in which the implied term of mutual trust and confidence can be breached by the employer, and a number of examples are given in **section 24.13** of *Blackstone's Employment Law Practice 2014*.

10.37 Not all breaches of contract by the employer are fundamental. If the breach in question is not fundamental, then it will not entitle the employee to resign. However, conduct which constitutes a breach of the mutual duty of trust and confidence is always fundamental, so that it repudiates the contract: *Morrow v Safeway Stores plc* [2002] IRLR 9 (EAT).

10.38 If an employee continues to work after a breach of contract, the situation may arise where there are later breaches which will cumulatively amount to a breach of the mutual duty of trust and confidence or some other term of the contract. An employee is then entitled to argue that the breaches should be treated cumulatively. Even if the later breach is not serious enough in itself to constitute a fundamental breach, it may be the 'last straw' which brings about the resignation and can provide the basis for a constructive dismissal: *Lewis v Motorworld Garages Ltd* [1985] IRLR 465 (CA). This principle is also relevant to the question of delay (see 10.42).

Resignation in response to the breach

10.39 The resignation must have been in response to the breach. If the employee was seeking new employment independently of the fundamental breach of contract, then the resignation may not be in response to the breach. As far as the tribunal is concerned, it is likely to give weight to the words written or spoken by the employee at the time that he or she resigned. For example, if there is a resignation letter, does it cite the employer's breach of contract? If so, it will provide important evidence of causation, although it is always possible that the tribunal will conclude that the resignation letter does not reflect the reality of the claimant's motivation. Conversely, if the breach is not mentioned in the resignation letter, that will be evidence against the claim of constructive dismissal. Again, however, it is possible that the absence of any mention of the breach will not be conclusive, eg because the claimant was concerned to preserve relations with the employer in order to obtain a favourable reference.

The effect of delay

10.40   There should not be such delay as to constitute acceptance of the employer's repudiation of the contract. As it was put by Lord Denning in *Western Excavating* (see 10.34): 'The employee must make up his mind soon after the conduct of which he complained; for if he continues for any length of time without leaving, he will lose his right to treat himself as discharged.'

10.41   The question is sometimes posed: 'how long a delay will mean acceptance?' It is not possible to answer such a question without looking at the facts as a whole. If the employee attends work and accepts pay for it at a later date, that will be a strong argument in favour of acceptance. But if he or she makes clear their objection to what is being done, eg by pursuing the grievance procedure, they will not be regarded as having accepted the breach by attending and accepting pay for a limited period of time, eg until the grievance is resolved.

10.42   Where the 'last straw' principle applies, then the tribunal may well choose to focus on the delay between the occurrence of the last straw event and the resignation of the employee, rather than any delay from the preceding fundamental breach of contract.

Constructive dismissal and fairness

10.43   The fact that an employee is constructively dismissed does not necessarily mean that the dismissal is unfair. All that has been done is to conclude that the claimant has been dismissed. The tribunal will then need to go on to consider whether that dismissal was fair or unfair. Of course, the fact that the employer will have been found responsible for a fundamental breach of contract means it is unlikely that the dismissal was fair, but the further steps which are set out in the following sections must still be considered.

Reason for dismissal

10.44 Once it has been determined that the claimant was dismissed by any of the three routes specified in s 95 of the ERA 1996, the next point to consider is the reason for the dismissal. It is for the employer to establish what the reason for dismissal was. According to *Abernethy v Mott, Hay and Anderson* [1974] IRLR 213 (CA), the reason for dismissal is the set of facts known to the employer, or beliefs which are held by the employer which cause it to dismiss the employee. It is not the label which the employer attaches to those beliefs.

10.45 The employee must be made aware of the nature of the allegations during the process of dismissal, even if an erroneous label is attached to those allegations. If the employee is not aware of the allegations, then he or she would not have had a proper opportunity to dispute them. For example, if the employee is told that she is subject to disciplinary proceedings for failing to handle and record the till takings correctly, but the real reason for dismissal is dishonesty, that will not be a mere change of label. That will be a material discrepancy in the facts upon which the employer is acting, with the result that the employee is not in a position to answer the charge properly: *Hotson v Wisbech Conservative Club* [1984] IRLR 422 (EAT).

10.46 It is the employer's state of mind at the time of dismissal which is important in identifying the reason for dismissal: *WT Devis & Sons v Atkins* [1977] IRLR 314 (HL). In that case, it was held that the employer could not rely upon evidence of dishonest conduct discovered after dismissal, even though the conduct in question had taken place before dismissal. In deciding the question of whether a dismissal was fair, the House of Lords determined that the tribunal could not consider facts which were not known to the employer at the time. However, the matters which had been discovered after dismissal could be taken into account in determining compensation. In this particular case, it was held that it was just and equitable to make no compensatory award, as there had been no injustice suffered by the employee.

10.47 Whilst the reason for, and fairness of dismissal are primarily determined by what is in the employer's mind at the time of the decision to dismiss, in exceptional cases the employer may have to take into account events which occurred during the notice period, eg where an employee is dismissed for redundancy, but the employer obtains a new contract requiring more workers during the notice period, it would be unfair not to consider offering one of the new posts to the redundant employee: *Stacey v Babcock Power Ltd* [1986] IRLR 3 (EAT).

Written reasons

10.48 An employee who has been dismissed is entitled to written reasons for the dismissal from his or her employer. The employee will only qualify for this right after two years' continuous employment, ie on the same basis as the right not to be unfairly dismissed. Where an employee is dismissed whilst pregnant or on maternity leave, however, this right is acquired regardless of length of service.

10.49 In order to trigger the employer's duty to supply reasons, the employee must request them. Unlike the reasons, the request does not have to be in writing. The right is set out in s 92 of the ERA 1996:

> 92 (1) An employee is entitled to be provided by his employer with a written statement giving particulars of the reasons for the employee's dismissal—
>   (a) if the employee is given by the employer notice of termination of his contract of employment,
>   (b) if the employee's contract of employment is terminated by the employer without notice, or
>   (c) if the employee is employed under a limited-term contract and the contract terminates by virtue of the limiting event without being renewed under the same contract.
>   (2) Subject to [subsections (4) and (4A)], an employee is entitled to a written statement under this section only if he makes a request for one; and a statement shall be provided within fourteen days of such a request.
>   (3) Subject to [subsections (4) and (4A)], an employee is not entitled to a written statement under this section unless on the effective date of termination he has been, or will have been, continuously employed for a period of not less than [two years] ending with that date.
>   (4) An employee is entitled to a written statement under this section without having to request it and irrespective of whether she has been continuously employed for any period if she is dismissed—
>   (a) at any time while she is pregnant, or
>   (b) after childbirth in circumstances in which her [ordinary or additional maternity leave period] ends by reason of the dismissal.
>   (4A) An employee who is dismissed while absent from work during an ordinary or additional adoption leave period is entitled to a written statement under this section without having to request it and irrespective of whether he has been continuously employed for any period if he is dismissed in circumstances in which that period ends by reason of the dismissal.
>   (5) A written statement under this section is admissible in evidence in any proceedings. . . .

10.50 The employer will not be able to argue that no written reasons need be given because the employee knows why they were dismissed. The basis for granting the right is so that the reason for dismissal is documented, and can be shown to third parties or used in court or tribunal proceedings: *McBrearty v Thomson t/a Highfield Mini-market* (EAT653/90). However, the employer may discharge the obligation by referring the employee to documents which are available to him or her: *Kent County Council v Gilham* [1985] IRLR 16 (CA). In view of the *Abernethy* case (see 10.44) the written reasons should contain a set of facts known to the employer, or beliefs held by it, which have caused it to dismiss the employee. A brief statement of those facts should suffice, but it will not be sufficient to merely state the statutory label, eg capability.

10.51 The remedy for failure to provide written reasons for dismissal is set out in s 93 of the ERA 1996. It is the payment of two weeks' pay.

Potentially fair reasons

10.52 The potentially fair reasons for deciding to dismiss an employee are set out in s 98 of the ERA 1996. The relevant parts read as follows:

> 98 (1) In determining for the purposes of this Part whether the dismissal of an employee is fair or unfair, it is for the employer to show—
> > (a) the reason (or, if more than one, the principal reason) for the dismissal, and
> > (b) that it is either a reason falling within subsection (2) or some other substantial reason of a kind such as to justify the dismissal of an employee holding the position which the employee held.
> (2) A reason falls within this subsection if it—
> > (a) relates to the capability or qualifications of the employee for performing work of the kind which he was employed by the employer to do,
> > (b) relates to the conduct of the employee,
> > (c) is that the employee was redundant, or
> > (d) is that the employee could not continue to work in the position which he held without contravention (either on his part or on that of his employer) of a duty or restriction imposed by or under an enactment.
> (3) In subsection (2)(a)—
> > (a) 'capability', in relation to an employee, means his capability assessed by reference to skill, aptitude, health or any other physical or mental quality, and 'qualifications', in relation to an employee, means any degree, diploma or other academic, technical or professional qualification relevant to the position which he held.

Capability or qualifications

10.53 Most tribunal cases where this reason is put forward deal with capability rather than qualifications. However, a lack of qualifications in the sense of an 'academic technical or professional qualification relevant to the position' (s 98(3)(b)) does constitute a potentially fair reason in terms of the statute, eg lack of a clean driving licence: *Tayside Regional Council v McIntosh* [1982] IRLR 272 (EAT).

10.54 As far as 'capability' is concerned, it may apply to competence. For example, an employer may decide to terminate employment because of a poor production rate or a failure to meet sales targets.

10.55 In addition, 'capability' may apply to ill-health. As stated in s 98(3)(a), capability is 'assessed by reference to skill, aptitude, health or any other physical or mental quality'. Repeated short absences from work, for example, may lead an employer to conclude that an employee is not capable of performing the job, with the result that it decides to dismiss. Alternatively, a prolonged absence with no prospect of early return may lead to a similar conclusion. In either of these cases, the employer could put forward the potentially fair reason of 'capability'.

10.56 It is worth stressing that, at present, we are dealing only with whether there is a potentially fair reason for dismissal. If there is, the tribunal must still consider reasonableness (see 10.65).

Conduct

10.57 If the reason for dismissal 'relates to the conduct of the employee' then it is potentially fair. A dismissal relating to conduct must, of course, be based upon the misconduct of the employee. It can cover issues ranging from dishonesty, lateness, or failure to obey a lawful order, to computer misuse. For a list of examples of misconduct which might, in appropriate circumstances, lead to dismissal, reference should be made to **sections 24.41** to **24.47** of *Blackstone's Employment Law Practice 2014*.

10.58 The fact that an employee has committed misconduct will not always justify dismissal. The decision of the employer to dismiss must be reasonable, and the question of reasonableness in relation to conduct dismissals is dealt with at 10.67 and 10.68.

Redundancy

10.59 The employer may put forward redundancy as the reason for dismissal. In order to establish this, however, there must be what is frequently referred to as 'a redundancy situation'. Further, the employer must show that redundancy was the reason (or the principal reason) for the dismissal of the employee.

10.60 The definition of redundancy is set out in s 139 of the ERA 1996, which reads in part as follows:

> 139 (1) For the purposes of this Act an employee who is dismissed shall be taken to be dismissed by reason of redundancy if the dismissal is wholly or mainly attributable to—
> (a) the fact that his employer has ceased or intends to cease—
> (i) to carry on the business for the purposes of which the employee was employed by him, or
> (ii) to carry on that business in the place where the employee was so employed, or

> (b) the fact that the requirements of that business—
>   (i) for employees to carry out work of a particular kind, or
>   (ii) for employees to carry out work of a particular kind in the place where the employee was employed by the employer,
> have ceased or diminished or are expected to cease or diminish.

10.61 The employer must show that one of these conditions is satisfied in order to establish that there was a redundancy situation. The words of the statute make it clear that it is the requirements of the business which determine whether there is a redundancy situation, and it has repeatedly been held that it is a matter for the employer to decide what the requirements of the business are. The issue is not whether the employer should have decided to end or reduce its requirement for workers, but whether it in fact did so decide. To put it another way, 'there cannot be any investigation into the reasons for creating redundancies or into the rights and wrongs of the declared redundancy': *Moon v Homeworthy Engineering (Northern) Ltd* [1977] IRLR 298 (EAT). However, if the case for the claimant is that the redundancy was a sham, in order to cover up some other reason for getting rid of him or her, then the tribunal will have to look into the question of whether the redundancy was genuine, which will almost inevitably mean some investigation into the reasons why it took place.

10.62 As with the other potentially fair reasons for dismissal, the fact that the employee was dismissed for redundancy does not end the matter. The tribunal will still need to look at whether the employer acted reasonably or unreasonably. In considering that, it will look at, for example, whether there was proper consultation, whether there was a fair selection process, and whether there was a search for alternative employment.

Statutory illegality

10.63 If it would contravene a statutory provision for the employee to continue doing their job, that will be a potentially fair reason for dismissal, eg where a driving licence is necessary to do the job, and the employee is disqualified.

Some other substantial reason

10.64 This provides a potentially fair reason for dismissal, by virtue of s 98(1)(b) of the ERA 1996. Although it sounds like a sweeping-up provision, apt to cover anything, in practice the tribunal is likely to examine with care any argument by the employer that the reason in question falls under this provision. Nevertheless, there are a number of categories which have been held to fall within 'some other substantial reason'. In particular, the following crop up from time to time:

(a) a business reorganization which does not fall within the definition of redundancy: *Hollister v National Farmers' Union* [1979] IRLR 238 (CA);

(b) pressure by a third party, eg a customer, to dismiss: *Dobie v Burns International Security Services (UK) Ltd* [1984] IRLR 329 (CA);

(c) A personality clash with other employees: *Treganowan v Robert Knee & Co Ltd* [1975] IRLR 247 (HC).

Reasonableness

10.65 If the employer has shown that the reason for dismissal was a potentially fair one, the next issue is set out in s 98 (4) of the ERA 1996:

> 98 (4) Where the employer has fulfilled the requirements of subsection (1), the determination of the question whether the dismissal is fair or unfair (having regard to the reason shown by the employer)—
>
> (a) depends on whether in the circumstances (including the size and administrative resources of the employer's undertaking) the employer acted reasonably or unreasonably in treating it as a sufficient reason for dismissing the employee, and
>
> (b) shall be determined in accordance with equity and the substantial merits of the case.

10.66 As indicated earlier, the burden of proof is on the employer to show the reason for dismissal, and that it was a potentially fair reason. Now that the inquiry shifts to the question of reasonableness, however, it is for the tribunal to decide, taking into account all the relevant circumstances, and whether the employer acted reasonably or unreasonably. This is sometimes expressed by saying that the burden is neutral on this question.

10.67 As to the factors which need to be taken into account in determining reasonableness, they will vary depending upon the reason for dismissal. Dismissals for misconduct should always be considered in the light of the statutory ACAS Code of Practice: Disciplinary and Grievance Procedures (2009), which is reproduced in Appendix 1. In addition, the leading case of *British Home Stores Ltd v Burchell* [1978] IRLR 379 (EAT) sets out clear guidance for the tribunal in determining whether a misconduct dismissal is fair. The tribunal should consider the following questions:

(1) Did the employer have a genuine belief that the employee had committed the misconduct in question?

(2) Was that belief based upon reasonable grounds?

(3) Was it formed after a reasonable investigation?

10.68 In addition to the preceding questions, the tribunal will ask whether the decision to dismiss was a reasonable sanction for the misconduct in question.

10.69 Whilst these are the questions on which the tribunal will focus in relation to misconduct dismissals, in other categories of reason for dismissal, there will be different tests. For example, the ACAS Code of Practice does not apply to redundancy dismissals, where the tribunal will rather take into account the guidelines set out in the leading case of *Williams v Compair Maxam* [1982] IRLR 83 (EAT). In that and other cases, it has been made clear that the criteria in determining the fairness of a redundancy dismissal will include:

(1) adequate consultation with the employee;
(2) fair selection criteria;
(3) a fair selection procedure, based upon those criteria;
(4) a search by the employer for suitable alternative employment.

10.70 Similarly, case law has set out factors to be considered in relation to the other potentially fair reasons—see **chapter 24** of *Blackstone's Employment Law Practice 2014*.

The band of reasonable responses

10.71 In determining whether the decision of the employer to dismiss was reasonable or unreasonable, the tribunal must not substitute its own judgment for that of the employer. In other words, the decision for the tribunal is not: 'Would we have dismissed in the circumstances?' It is rather: 'Does the decision of the employer to dismiss fall within the band of reasonableness?'

10.72 Hence, in an unfair dismissal case where the reason for dismissal is misconduct, the question is not whether the employee actually committed the misconduct in question. The issue is rather whether the employer acted reasonably or not in deciding to dismiss. This principle was reaffirmed in *Post Office v Foley* [2000] IRLR 827 (CA). The test of whether the employer acted within the band of reasonableness applies not only to whether dismissal was appropriate in the circumstances of the misconduct, but will also be relevant when the tribunal is looking at the procedure which the employer adopted. According to *Sainsbury Supermarkets Ltd v Hitt* [2003] IRLR 23 (CA): 'the objective standards of the reasonable employer must be applied to all aspects of the question whether an employee was fairly and reasonably dismissed'. This means, for example, that in considering whether an investigation was reasonable, the tribunal must have regard to the band of reasonableness, rather than its own view as to what should have been done.

10.73   The wording of s 98(4) of the ERA 1996 recognizes that small employers will not always be as able to implement such an elaborate disciplinary procedure as the larger employer. This does not mean that the smaller employer has leeway to act unfairly; rather, it means that it may not always have the resources to carry out, for example, such a detailed investigation, or a completely independent appeals process.

'No difference' dismissals

10.74   If the employer has acted unreasonably in dealing with the disciplinary process, it is not sufficient for it to argue that a fair procedure would have made no difference. The dismissal will still be unfair, but the fact that the result would have been the same after a fair procedure will affect compensation (see Chapter 20 on Remedies for Unfair Dismissal).

11 Redundancy

Introduction

11.01 Redundancy is a form of dismissal. Most tribunal cases which involve redundancy deal with one or more of the following issues:

(1) whether the claimant or claimants concerned were actually redundant;
(2) whether any dismissal for redundancy was carried out fairly;
(3) whether the claimant is entitled to a redundancy payment;
(4) whether the employer carried out the duty to consult collectively where there were 20 or more redundancies.

When is a person redundant?

11.02 In determining whether an individual is redundant for the purposes of a redundancy payment or unfair dismissal, the definition which appears in s139 of the Employment Rights Act 1996 (ERA 1996) must be applied:

> 139 (1) For the purposes of this Act an employee who is dismissed shall be taken to be dismissed by reason of redundancy if the dismissal is wholly or mainly attributable to—
>
> (a) the fact that his employer has ceased or intends to cease—
> (i) to carry on the business for the purposes of which the employee was employed by him, or
> (ii) to carry on that business in the place where the employee was so employed, or
>
> (b) the fact that the requirements of that business—
> (i) for employees to carry out work of a particular kind, or
> (ii) for employees to carry out work of a particular kind in the place where the employee was employed by the employer,
> have ceased or diminished or are expected to cease or diminish.
>
> (2) For the purposes of subsection (1) the business of the employer together with the business or businesses of his associated employers shall be treated as one (unless either of the conditions specified in paragraphs (a) and (b) of that subsection would be satisfied without so treating them).

11.03 One therefore needs to look at whether the employer:

(1) has closed down, or intends to close down, the business where the employee works—if so, all those employed in the business are potentially redundant;

(2) has decided to reduce the number of employees required to carry out work of a particular kind—if so, employees carrying out that work will be in a pool of those who may be redundant;

(3) no longer needs employees to carry out work of a particular kind in a particular place—if so, employees carrying out that work at that place will be potentially redundant;

(4) has decided to reduce the number of employees required to carry out work of a particular kind in a particular place—if so, employees carrying out that work at that place will be in a pool of those who may be redundant.

11.04   Where a business ceases completely, there is unlikely to be a dispute over whether the employees working there are redundant, as the position is clear-cut. Where the business is taken over by another company, then the Transfer of Undertakings (Protection of Employment) Regulations 2006 will be relevant (see Chapter 19).

11.05   If the business ceases at the employee's workplace, then his or her dismissal will be on grounds of redundancy, even if the business of the employer continues elsewhere (see s 139(1)(a)(ii) of the ERA 1996). Occasionally, there is an issue about the place of work of an employee. As far as the redundancy provisions are concerned, the test is a factual one rather than a contractual one. In other words, even if the employee's contract contains a mobility clause saying that they can be transferred to another location, the question of whether they are redundant will normally be determined by where they actually work: *High Table Ltd v Horst* [1997] IRLR 513. However, an employee will not be made redundant if he or she has a mobility clause in their contract, and is genuinely relocated in accordance with this clause, with advance notice as part of the redundancy consultation procedures: *Home Office v Evans* [2008] IRLR 59 (CA).

11.06   Frequently in the tribunal the argument is about whether there has been a reduction in the requirement for employees to perform work of a particular kind, either in the business generally or in a particular workplace (s 139(1)(b)). Crucially, it is not necessary for the *work* to have diminished. The employer is entitled to decide that the same amount of work should be done by *fewer people*. Those whose dismissal is attributable to that decision are then redundant. There will not usually be 'any investigation into the rights and wrongs of the declared redundancy': *Moon v Homeworthy Furniture* [1976] IRLR 298 (EAT). By this is meant that tribunals will not usually revisit the employer's decision that there ought to be redundancies, provided that the decision is a genuine one. In order to show that there was a genuine redundancy situation, the employer may need to put forward evidence of the state of the business, eg a fall in demand, or a new technological development. But in considering that evidence, the tribunal should not be looking at whether the redundancies were inevitable, or even whether they were reasonable. It rather has to decide whether the requirements of the employer for employees had ceased or diminished. Was it, in other words, a genuine redundancy situation?

Unfair dismissal for redundancy

11.07 Redundancy is a potentially fair reason for dismissal. However, for a dismissal to be fair, it must not only be for a fair reason, but the employer must have acted 'reasonably' rather than 'unreasonably' in treating it (redundancy) as a fair reason for dismissal. The statutory test is contained in s 98(4) of the ERA 1996, which reads in part:

> 98 (4) ... the determination of the question whether the dismissal is fair or unfair (having regard to the reason shown by the employer)—
>
> (a) depends on whether in the circumstances (including the size and administrative resources of the employer's undertaking) the employer acted reasonably or unreasonably in treating it as a sufficient reason for dismissing the employee, and
>
> (b) shall be determined in accordance with equity and the substantial merits of the case.

11.08 For the majority of unfair dismissal claims which are heard by the employment tribunal, assistance in deciding what is 'reasonable' is provided by the ACAS Code of Practice on Disciplinary and Grievance Procedures (2009)—see Appendix 1. But no such help is provided in the case of redundancy dismissals. As stated in the Foreword to the Code of Practice:

> The Code does not apply to dismissals due to redundancy or the non-renewal of fixed term contracts on their expiry. Guidance on handling redundancies is contained in Acas' advisory booklet on redundancy handling.

11.09 Some guidance as to fairness in relation to redundancy is provided by the case law, however. The leading case on what is reasonable in a redundancy situation is *Williams v Compair Maxam* [1982] IRLR 83 (EAT). Strictly speaking, it deals with the situation where employees are represented by a trade union recognized by the employer. Nevertheless, the principles which it lays down are of more general application, and can be summarized as follows:

(1) The employer must give as much warning as possible of impending redundancies.

(2) There should be consultation as to how the desired management outcome can be achieved with as little hardship as possible to the employees, particularly with regard to the criteria to be applied in selecting for redundancy.

(3) Fair criteria should be established which, so far as possible, can be objectively checked, eg against attendance record, efficiency, experience, length of service.

(4) Selection should be in accordance with these criteria and consideration of representations as to the selection process.

(5) The employer should seek to see whether alternative employment is available, so as to avoid dismissing the employee.

11.10 Failure to follow one or other of these principles will not automatically lead to a finding of unfairness. However, the principles should only be departed from with good reason.

The pool

11.11 The determination of the pool from which those to be made redundant will be selected is obviously a crucial part of the process.

11.12 In *Taymech v Ryan* (UKEAT 663/94), the EAT dealt with this problem, declaring:

> The question of how the pool should be defined is primarily a matter for the employer to determine. It would be difficult for the employee to challenge it where the employer has genuinely applied his mind [to] the problem (per Mummery J).

11.13 *Taymech* was applied in *Capita Hartshead v Byard* (UKEAT 0171/11), where the employer had decided on a pool of one, with the virtually inevitable consequence that the claimant was declared redundant. The EAT emphasized that the respondent had to apply its mind genuinely to the determination of the pool, and that the tribunal had a role in considering genuineness. A pool of one was not automatically unfair, but in this case the tribunal was entitled to find on the facts that the employer had not genuinely applied its mind to pool selection. As a result, the value of any consultation was undermined and the dismissal was unfair.

Bumping

11.14 One of the aspects of the determination of the pool is whether the employer should consider 'bumping', ie defining the pool broadly so as to encompass a number of different teams or job titles. The consequence of such a course of action may be that the employee eventually considered redundant is not the one whose job has disappeared. Rather he or she has been 'bumped' into redundancy by someone from another team whom management wishes to retain in the business.

11.15 It was made clear in *Murray v Foyle Meats* [1999] IRLR 562 (HL) that dismissal of an employee can be attributable to a diminution in the need for employees to do work of a particular kind within the meaning of the s 139 ERA definition of redundancy, regardless of their contractual terms or their function in the workplace. This opens the door to 'bumping' redundancies.

Scrutiny of criteria and the scoring process

11.16 It is for the employer to determine a set of criteria which will be used to select employees for redundancy. Commonly, this is done by way of a matrix, which sets out a list of criteria. Each employee receives a score against each criterion. Some criteria may receive a weighting if they are considered more important, so that they will count for more when the total is counted up.

11.17 To what extent should the employment tribunal consider and adjudicate upon the criteria and the scoring process adopted by the employer? *British Aerospace v Green* [1995] IRLR 437 (CA) aims to keep any such process within boundaries. In that case, which concerned the question of disclosure of documents in the context of a very substantial redundancy exercise, Waite LJ said:

> Employment law recognises, pragmatically, that an over-minute investigation of the selection process by the tribunal members may run the risk of defeating the purpose which the tribunals were called into being to discharge, namely a swift, informal disposition of disputes arising from redundancy in the workplace. So in general the employer who sets up a system of selection which can reasonably be described as fair and applies it without any overt signs of conduct which mars its fairness will have done all that the law requires of him.

11.18 Applying this pragmatic line of reasoning, the Court of Appeal overturned an order of the employment tribunal for discovery where the employer was declaring some 530 redundancies from a pool of 7000.

11.19 In *FDR Ltd v Holloway* [1995] IRLR 400 (EAT), however, where one employee was to be declared redundant out of eight, discovery of all eight assessments was ordered, to see whether the criteria had been fairly applied. In that case, an issue had arisen as to the fairness of the procedure, as an employee with less service and a poorer record than the claimant had been retained while the claimant was dismissed. In that sense, it dealt with a different situation from that in *British Aerospace*.

11.20 In *Nicholls v Rockwell Automation Ltd* (UKEAT/0540/11), the EAT emphasized that when considering whether selection for redundancy was unfair because of the application of the criteria, the tribunal must look at whether the process was within the band of reasonable responses. What were the respondent's reasons for the selection, and were those reasons reasonable? It stressed that it was an error in law for the tribunal to embark on a detailed critique of individual items of scoring. Close scrutiny was stated to be wrong 'once improper motivation had been rejected'.

11.21 It appears that close scrutiny is legitimate, however, when one is deciding on the integrity of the scoring process. Sometimes the claimant argues that the scoring process was not a genuine one, eg that he or she had been earmarked by the employer for redundancy, and the result was pre-determined on the basis of prejudice. If so, the tribunal has to look at the issue of genuineness first, adopting close scrutiny if necessary.

11.22 There is no need for *all* the criteria which the employer adopts to be objective. However, it is worth returning to *Williams v Compair Maxam* [1982] IRLR 83 (EAT) and what was said there about criteria:

> The purpose of having, so far as possible, objective criteria is to ensure that redundancy is not used as a pretext for getting rid of employees who some manager wishes to get rid of for other reasons. Except in cases where the criteria can be applied automatically (eg last in first out), in any selection for redundancy elements of personal judgment are bound to be required thereby involving the risk of judgment being clouded by personal animosity. Unless some objective criteria are included, it is extremely difficult to demonstrate that the choice was not determined by personal likes and dislikes alone.

11.23 As a matter of practice it would seem that an employer will be acting reasonably if the criteria which are adopted constitute a mixture of the objective and the subjective. That is what most employers do in practice, and it is fair to say that such a mixture will in itself usually be reasonable (subject to the criteria themselves being reasonable, quite apart from the question of whether they are subjective or objective).

11.24 Where criteria have been fixed, it is likely to be unfair to depart from them in any significant way: *Watkins v Crouch t/a Temple Bird Solicitors* [2011] IRLR 382 (EAT).

Redundancy scoring and discrimination

11.25 It is apparent from the cases just mentioned that the limits on close scrutiny of the criteria and the scoring process are subject to the proviso that they can be examined with care when an improper motive is alleged.

11.26 In particular this will be the case where what is alleged is that the claimant was selected for a discriminatory reason. The reverse burden of proof applies (see Chapter 16 on Discrimination).

Where the employee establishes facts from which discrimination can be inferred, the employer is obliged to provide a non-discriminatory explanation for those facts.

Individual consultation

11.27 The employer must warn and consult an employee who is at risk of being made redundant. This can only be avoided if the employer is able to show that consultation would be 'an utterly futile exercise': *Mugford v Midland Bank* [1997] IRLR 209 (EAT).

11.28 As far as warning is concerned, it is best practice to warn all employees in the pool that they are at risk of redundancy before the process of selection begins.

11.29 What does consultation involve? In *King v Eaton Ltd* [1996] IRLR 199, the following definition was adopted by the Scottish Court of Session:

… fair consultation means (a) consultation when the proposals are still at a formative stage; (b) adequate information on which to respond; (c) adequate time in which to respond; and (d) conscientious consideration by an authority of a response to consultation.

11.30 The following matters ought to be covered in a consultation meeting:

- the employee should be told of the reasons why redundancies are being considered if this has not been done previously;
- an explanation of why his or her job is at risk should be given;
- the selection criteria, and why the employee has been selected on the basis of those criteria should be explained—the employee should be shown his or her own score, but need not normally be shown the scores of other employees;
- the possibility of alternative jobs which may be available may be mentioned. However, it may be premature to deal with this matter in any detail prior to the consideration of representations made by the employee about the prospect of redundancy;
- any financial arrangements in relation to redundancy pay, etc should be explained.

11.31 The employee must be given the opportunity to comment and respond before any final decision is taken: *R v British Coal Corporation, ex p Price* [1994] IRLR 72 (HC). Preferably, a meeting should be fixed to discuss any such response.

Alternative employment

11.32 The employer has a duty, if someone has been provisionally selected for redundancy, to take reasonable steps to seek alternative employment for that employee. Such alternative employment may be within the company, or with any associated company of the employer (see s 139(2) of the ERA 1996 set out at 11.02). The duty may be summarized as follows:

(1) the employer must find out what vacancies exist;

(2) the employer must give the employee available information about the proposed salary and other terms attaching to such vacancies;

(3) such vacancies ought to be brought to the attention of the employee even if they are of lower status or carry lower wages than the employee's current job.

11.33 The duty to search for alternative employment is one of the crucial points in determining whether the employer acted reasonably in dismissing the employee. The job which the employee does may be redundant, but it may be possible for him or her to continue to work for the employer, thus avoiding dismissal. The failure to carry out a search for alternative employment is likely to lead to the conclusion that the dismissal was unfair: *Vokes Ltd v Bear* [1973] IRLR 363 (EAT). However, the duty is not to find alternative employment, but to make a serious search.

11.34 If the employer is able to identify suitable alternative work and makes an offer of such work to the potentially redundant employee, the employer is likely to escape liability to make a redundancy payment. See **sections 25.24** to **25.28** of *Blackstone's Employment Law Practice 2014* for details of the consequences of such an offer, including trial periods, suitability, and reasonableness.

Automatic unfairness

11.35 If a dismissal for redundancy is made on certain specified grounds, it will be automatically unfair. Many of the grounds in question are set out in s 105 of the ERA 1996. Among them are:

(1) membership or non-membership of a trade union (this appears in s 153 of the Trade Union and Labour Relations (Consolidation) Act 1992 (TULR(C)A 1992);

(2) assertion of a statutory right;

(3) requesting flexible working;

(4) being the trustee of an occupational pension scheme.

11.36 If an employee is absent on maternity leave when her job becomes redundant, she must be offered alternative employment if any suitable vacancy exists. Such an offer:

• must be made before the old employment ends;

• must start immediately after the old employment ends;

- must involve suitable and appropriate work for the employee; and
- must not be on terms which are substantially less favourable than the old employment.

11.37 If such a vacancy exists, and the employer does not comply with these provisions, the dismissal will be automatically unfair (Maternity and Parental Leave etc Regulations 1999, regs 10 and 20).

Redundancy payments

11.38 If an employee is dismissed for redundancy, he or she will be entitled to a statutory redundancy payment if they have two or more years' employment with that employer. Redundancy pay is calculated in accordance with the formula set out in s 162 of the ERA 1996, which reads in part as follows:

> 162 (1) The amount of a redundancy payment shall be calculated by—
> (a) determining the period, ending with the relevant date, during which the employee has been continuously employed,
> (b) reckoning backwards from the end of that period the number of years of employment falling within that period, and
> (c) allowing the appropriate amount for each of those years of employment.
> (2) In subsection (1)(c) 'the appropriate amount' means—
> (a) one and a half weeks' pay for a year of employment in which the employee was not below the age of forty-one,
> (b) one week's pay for a year of employment (not within paragraph (a)) in which he was not below the age of twenty-two, and
> (c) half a week's pay for each year of employment not within paragraph (a) or (b).
> (3) Where twenty years of employment have been reckoned under subsection (1), no account shall be taken under that subsection of any year of employment earlier than those twenty years.

There is an online calculator to calculate statutory redundancy pay at <https://www.gov.uk/calculate-your-redundancy-pay>.

11.39 The week's pay upon which the calculation is based is gross (before tax) and is subject to a statutory limit of £464 with effect from 6 April 2014 (revised annually).

11.40 Where there is a dispute in a claim for a redundancy payment over whether dismissal was for redundancy, the presumption is that it was, in accordance with s 163(2) of the ERA 1996:

> 163(2) For the purposes of any such reference [of a claim for a statutory redundancy payment], an employee who has been dismissed by his employer shall, unless the contrary is proved, be presumed to have been so dismissed by reason of redundancy.

11. Redundancy

11.41 This presumption does not apply in other contexts, eg unfair dismissal.

11.42 In addition to the statutory redundancy payment, an employee may have a contractual entitlement to severance pay at a higher level than the statutory minimum. (For details see **section 25.32** of *Blackstone's Employment Law Practice 2014*.)

Claiming redundancy payment

11.43 If the employer fails to pay the amount due, the employee should claim his or her entitlement in writing. In the event of continued failure to receive the payment, a claim should be made to the employment tribunal within six months from the date of termination, subject to a further extension of six months if just and equitable (see Chapter 6 on Time Limits for further details).

11.44 If the employer is insolvent, and has not paid the statutory redundancy payment, the government will make the statutory payment (s 166 of the ERA 1996). An employee in this position should apply to their local Redundancy Payments Office. Certain other payments, eg statutory holiday pay, statutory notice pay, deductions from wages, are also payable by the government in such circumstances.

Collective consultation: the duty

11.45 In addition to consultation at the individual level, there is a duty on the employer to carry out collective consultation in certain circumstances. The duty is set out in s 188 of the TULR(C)A 1992, which reads in part as follows:

> 188 (1) Where an employer is proposing to dismiss as redundant 20 or more employees at one establishment within a period of 90 days or less, the employer shall consult about the dismissals all the persons who are appropriate representatives of any of the employees who may be affected by the proposed dismissals or may be affected by measures taken in connection with those dismissals.
>
> (1A) The consultation shall begin in good time and in any event—
> (a) where the employer is proposing to dismiss 100 or more employees as mentioned in subsection (1), at least 45 days, and
> (b) otherwise, at least 30 days,
> before the first of the dismissals takes effect.
>
> (2) The consultation shall include consultation about ways of—
> (a) avoiding the dismissals,
> (b) reducing the numbers of employees to be dismissed, and
> (c) mitigating the consequences of the dismissals,
> and shall be undertaken by the employer with a view to reaching agreement with the appropriate representatives.

(3) In determining how many employees an employer is proposing to dismiss as redundant no account shall be taken of employees in respect of whose proposed dismissals consultation has already begun.

(4) For the purposes of the consultation the employer shall disclose in writing to the appropriate representatives—

    (a) the reasons for his proposals,

    (b) the numbers and descriptions of employees whom it is proposed to dismiss as redundant,

    (c) the total number of employees of any such description employed by the employer at the establishment in question,

    (d) the proposed method of selecting the employees who may be dismissed, . . .

    (e) the proposed method of carrying out the dismissals, with due regard to any agreed procedure, including the period over which the dismissals are to take effect . . .

    (f) the proposed method of calculating the amount of any redundancy payments to be made (otherwise than in compliance with an obligation imposed by or by virtue of any enactment) to employees who may be dismissed,

    (g) the number of agency workers working temporarily for and under the supervision and direction of the employer,

    (h) the parts of the employer's undertaking in which those agency workers are working, and

    (i) the type of work those agency workers are carrying out.

11.46   In summary, the duty arises where the employer proposes to dismiss 20 or more employees at one establishment within a period of 90 days or less. Where between 20 and 99 redundancies are planned, such consultation must begin in good time, and at least 30 days before the first of the dismissals takes effect. Where it is proposed to dismiss 100 or more employees, the minimum period is 45 days.

11.47   The TULR(C)A 1992 provisions are intended to implement the Collective Redundancies Directive of the European Union (98/59/EC), the relevant parts of Arts 1 and 2 of which read as follows:

Article 1

For the purposes of this Directive—

'collective redundancies' means dismissals effected by an employer for one or more reasons not related to the individual workers concerned where, according to the choice of the Member States the number of redundancies is

(i) [not adopted by the United Kingdom];

(ii) . . . over a period of 90 days, at least 20, whatever the number of workers normally employed at the establishments in question . . .

Article 2

Where an employer is contemplating collective redundancies, he shall begin consultation with the workers' representatives in good time with a view to reaching an agreement.

What triggers the duty?

11.48 As will be seen from the wording of the statute and the Directive, the TULR(C)A 1992 refers to the employer 'proposing' redundancies, whereas the European Directive talks about the employer 'contemplating' dismissals. In *MSF v Refuge Assurance plc* [2002] IRLR 324, the EAT considered this difference. It held that s 188 of the TULR(C)A 1992 could not be interpreted in accordance with the requirements of the Directive. As a result, the duty to consult under UK law is not triggered merely by the contemplation of collective redundancies. The employer does not have to start consulting until the stage has been reached when there are proposals to be made.

What is the duty?

11.49 Both the TULR(C)A 1992 and the Directive refer to 'consultation'. Consultation was defined in *King v Eaton Ltd* (see 11.29). However, s 188(2) of the TULR(C)A 1992 states that this is 'with a view to reaching agreement'. This is a formula which really equates to negotiation, and this interpretation is in accordance with the case of *Junk v Kuhnel* [2005] IRLR 310 (ECJ). The process must be entered into with a view to achieving agreement, although if no agreement is reached, management can impose its will.

11.50 In order for consultation to be meaningful, the employer must give to the employee representatives the information which is set out in s 188(4) (see 11.45). As to the content of the consultation, as stated in s 188(2) it includes consultation about ways of avoiding the dismissals, reducing the number of redundancies, and mitigating the consequences of those redundancies.

With whom must the employer consult?

11.51 The employer must consult with 'appropriate representatives' as defined in s 188(1B) of the TULR(C)A 1992, which reads as follows:

> 188 (1B) For the purposes of this section the appropriate representatives of any affected employees are—
> (a) if the employees are of a description in respect of which an independent trade union is recognised by their employer, representatives of the trade union, or
> (b) in any other case, whichever of the following employee representatives the employer chooses—
> (i) employee representatives appointed or elected by the affected employees otherwise than for the purposes of this section, who (having regard to the purposes for and the method by which they were appointed or elected) have

> authority from those employees to receive information and to
> be consulted about the proposed dismissals on their behalf;
> (ii) employee representatives elected by the affected employ-
> ees, for the purposes of this section, in an election satisfying
> the requirements of section 188A(1).

11.52 This means that, where there is a recognized trade union, that
will be the body with which the employer consults. If there is not, then
the employer has a choice either to consult with representatives of the
affected employees who already have authority for this purpose, or to consult with representatives elected by those employees in accordance with
s 188A(1) of the TULR(C)A 1992. The latter provision reads as follows:

> 188A (1) The requirements for the election of employee representatives
> under section 188(1B)(b)(ii) are that—
> (a) the employer shall make such arrangements as are reasonably
> practical to ensure that the election is fair;
> (b) the employer shall determine the number of representatives to
> be elected so that there are sufficient representatives to repre-
> sent the interests of all the affected employees having regard
> to the number and classes of those employees;
> (c) the employer shall determine whether the affected employ-
> ees should be represented either by representatives of all the
> affected employees or by representatives of particular classes
> of those employees;
> (d) before the election the employer shall determine the term of
> office as employee representatives so that it is of sufficient
> length to enable information to be given and consultations
> under section 188 to be completed;
> (e) the candidates for election as employee representatives are
> affected employees on the date of the election;
> (f) no affected employee is unreasonably excluded from standing
> for election;
> (g) all affected employees on the date of the election are entitled
> to vote for employee representatives;
> (h) the employees entitled to vote may vote for as many candidates
> as there are representatives to be elected to represent them or, if
> there are to be representatives for particular classes of employees,
> may vote for as many candidates as there are representatives to
> be elected to represent their particular class of employee;
> (i) the election is conducted so as to secure that—
> (i) so far as is reasonably practicable, those voting do so in secret, and
> (ii) the votes given at the election are accurately counted.

Who is included in the numbers?

11.53 As the duty of the employer depends upon the number of
redundancies proposed, it is important to be clear about how those

numbers are calculated. There are two issues. First, what categories of employee are included in the calculation? Second, what is the significance of the phrase 'at one establishment' in s 188 of the TULR(C)A 1992?

11.54 If the employer calls for volunteers in order to avoid compulsory redundancies, those who volunteer must be included in the calculation: *Optare Group Ltd v TGWU* [2007] IRLR 931 (EAT).

11.55 Those whom the employer plans to redeploy elsewhere in the business must also be included in counting those who are potentially redundant: *Hardy v Tourism South East* [2005] IRLR 242 (EAT).

11.56 Those who are employed under fixed-term contracts which are set to expire do not count in the calculation of redundancies. They must, however, be counted if they are to be dismissed before the expiry of such contracts.

'At one establishment'

11.57 This phrase, used in s 188(1) of the TULR(C)A 1992, has caused considerable controversy. From the point of view of the employer, the advantage lies in interpreting 'establishment' as narrowly as possible, with the result that the duty is less likely to be triggered. Conversely, from the employee's perspective, a broad interpretation is helpful in ensuring that the duty is brought into play more frequently.

11.58 In *Renfrewshire Council v Educational Institute of Scotland* [2013] IRLR 76 (EAT), the teacher claimants argued that the word should be construed widely, so that it covered the whole of the education and leisure service run by the council. The council argued that each individual school was an establishment at which the claimants were employed. On appeal, it was held that the phrase 'at an establishment' denoted a physical presence rather than being used in an organizational sense. It was further held that no regard should be paid to the scope of any contractual mobility clause, and that it was the factual, rather than the contractual, position which mattered. The conclusion of the tribunal that an individual school could not be a distinct entity for collective consultation was held to be perverse, and the appeal succeeded.

11.59 By contrast, in the case of *USDAW v Ethel Austin Ltd* [2013] IRLR 686 (EAT), the EAT held that priority must be given to obligations under the EU Collective Redundancies Directive (see 11.47). This states that the duty to inform and consult arises wherever the number of redundancies is 'over a period of 90 days, at least 20, whatever the number of workers normally employed at the establishments in question'. It does not state that the minimum 20 workers have to be employed at the same establishment. The EAT held that the obligation was triggered irrespective of whether the employees worked at the same or different establishments. As far as s 188 of the TULR(C)A 1992 was concerned, the EAT held that the words 'at one establishment' are to be treated as deleted.

11.60　The *USDAW* case (see 11.59) was appealed to the Court of Appeal, which has referred it to the CJEU.

Special circumstances

11.61　Section 188(7) of the TULR(C)A 1992 makes reference to 'special circumstances which render it not reasonably practicable for the employer to comply with' the duty to consult and inform. It is clear that such circumstances will be exceptional, and they should be specific to the case in question, eg it is not sufficient to cite insolvency as 'special circumstances', but it will rather be necessary to specify the particular special issues which arose in the insolvency in question. In any event, the statutory provision makes it clear that the employer must take such steps as are reasonably practicable in the circumstances.

Remedies

11.62　Where the employer has failed to comply with its duties under s 188 or s 188A of the TULR(C)A 1992, a claim may be presented to the tribunal by the employee representatives or, where the appointment of appropriate representatives is at issue, by any of the redundant employees. The claim is for a protective award, which orders the employer to pay the wages of redundant employees for a protected period of up to 90 days. If an employee is covered by a protective award, he or she will be entitled to gross wages for the protected period. Any such award will be additional to any other compensation which the employee receives, eg an award for unfair dismissal, or a redundancy payment. Section 189 of the TULR(C)A 1992 (reproduced in part) sets out this right:

> 189 (1) Where an employer has failed to comply with a requirement of section 188 or section 188A, a complaint may be presented to an employment tribunal on that ground—
>
> (a) in the case of a failure relating to the election of employee representatives, by any of the affected employees or by any of the employees who have been dismissed as redundant;
>
> (b) in the case of any other failure relating to employee representatives, by any of the employee representatives to whom the failure related,
>
> (c) in the case of failure relating to representatives of a trade union, by the trade union, and
>
> (d) in any other case, by any of the affected employees or by any of the employees who have been dismissed as redundant.

> (1A) If on a complaint under subsection (1) a question arises as to whether or not any employee representative was an appropriate representative for the purposes of section 188, it shall be for the employer to show that the employee representative had the authority to represent the affected employees.
>
> (1B) On a complaint under subsection (1)(a) it shall be for the employer to show that the requirements in section 188A have been satisfied.
>
> (2) If the tribunal finds the complaint well-founded it shall make a declaration to that effect and may also make a protective award.
>
> (3) A protective award is an award in respect of one or more descriptions of employees—
>
> (a) who have been dismissed as redundant, or whom it is proposed to dismiss as redundant, and
>
> (b) in respect of whose dismissal or proposed dismissal the employer has failed to comply with a requirement of section188,
>
>   ordering the employer to pay remuneration for the protected period.
>
> (4) The protected period—
>
> (a) begins with the date on which the first of the dismissals to which the complaint relates takes effect, or the date of the award, whichever is the earlier, and
>
> (b) is of such length as the tribunal determines to be just and equitable in all the circumstances having regard to the seriousness of the employer's default in complying with any requirement of section 188;
>
>   but shall not exceed 90 days....

11.63 In *Susie Radin Ltd v GMB* [2004] IRLR 400 (CA), it was held that the protective award is punitive. The tribunal should focus upon the seriousness of the employer's default, start with the maximum award of 90 days, and reduce for mitigating circumstances. In so doing, it should take into account whether any breach was merely technical, whether it was deliberate, and the availability of legal advice. It is also clear that where the employer has taken some steps (even though inadequate) towards consultation, the starting point will be somewhat below the full 90-day maximum. The award is not subject to the statutory limit of £464 per week (updated annually) which applies to redundancy payments, etc.

Notifying the government

11.64 In addition to its duty to inform and consult representatives of the workforce, the employer has an obligation to notify the Secretary of State for Business, Industry and Skills. The time limits in question are the same as those for consulting the workforce, and a copy of the form must be given to the appropriate representatives, as part of the information required under the duty to consult.

12 Whistleblowers and Protected Disclosure

Introduction

12.01 Whistleblowers are given protection under employment law in three ways. First, a *worker* may not be subjected to a detriment as a result of having made a protected disclosure. Second, an *employee* may not be dismissed as a result of having made a protected disclosure. Third, any provision in a contract purporting to prevent a worker from making a protected disclosure is void.

12.02 Protection from detriment is given to workers by s 47B of the Employment Rights Act 1996 (ERA 1996):

> 47B (1) a worker has the right not to be subjected to any detriment by any act, or any deliberate failure to act, by his employer done on the ground that the worker has made a protected disclosure.
>
> (2) ... This section does not apply where—
>
> (a) the worker is an employee, and
>
> (b) the detriment in question amounts to a dismissal ...

12.03 The issues in a claim for detriment suffered as a result of whistleblowing are set out in **Figure 12.1**.

12.04 Protection from unfair dismissal is given to employees by s 103A of the ERA 1996:

> 103A An employee who is dismissed shall be regarded for the purposes of this part as unfairly dismissed if the reason (or, if more than one, the principal reason) for the dismissal is that the employee made a protected disclosure.

12.05 The protection for unfair dismissal applies from the beginning of employment. In other words, there is no need for the employee to show any qualifying period of employment.

12.06 Further, any dismissal for whistleblowing because of a protected disclosure is automatically unfair, so that once it is established, the tribunal will not consider whether the actions of the employer were reasonable or unreasonable (see Chapter 5 on Evidence). The issues arising in a claim for unfair dismissal as a result of whistleblowing are set out in **Figure 12.2**.

12.07 Similarly, the protection from detriment will also apply from day one of the worker's employment.

12. Whistleblowers and Protected Disclosure

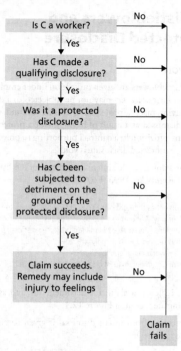

C = Claimant

Figure 12.1 Whistleblowing: detriment (s 103A of the ERA 1996)

12.08 Finally, s 43J of the ERA 1996 prohibits any clause which aims to gag a whistleblower:

> 43J (1) Any provision in an agreement to which this section applies is void in so far as it purports to preclude the worker from making a protected disclosure.
>
> (2) This section applies to any agreement between a worker and his employer (whether a worker's contract or not), including an agreement to refrain from instituting or continuing any proceedings under this Act or any proceedings for breach of contract.

Eligibility: employee and worker

12.09 As appears from the preceding section, the right to claim unfair dismissal is confined to employees. For the definition of an employee, reference should be made to Chapter 9 on Employment Status.

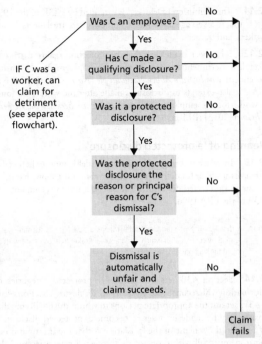

IF C was a worker, can claim for detriment (see separate flowchart).

C = Claimant

Figure 12.2 Whistleblowing: unfair dismissal (s 47B of the ERA 1996)

12.10 The right to claim detriment, however, has a broader ambit, being available to 'workers', who are defined more broadly than they are for other purposes. The core definition of 'worker' is to be found in s 230(3) of the ERA 1996 (see 9.15) and covers those who work under:

> 230 (3) (a) a contract of employment, or
> (b) any other contract, whether express or implied and (if it is express) whether oral or in writing, whereby the individual undertakes to do or perform personally any work or services for another party to the contract whose status is not by virtue of the contract that of a client or customer of any profession or business undertaking carried on by the individual;
>
> and any reference to a worker's contract shall be construed accordingly.

12.11　This definition of 'worker' is extended by s 43K of the 1996 Act so that it covers agency workers, homeworkers, freelancers, health workers, and trainees.

12.12　It has been made clear that the protection against detriment extends to detrimental treatment after the employment relationship has ended: *Woodward v Abbey National plc (No 1)* [2006] IRLR 634 (CA). It also extends to disclosures made after the worker no longer works for the employer: *Onyango v Adrian Berkeley t/a Berkeley Solicitors* [2013] IRLR 338 (EAT).

Meaning of 'a protected disclosure'

12.13　In order to bring a claim for whistleblowing (whether for unfair dismissal or for detriment), the claimant must show that he or she made a protected disclosure. The brief definition is contained in s 43A of the ERA 1996.

> 43A In this Act a 'protected disclosure' means a qualifying disclosure (as defined by section 43B) which is made by a worker in accordance with any of the sections 43C to 43H.

12.14　Section 43B sets out particular protected categories of information which constitute a 'qualifying disclosure'. Sections 43C to 43H set out the appropriate persons to whom the qualifying disclosure may be made in order to become a 'protected disclosure'. As a result, the scheme of the legislation is that the information in question must fall within one of the protected categories, and the way in which it is disclosed must also be one which is protected by the statute.

'In good faith'

12.15　Historically, for a qualifying disclosure to acquire protection, it had to be made 'in good faith'.

12.16　However, the Enterprise and Regulatory Reform Act 2013 abolished this requirement with regard to disclosures made on or after 25 June 2013. In its place, there is now a provision for the employment tribunal to reduce the compensation award by up to 25 per cent where it considers that the disclosure was not made in good faith (see ss 49(6A) and 123(6A) of the ERA 1996).

'Qualifying disclosures'

12.17　The six categories of information which qualify for protection are set out in s 43B of the ERA 1996:

43B (1) in this Part a 'qualifying disclosure' means any disclosure of information which, in the reasonable belief of the worker making the disclosure, is made in the public interest and tends to show one or more of the following—

   (a) that a criminal offence has been committed, is being committed or is likely to be committed,

   (b) that a person has failed, is failing or is likely to fail to comply with any legal obligation to which he is subject,

   (c) that a miscarriage of justice has occurred, is occurring or is likely to occur,

   (d) that the health and safety of any individual has been, is being or is likely to be endangered,

   (e) that the environment has been, is being or is likely to be damaged, or

   (f) that information tending to show any matter falling within one of the preceding paragraphs has been, or is likely to be deliberately concealed.

(2) for the purposes of subsection (1), it is immaterial whether the relevant failure occurred, occurs or would occur in the United Kingdom or elsewhere, and whether the law applying to it is that of the United Kingdom or of any other country or territory.

(3) a disclosure of information is not a qualifying disclosure if the person making the disclosure commits an offence by making it.

(4) disclosure of information in respect of which a claim to legal professional privilege (or, in Scotland, to confidentiality as between client and professional legal adviser) could be maintained in legal proceedings is not a qualifying disclosure if it is made by a person to whom the information had been disclosed in the course of obtaining legal advice.

12.18   The disclosure must contain *information*. It will not qualify so as to acquire protection if it is merely an allegation: *Cavendish Munro Professional Risks Management Ltd v Geduld* [2010] IRLR 38 (EAT).

12.19   A qualifying disclosure does not have to be about a failing of the employer. It could be about a fellow worker, a client, or other third party: *Hibbin v Hesters Way Neighbourhood Project* [2009] IRLR 198 (EAT)

12.20   Among the other issues which commonly arise in interpreting these provisions are 'reasonable belief', 'in the public interest', 'criminal offences', and 'legal obligations'. These phrases are dealt with in the subsequent three sections.

Reasonable belief

12.21   Section 43B (1) of the ERA 1996 requires that the worker making the disclosure should have a reasonable belief in the information disclosed, rather than a belief which is merely genuine. However, it is not necessary that the factual basis of what is disclosed should be true, merely that the worker reasonably believes that it is: *Darnton v University of Surrey* [2003] IRLR 133 EAT.

In the public interest

12.22   The requirement that a disclosure should be (in the reasonable belief of the worker) 'in the public interest' in order to qualify for protection was introduced by s 17 of the Enterprise and Regulatory Reform Act 2013. It applies to disclosures made on or after 25 June 2013. There is no statutory guidance as to what constitutes 'in the public interest'. It is clear, however, that the worker is also entitled to have a personal interest in the disclosure, provided that he or she also has a reasonable belief that it is in the public interest.

Criminal offences

12.23   Any disclosure which, in the reasonable belief of the worker making it, tends to show that a criminal offence has been or is being committed, or is likely to be committed, will amount to a qualifying disclosure, provided that the worker also believes that the disclosure is in the public interest. What if the worker believes that the information disclosed relates to such an offence, but is mistaken as to the existence or scope of the offence? In *Babula v Waltham Forest College* [2007] IRLR 346, the Court of Appeal held that the worker will be protected, even if mistaken as to the existence of a criminal offence.

Legal obligations

12.24   A disclosure which, in the reasonable belief of the worker making it, tends to show breach of a legal obligation will amount to a qualifying disclosure if the worker also reasonably believes that disclosure is in the public interest. In practice, this is the most common type of information which is relied upon in claims by whistleblowers. It covers both statutory and common law obligations. As is the case in relation to criminal offences (see 12.23), an employee is not expected to have an encyclopaedic knowledge of the law, provided that their belief in the underlying facts is genuine: *Babula v Waltham Forest College* [2007] IRLR 346 (CA).

Which qualifying disclosures are protected?

12.25   Not all qualifying disclosures acquire the protection of the statute. As is indicated at 12.17, the content of the disclosure is important, and gives it 'qualifying' status. In addition, however, the way in which the information is disclosed must comply with the provisions of the statute. There are seven methods by which a qualifying disclosure will become protected. These are (section numbers refer to the ERA 1996):

- disclosure to the employer—s 43C(1)(a);
- disclosure to the person believed to be responsible for the failing in question—s 43C(1)(b);
- disclosure to a legal adviser—s 43D;
- disclosure to a Minister of the Crown—s 43E;
- disclosure to a prescribed person—s 43F;
- external disclosure in other cases—s 43G;
- disclosure of exceptionally serious failures—s 43H.

12.26   Each of these alternatives is dealt with in one of the sections which follows, and the relevant statutory provision is reproduced.

12.27   In general, the method by which the disclosure is made will determine whether the worker will gain protection. Additional obligations are imposed depending upon the remoteness of the recipient of the information from the employer.

Disclosure to the employer or designated person

12.28   A disclosure made to the employer, or someone whom the employer has designated for the purpose, is authorized by s 43C(1)(a) and (2) of the ERA 1996, and no additional obligations are laid down for the worker to meet:

> 43C (1) A qualifying disclosure is made in accordance with this section if the worker makes the disclosure—
>
> (a) to his employer
>
> ...
>
> (2) a worker who, in accordance with the procedure whose use by him is authorised by his employer, makes a qualifying disclosure to a person other than his employer, is to be treated for the purposes of this Part as making the qualifying disclosure to his employer.

Disclosure to a person responsible for the failing

12.29   The authority laid down for a disclosure in these circumstances is similar to that where it is made to the employer, but the focus is upon a third party whom the worker believes to be responsible for the relevant failing about which he or she makes the disclosure. The relevant provision is set out in s 43C(1)(b):

> 43C (1) a qualifying disclosure is made in accordance with this section if the worker makes the disclosure—
>
> ...

> (b) where the worker reasonably believes that the relevant failure relates solely or mainly to—
>   (i) the conduct of a person other than his employer, or
>   (ii) any other matter for which a person other than his employer has legal responsibility, to that other person.

Disclosure to a Minister of the Crown

12.30   Where the worker's employer is an individual or an organization appointed under any enactment, any qualifying disclosure will acquire protection if it is made to a Minister of the Crown. It would seem that the disclosure could be made to any appropriate person within the Minister's Department:

> 43E A qualifying disclosure is made in accordance with this section if—
>   (a) the worker's employer is—
>   (i) an individual appointed under any enactment (including any enactment comprised in, or in an instrument made under, an act of the Scottish Parliament), or
>   (ii) a body any of whose members are so appointed, and
>   the disclosure is made to a Minister of the Crown or a member of the Scottish Executive.

Disclosure to a prescribed person or body

12.31   A further route for a qualifying disclosure to acquire protection is provided by s 43F of the ERA 1996. This deals with disclosure to 'prescribed persons' of matters which they are designated to deal with. The 'persons' in question consist of a number of bodies, most of which have some sort of regulatory function, eg the Audit Commission, the Commissioners of Customs and Excise and the Inland Revenue, and authorities which are responsible for the enforcement of consumer protection legislation and health and safety standards. The list is a long one, and is set out in the Schedule to the Public Interest Disclosure (Prescribed Persons) Order 1999, SI 1999/1549, as amended by SI 2009/2457.

12.32   The conditions which are laid down for a qualifying disclosure to acquire protection when it is made by this route are rather more stringent than those which apply when disclosure is made to the employer. However, they are less demanding than those which are made to an external body:

> 43F (1) A qualifying disclosure is made in accordance with this section if the worker—
>   (a) makes the disclosure to a person prescribed by an order made by the Secretary of State for the purposes of this section, and

(b) reasonably believes—
   (i) that the relevant failure falls within any description of matters in respect of which that person is so prescribed, and
   (ii) that the information disclosed, and any allegation contained in it, are substantially true.

Other external disclosure

12.33 A qualifying disclosure may, subject to stringent conditions, acquire protection even if it is not made to the employer or one of the prescribed bodies set out in the previous sections. Such external bodies might include, to take a few random examples, the press, a professional body or trade union, a shareholder in the employer company, the relatives of a patient at risk, or a client of the employer.

12.34 These situations are covered by the provisions of s 43G of the ERA 1996:

43G (1) A qualifying disclosure is made in accordance with this section if—
   (a) [repealed]
   (b) the worker reasonably believes that the information disclosed, and any allegation contained in it, are substantially true,
   (c) he does not make the disclosure for purposes of personal gain,
   (d) any of the conditions in subsection (2) is met, and
   (e) in all the circumstances of the case, it is reasonable for him to make the disclosure.
(2) The conditions referred to in subsection (1)(d) are—
   (a) that, at the time he makes the disclosure, the worker reasonably believes that he will be subjected to a detriment by his employer if he makes a disclosure to his employer or in accordance with section 43F,
   (b) that, in a case where no person is prescribed for the purposes of section 43F in relation to the relevant failure, the worker reasonably believes that it is likely that evidence relating to the relevant failure will be concealed or destroyed if he makes a disclosure to his employer, or
   (c) that the worker has previously made a disclosure of substantially the same information—
      (i) to his employer, or
      (ii) in accordance with section 43F.
(3) In determining for the purposes of subsection (1) (e) whether it is reasonable for the worker to make the disclosure, regard shall be had, in particular, to—
   (a) the identity of the person to whom the disclosure is made,
   (b) the seriousness of the relevant failure,
   (c) whether the relevant failure is continuing or is likely to occur in the future,
   (d) whether the disclosure is made in breach of a duty of confidentiality owed by the employer to any other person,

> (e) in a case falling within subsection (2) (c) (i) or (ii), any action which the employer or the person to whom the previous disclosure in accordance with section 43F was made has taken or might reasonably be expected to have taken as a result of the previous disclosure, and
>
> (f) in a case falling within subsection (2) (c) (i), whether in making the disclosure to the employer the worker complied with any procedure whose use by him was authorised by the employer.
>
> (4) For the purposes of this section a subsequent disclosure may be regarded as the disclosure of substantially the same information as that disclosed by a previous disclosure as mentioned in subsection (2) (c) even though the subsequent disclosure extends to information about action taken or not taken by any person as a result of the previous disclosure.

12.35   An analysis of this section shows that, in order to acquire protection, the person making the qualifying disclosure must satisfy a series of conditions.

12.36   First, he or she must believe that the information disclosed, including any allegation within it, is substantially true. Second, the disclosure must not have been made for the purposes of personal gain. This would exclude, for example, a case where the primary purpose of the person making the disclosure was to receive payment from a journalist. Third, one of the conditions contained in s 43G(2) must be met—this requirement is elaborated in the following paragraph.

12.37   As to the additional conditions contained in s 43G(2), these require either a threat to the worker, a threat to the relevant evidence, or being able to show that the information is not being disclosed for the first time.

12.38   With regard to the requirement that disclosure through this route should be reasonable in all the circumstances, reasonableness must be assessed taking into account the six criteria which are contained in s 43G(3).

Disclosure in exceptionally serious cases

12.39   Where the relevant failure is of an 'exceptionally serious nature', the required conditions for a qualifying disclosure are somewhat less stringent:

> 43H (1) A qualifying disclosure is made in accordance with this section if—
>
> (a) [repealed]

(b) the worker reasonably believes that the information disclosed, and any allegation contained in it, are substantially true,

(c) he does not make the disclosure for purposes of personal gain,

(d) the relevant failure is of an exceptionally serious nature, and

(e) in all the circumstances of the case, it is reasonable for him to make the disclosure.

(2) In determining for the purposes of subsection (1) (e) whether it is reasonable for the worker to make the disclosure, regard shall be had, in particular, to the identity of the person to whom the disclosure is made.

12.40 No guidance is given in the statute as to what constitutes 'exceptionally serious', and there is no definitive appellate guidance on this point.

Causation in an unfair dismissal claim

12.41 Frequently causation is the crucial point for a tribunal in determining whether a claimant was unfairly dismissed for making a protected disclosure.

12.42 The statutory test is to be found in s 103A of the ERA 1996:

103A An employee who is dismissed shall be regarded for the purposes of this Part as unfairly dismissed if the reason (or, if more than one, the principal reason) for the dismissal is that the employee made a protected disclosure.

12.43 If it falls within this section, the dismissal will be automatically unfair, and the tribunal will not enquire into whether the employer acted reasonably or unreasonably.

12.44 The onus of proof in such a case was dealt with in *Maund v Penwith District Council* [1984] IRLR 24 (CA). Where the claimant has the requisite period of continuous employment to qualify for 'ordinary' unfair dismissal (one year if employment began before 6 April 2012, two years if it began thereafter) then the position is as follows:

(a) Has the employee shown that there is a real issue as to whether the reason put forward by the employer for the dismissal was not the true reason, ie has he raised some doubt as to that reason by advancing a public interest disclosure reason?

(b) If so, has the employer proved its reason for dismissal?

(c) If not, has the employer disproved the public interest disclosure reason advanced by the employee?

(d) If not, dismissal is for the public interest disclosure reason.

12.45 The position is different if the employee does not have the necessary period of continuous employment to qualify for 'ordinary' unfair dismissal. If this is the case, the onus will be on the employee to prove that the principal reason for the dismissal was the protected disclosure.

12.46 Sometimes the tribunal will have to deal with the situation where a protected disclosure is related to an act of misconduct. For example, in *Bolton School v Evans* [2007] IRLR 140 (CA), a teacher hacked into his employer's computer system in order to show that it was unsafe. It was held that this was an act of misconduct which could not be regarded as part of the disclosure.

12.47 The onus of proof where there is a claim for detriment because of a public interest disclosure is dealt with in the following section.

Causation in a detriment claim

12.48 Where a worker claims that he or she has been subjected to a detriment because of a protected disclosure, the burden of proof is determined in accordance with s 48(2) of the ERA 1996:

> 48(2) On such a complaint it is for the employer to show the ground on which any act, or deliberate failure to act, was done.

12.49 According to the Court of Appeal in *NHS Manchester v Fecitt* [2012] IRLR 64, the employer must prove on the balance of probabilities that the detriment to which the worker was subjected was not on the grounds that the employee had done the protected act. This means that it must show that the protected act did not materially influence (in the sense of being more than a trivial influence) the employer's treatment of the whistleblower.

12.50 It will be seen that the provision with respect to the burden of proof in a detriment case is similar to that in a discrimination case, and is more favourable to the claimant than in an unfair dismissal case.

Detrimental treatment by co-workers

12.51 The Enterprise and Regulatory Reform Act 2013 has inserted a new subsection (1A) in s 47B of the ERA 1996. Where a worker is subjected to detrimental treatment by a co-worker because he or she made a protected disclosure, and the co-worker acts in the course of their employment, that treatment will be a legal wrong. Any claim will be actionable against both the employer and the co-worker. A similar liability will attach to the actions of an agent. However, the employer will be able to rely on the defence that they took all reasonable steps to prevent the co-worker or agent from subjecting the whistleblower to a detriment. In other words, the position will be similar to that which applies to acts of discrimination (see 16.14). These provisions came into effect for acts on or after 25 June 2013:

> 47B (1A) A worker ('W') has the right not to be subjected to any detriment by any act, or any deliberate failure to act, done—
>
> > (a) by another worker of W's employer in the course of that other worker's employment, or
> >
> > (b) by an agent of W's employer with the employer's authority,
> >
> > on the ground that W has made a protected disclosure.
>
> (1B) Where a worker is subjected to detriment by anything done as mentioned in subsection (1A), that thing is treated as also done by the worker's employer.
>
> (1C) For the purposes of subsection (1B), it is immaterial whether the thing is done with the knowledge or approval of the worker's employer.
>
> (1D) In proceedings against W's employer in respect of anything alleged to have been done as mentioned in subsection (1A) (a), it is a defence for the employer to show that the employer took all reasonable steps to prevent the other worker—
>
> > (a) from doing that thing, or
> >
> > (b) from doing anything of that description.
>
> (1E) A worker or agent of W's employer is not liable by reason of subsection (1A) for doing something that subjects W to detriment if—
>
> > (a) the worker or agent does that thing in reliance on a statement by the employer that doing it does not contravene this act, and
> >
> > (b) it is reasonable for the worker or agent to rely on the statement.
> >
> > But this does not prevent the employer from being liable by reason of subsection (1B).

Procedure in protected disclosure cases

12.52 The tribunal will frequently require a preliminary hearing in order to identify the issues in the case of an alleged protected disclosure: *ALM Medical Services Ltd v Bladon* [2002] IRLR 807. This is because the protected disclosure provisions set out previously require a number of different elements to be established, and it is necessary to ascertain which of those are in dispute.

Remedies

12.53 As far as automatic unfair dismissal under s 103A of the ERA 1996 is concerned, the remedies are the same as those which are awarded in 'ordinary' unfair dismissal cases (see Chapter 20 on Remedies for Unfair Dismissal). However, there is no statutory cap on the compensatory award (s 124(1A) of the ERA 1996).

12.54 With respect to compensation for detriment suffered as a result of a protected disclosure, an injury to feelings award can be made: *Virgo Fidelis Senior School v Boyle* [2004] IRLR 268 (EAT). This would be assessed in accordance with the guidelines set out for determining injury to feelings awards in discrimination cases (see 21.23).

12.55 For protected disclosures made on or after 25 June 2013, where a claim can successfully be made even where the disclosure was not in good faith (see 'In good faith' at 12.16), the employment tribunal has the power to reduce compensation by up to 25 per cent if the protected disclosure was not made in good faith, and they consider it just and equitable to do so. In the case of unfair dismissal, the discretion to reduce will apply only to the compensatory award, and not to the basic award.

12.56 In an unfair dismissal claim, however, there can be no compensation for non-financial loss such as injury to feelings: *Dunnachie v Kingston-upon-Hull City Council* [2004] IRLR 727 (HL).

12.57 Where the facts justify it, a claimant can claim for both detriment and unfair dismissal, eg where what is alleged is detrimental treatment leading to resignation and constructive dismissal. In such a case, an award for injury to feelings could be claimed for the period up to the effective date of termination.

Detriment and unfair dismissal claims distinguished

12.58 As set out earlier, the following are the major differences between a claim for detriment and a claim for unfair dismissal because of public interest disclosure:

(1) *Eligibility*. Only employees can claim unfair dismissal; all workers (including those within an extended definition) can claim detriment.

(2) *Burden of proof*. This is more difficult for the employer to discharge in a detriment case.

(3) *Remedies*. For unfair dismissal, the remedies of reinstatement and re-engagement are available.

(4) *Compensation*. For detriment, compensation can include an award for injury to feelings. There is no statutory cap on compensation for unfair dismissal, or for detriment, because of a protected disclosure.

13 Contractual Claims and Wrongful Dismissal

Introduction

13.01   If an employee is dismissed without full notice, or money in lieu of notice, he or she will have been wrongfully dismissed, unless they are in repudiatory breach of contract. Where the employee has committed gross misconduct, that will be a repudiatory breach, and the employer will be entitled to terminate their contract without notice or payment in lieu of notice. Similarly, there will be no obligation on the part of the employer to give notice where the employee has committed some other serious breach of the contract of employment, such as dishonesty or setting up in competition with the employer.

13.02   An employee is entitled, in normal circumstances, to whichever is the better of the period of notice laid down in the contract, or that which is set out in the statute. As far as the contractual entitlement is concerned, this may be expressly spelt out in the contract. Alternatively, if it is not, the period of notice would be that which is reasonable in the relevant field of employment for someone in the employee's position.

13.03   The statutory entitlement is set out in s 86 of the Employment Rights Act 1996 (ERA 1996), which reads in part as follows:

> 86 (1) The notice required to be given by an employer to terminate the contract of employment of a person who has been continuously employed for one month or more—
>   (a) is not less than one week's notice if his period of continuous employment is less than two years,
>   (b) is not less than one week's notice for each year of continuous employment if his period of continuous employment is two years or more but less than twelve years, and
>   (c) is not less than twelve weeks' notice if his period of continuous employment is twelve years or more.
> (2) The notice required to be given by an employee who has been continuously employed for one month or more to terminate his contract of employment is not less than one week.
> (3) Any provision for shorter notice in any contract of employment with a person who has been continuously employed for one month or more has effect subject to subsections (1) and (2); but this section does not prevent either party from waiving his right to notice on any occasion or from accepting a payment in lieu of notice.

> (4) Any contract of employment of a person who has been continuously employed for three months or more which is a contract for a term certain of one month or less shall have effect as if it were for an indefinite period; and, accordingly, subsections (1) and (2) apply to the contract.
> ...
> (6) This section does not affect any right of either party to a contract of employment to treat the contract as terminable without notice by reason of the conduct of the other party.

Compensation for wrongful dismissal

13.04   In a claim for wrongful dismissal, the usual measure of damages is payment for the period of notice. In some cases, however, there may be contractual procedures which the employer was obliged to follow, but it failed to do so. In such a case, damages will be available for whatever period it would have taken the employer to terminate the contract in accordance with those contractual procedures.

13.05   Once the period for damages is determined, the next question is: 'What is the entitlement of the employee during that period?' This may include benefits other than pay, such as commission, the use of a company car, etc. Similar principles apply in this area to those which apply in determining compensation for unfair dismissal (see Chapter 20 on Remedies for Unfair Dismissal). In particular, there is a duty to mitigate any loss from a breach of contract. This means that there must be deducted from any award the amount which the employee received by way of mitigation (eg in alternative employment), or the amount which should have been received if reasonable efforts had been made.

Procedure

13.06   The procedure relating to contractual claims in the employment tribunal is dealt with in detail in **chapter 8** of *Blackstone's Employment Law Practice 2014*. In summary, an employee's contract claim must comply with the following conditions:

(1) The claim must be of one of the following types, in accordance with s 3(2) of the Employment Tribunals Act 1996 (ETA 1996):
   (a) a claim for damages for breach of a contract of employment or other contract connected with the employment;
   (b) a claim for a sum due under such a contract;
   (c) a claim for recovery of a sum in pursuance of any enactment relating to the terms of performance of such a contract.

(2) The claim must be within the jurisdiction of the courts in England, Wales, or Scotland.

(3) The claim must arise or be outstanding on the termination of the employee's employment (art 3(b) of the Employment Tribunals

Extension of Jurisdiction (England and Wales) Order 1994 ('the 1994 Order')).

13.07　It follows from these conditions that the jurisdiction of the tribunal is limited to money claims, and it has no jurisdiction to grant injunctions or order delivery up of property.

13.08　A settlement agreement entered into between an employer and an employee in respect of the latter's employment is a contract connected with employment. As a result, a party to the agreement may claim in the tribunal for damages for breach of the agreement: *Rock-It Cargo v Green* [1997] IRLR 581 (EAT).

13.09　Unlike a claim for unfair dismissal, a claim for breach of contract such as wrongful dismissal (in the form of failure to pay notice pay) requires no minimum qualifying period.

13.10　An important limitation on the jurisdiction of the tribunal is that the claim must be outstanding on the date of termination, or arise on that date. A claim cannot be brought while the employee is still employed. While there is no jurisdiction to hear a contract claim because employment has not been terminated, the claimant may be able to formulate the claim as one for an unlawful deduction from wages (see Chapter 14 on Wages). It should also be stressed that there is a limit of £25,000 to the amount which may be awarded by an employment tribunal for breach of contract. A claim for a larger amount should be brought in the ordinary courts. If it is brought in the tribunal, a maximum of £25,000 can be awarded, and the surplus cannot then be claimed in the courts.

13.11　As far as settlement agreements are concerned, where the agreement is made after the termination of employment, the claim does not arise, and is not outstanding, on the termination of employment. There is therefore no jurisdiction to hear a claim in relation to a contract of settlement where negotiations began prior to termination of employment, but were not concluded until after termination.

13.12　Certain claims are excluded, even if they constitute breach of a contractual term, by art 5 of the 1994 Order:

(1) a term by which the employer must provide living accommodation, or which imposes obligations in respect of living accommodation;

(2) a term relating to intellectual property;

(3) a term imposing an obligation of confidence;

(4) a covenant in restraint of trade.

Employer counterclaim

13.13　An employer may bring a counterclaim against an employee who has brought a claim for breach of contract. The conditions for doing so are similar to those for the employee, and are set out in art 4 of the 1994 Order. The counterclaim must fall within the terms of s 3(2) of the ETA 1996; it must not be excluded by art 5 of the 1994 Order, and it must arise or be outstanding on the termination of the employment of the employee.

13.14   The employer can only bring a counterclaim at a time when there is a contract claim by the employee which has not been settled or withdrawn. Once a counterclaim has been presented, however, the tribunal has jurisdiction to determine it, even if the claim by the employee is subsequently withdrawn or settled.

13.15   Since the counterclaim of the employer must be based upon a claim for breach of contract by the employee, important tactical considerations arise. If the employee claims only unfair dismissal, the employer will not be able to counterclaim for breach of contract. Where there is potential for a substantial counterclaim, therefore, the employee may be well advised not to claim for breach of contract if there is an alternative in the form of a claim for unfair dismissal. On the other hand, where no counterclaim is anticipated, the employee may regard a claim for breach of contract (eg for notice pay) as being a useful alternative in the event that the claim for unfair dismissal does not succeed.

14 Wages

Introduction

14.01 The entitlement of a worker to be paid is governed in general by the contract of employment. However, statute intervenes in several important respects, two of which are dealt with in this chapter. They are:

(a) an employer's right to make deductions from wages is limited by statute—ss 13 to 27 of the Employment Rights Act 1996 (ERA 1996); and

(b) a minimum level of pay prescribed by the National Minimum Wage Act 1998 (NMWA 1998) and the National Minimum Wage Regulations 1999 (NMWR 1999).

Itemized pay statement

14.02 An employee is entitled to receive certain documentation in relation to their pay. The employer must give to an employee (but need not give to a worker who is not an employee) an itemized pay statement which shows their gross pay, and specified deductions. This right is set out in s 8 of the ERA 1996:

> 8 (1) an employee has the right to be given by his employer, at or before the time at which any payment of wages or salaries is made to him, a written itemised pay statement.
>
> (2) The statement shall contain particulars of—
>
> (a) the gross amount of the wages or salary,
>
> (b) the amounts of any variable, and (subject to section 9) any fixed, deductions from that gross amount and the purposes for which they are made,
>
> (c) the net amount of wages or salary payable, and
>
> (d) where different parts of the net amount are paid in different ways, the amount and method of payment of each part-payment.

14.03 Section 9 sets out an exception in relation to certain fixed deductions, which may be dealt with by a standing statement of fixed deductions.

14.04 This right enables the employee to check whether he or she is receiving the wages to which they are entitled. Where the employer fails to comply with s 8, a claim may be made to the employment tribunal. If it is successful, compensation is not payable, but the tribunal has the power to make a declaration as to what the pay statement should contain. In addition, it will order the employer to pay any wages which should have been paid in accordance with the terms of the statement (ss 11 and 12 of the ERA 1996).

The right not to have deductions made from wages

14.05 The deductions which an employer can make from a worker's wages are limited, and are set out in the following section. If any other deduction is made, it is unlawful, and a claim can be made for an unlawful deduction from wages. As to what constitutes a unauthorized deduction, that is dealt with in s 13(3) and (4) of the ERA 1996:

> 13 (3) Where the total amount of wages paid on any occasion by an employer to a worker employed by him is less than the total amount of wages properly payable by him to the worker on that occasion (after deductions), the amount of the deficiency shall be treated for the purposes of this Part as a deduction made by the employer from the worker's wages on that occasion.
>
> (4) Subsection (3) does not apply insofar as the deficiency is attributable to an error of any description on the part of the employer affecting the computation by him of the gross amount of the wages properly paid by him to the worker on that occasion.

14.06 It follows that the term 'deduction' covers any deficiency in what is properly payable to the worker, except where the deficiency arises from an error of computation in relation to gross wages. A failure to pay the worker any wages at all is therefore a 'deduction' in terms of the statute, although this would not be normal everyday usage.

What deductions are lawful?

14.07 The deductions which an employer can make from a worker's wages are limited to the following (references are to the ERA 1996):

(a) deductions required or authorized to be made by virtue of a statutory provision such as PAYE or National Insurance contributions (s 13(1)(a));

(b) any deduction required or authorized to be made by virtue of a relevant provision of the worker's contract (s 13(1)(a));

(c) any deduction to which the employee has consented in writing prior to its being made (s 13(1)(b));

(d) any payment to a third party to which the employee has consented in writing (s 14(4));

(e) any deductions made for reimbursement of previous overpayments of wages or expenses (s 14(1));

(f) any deduction made as a consequence of any disciplinary proceedings if those proceedings were held by virtue of a statutory provision (s 14(3));

(g) any deductions made on account of an employee's participation in industrial action (including not only pay but also any damages suffered by the employer as a result of the industrial action) (s 14(5));

(h) any payments the employer is required by statute to make to a public authority following an appropriate order (s 14(3));

(i) any sums the employer is required to pay pursuant to an attachment of orders of earnings order made by the court (s 14(6)).

14.08   As far as item (b) of the list at 14.07 is concerned, 'relevant provision' of a worker's contract is defined in s 13(2):

> 13 (2) in this section 'relevant provision', in relation to a workers contract, means a provision of the contract comprised—
>
> (a) in one or more written terms of the contract of which the employer has given the worker a copy on an occasion prior to the employer making the deduction in question, or
>
> (b) in one or more terms of the contract (whether express or implied and, if express, whether oral or in writing) the existence and effect, or combined effect, of which in relation to the worker the employer has notified to the worker in writing on such an occasion.

14.09   As to 'prior written consent' in item (c) of the list at 14.07, the consent must precede not only the deduction itself, but also the event which gave rise to the deduction: *Potter v Hunt Contracts Ltd* [1992] IRLR 108 (EAT).

What is meant by wages in this context?

14.10   Wages are widely defined by s 27 of the ERA 1996 so as to include fees, bonuses (including those which are non-contractual), commissions, holiday pay, statutory sick pay, statutory maternity, paternity, and adoption pay, guarantee payments, and a number of other statutory payments.

14.11   Section 27(2) excludes certain payments from the definition of wages. Advances on loans, payments for expenses, payments by way of pension or in connection with retirement or loss of office, redundancy payments, and any payment to the worker other than in his capacity as a worker are expressly excluded by this provision.

14.12   Pay in lieu of notice will not normally fall within the definition of wages: *Delaney v Staples* [1992] IRLR 191 (HL). Further, a discretionary bonus which has not yet been determined is not recoverable under these provisions: *Farrell Matthews & Weir v Hansen* [2005] IRLR 160.

Retail workers

14.13   Special provisions apply in the retail industry. In the case of retail workers, even if the worker has consented in writing to deductions being made, deductions in any period to compensate for stock deficiencies or cash shortages must not exceed 10 per cent of the worker's gross wages for the relevant period. The detailed provisions in relation to retail workers are contained within ss 17 to 22 of the ERA 1996.

Remedies for unlawful deduction from wages

14.14 Where the employer makes unlawful deductions from pay, or makes no payment at all, the worker may bring a claim to the employment tribunal within three months of the deduction in question, or three months of the last deduction in the series, seeking an order for payment of the sums due. As far as the time limit is concerned, that is dealt with in s 23(2) of the ERA 1996:

> 23 (2) subject to subsection (4), an employment tribunal shall not consider a complaint under this section unless it is presented before the end of the period of three months beginning with—
>
>   (a) in the case of a complaint relating to a deduction by the employer, the date of payment of the wages from which the deduction was made, or
>
>   ...
>
> (3) where a complaint is brought under this section in respect of—
> a series of deductions or payments,
>
>   ...
>
> the references in subsection (2) to the deduction or payment are to the last deduction or payment in the series...
>
>   ...
>
> (4) where the employment tribunal is satisfied that it was not reasonably practicable for a complaint under this section to be presented before the end of the relevant period of three months, the tribunal may consider the complaint if it is presented within such further period as the tribunal considers reasonable.

14.15 The remedy where the tribunal finds that the claim succeeds is set out in s 24. Essentially the tribunal must make a declaration to the effect that the complaint is well founded, and order the employer to pay to the worker the amount of the deduction.

14.16 A claim for unlawful deduction from wages will, in essence, be based upon a breach of the wages clause of the contract. It follows that, in theory, such claims could usually be brought as a claim for breach of contract. The right to bring a claim in the employment tribunal for unlawful deduction from wages, however, is one which can be exercised by current or former employees or workers. A claim for breach of contract, by contrast, is limited to a claim which is 'outstanding on the termination of the employee's employment' (art 3(c) of the Employment Tribunals Extension of Jurisdiction (England and Wales) Order 1994, SI 1994/1623). It is therefore limited to former employees.

14.17 In consequence, if the claimant is a worker and/or remains in employment, he or she should bring the claim as one of unlawful deduction from wages, rather than breach of contract. In addition, a claim for deduction from wages does not trigger a right on the part of the employer to bring a counterclaim for breach of contract, whereas a claim for breach of contract by the employee will open the door to such a counterclaim.

The right to a national minimum wage

14.18 The right to the national minimum wage is set out in s 1 of the NMWA 1998:

> 1 (1) A person who qualifies for the national minimum wage shall be remunerated by his employer in respect of his work in any pay reference period at a rate which is not less than the national minimum wage.
>
>   (2) A person qualifies for the national minimum wage if he is an individual who—
>
>   (a) is a worker;
>
>   (b) is working, or ordinarily works, in the United Kingdom under his contract; and
>
>   (c) has ceased to be of compulsory school age.

14.19 Section 54(3) of the NMWA 1998 defines 'worker':

> 54 (3) In this act 'worker' (except in the phrases 'agency worker' and 'homeworker') means an individual who has entered into or works under (or, where the employment has ceased, worked under)—
>
>   (a) a contract of employment; or
>
>   (b) any other contract, whether express or implied and (if it is express) whether oral or in writing, whereby the individual undertakes to do or perform personally any work or services for another party to the contract whose status is not by virtue of the contract that of a client or customer of any profession or business undertaking carried on by the individual;
>
>   and any reference to a worker's contract shall be construed accordingly.

14.20 Section 34 of the 1998 Act makes clear the entitlement of agency workers (as defined in that section) to the national minimum wage. Section 35 performs a similar function in relation to homeworkers.

Those excluded from the national minimum wage

14.21 Regulation 2(2) and (3) of the NMWR 1999 exclude certain workers from entitlement to the national minimum wage, in particular au pairs, certain categories of apprentice, voluntary workers, and those who work in a family business. Reference should be made to the regulation in question for the detailed provisions relating to these exceptions.

What is the national minimum wage rate?

14.22 With effect from 1 October 2014, the national minimum wage is as shown in **Table 14.1**:

Table 14.1 **National minimum wage**

For workers aged 21 or more	£6.50
For workers aged 18–20	£5.13
For workers aged 16–17	£3.79
For apprentices	£2.73

14.23 The rates in question are revised annually, and reference should be made to regs 11, 12, and 13 of the NMWR, as amended for the current amounts.

How are wages calculated?

14.24 The calculation of wages in order to determine whether the national minimum wage is being paid is a complicated one. Certain rules are set out for making the calculation, as follows (all references are to the NMWR 1999):

(a) the relevant period for the calculation is one month or, in the case of a worker paid by reference to a shorter period than a month, that shorter period (reg 10(1));

(b) only money payments, and not benefits in kind, are taken into account (regs 30 to 37);

(c) however, a certain amount in relation to accommodation may be taken into account, limited to £4.82 per day (increased annually: reg 36(1));

(d) loans, advances, pension and other retirement scheme payments, settlement payments, and redundancy payments must be excluded (regs 30 to 37);

(e) various reductions must then be made, eg shift premiums, premiums for work on bank holidays, and tips or service charges.

14.25 The method of calculating the national minimum wage will then be determined in accordance with the type of working arrangement which governs the worker, eg salaried, time work, output work, unmeasured work. Reference should be made to the relevant regulations in the NMWR 1999, where a calculation needs to be made (for salaried work, see regs 4, 16, 21, 22, and 23; for time work, see regs 3 and 15; for output work, see regs 5, 17, 24, 25, 26, and 26A; for unmeasured work, see regs 6, 18, 27, 28, and 29).

14.26 The calculation of the rate that the worker is paid can then be determined by dividing the amount paid over the reference period (eg a month) by the total number of hours worked over the reference period.

Records maintained by the employer

14.27 The employer must maintain records of hours worked and wages paid (reg 38 of the NMWR 1999). The employer must allow the worker to have access to these records if so requested (s 10 of the NMWA 1998).

Remedies

14.28 A worker who qualifies for the national minimum wage is entitled to bring a claim in the employment tribunal for the shortfall in his or her wages. Section 17(1) of the NMWA 1998 provides that if such a worker is paid at a rate which is less than the national minimum wage, the worker shall be entitled under his or her contract to be paid, as additional remuneration in respect of the relevant period, the greater of:

(1) the shortfall between the amount paid and the amount that should have been paid under the national minimum wage applicable at the time of the underpayment; and

(2) the sum payable if the rate of the national minimum wage applying at the time of the arrears being determined had been applicable throughout the relevant period.

14.29 This new method of calculating arrears has retrospective effect. It applies even where the worker's entitlement arose before the new provision came into force (s 8(8) of the Employment Act 2008).

14.30 Section 17 of the NMWA 1998 gives qualifying workers a contractual right to receipt of the national minimum wage. If an employer fails to pay it, that is a breach of contract. Where an employment tribunal makes an award in respect of another statutory right, the national minimum wage becomes the minimum payable to the employee in respect of a week's wages (eg in calculating a redundancy payment or the basic award in an unfair dismissal claim).

14.31 Any worker has the right not to be subjected to detriment by his or her employer on the ground that they asserted their right to the national minimum wage (s 23 of the NMWA 1998). This section does not apply to dismissal, but an employee dismissed for asserting their right to the national minimum wage will be automatically unfairly dismissed (s104A of the ERA

1996) and no qualifying period is required to bring a claim in these circumstances.

14.32 In addition, criminal offences cover refusal to pay the national minimum wage, failure to keep proper records, and obstruction of compliance officers. The details of and penalties for these offences are beyond the scope of this work.

15 Holiday Pay

Introduction

15.01 The worker's contract will lay down certain rights as to the amount of leave to which he or she is entitled, and the pay which they should receive with respect to that period. There is, in addition, a statutory entitlement to paid holiday under the Working Time Regulations 1998 (WTR 1998), which are based upon the EU Directive on Working Time (2003/88/EC).

15.02 In summary, the position is that the worker is entitled to the right to paid holiday which appears in his or her contract, or their statutory rights, whichever is the better.

What is the statutory right to holiday pay?

15.03 The worker is entitled to 5.6 weeks' annual leave in each leave year. If the worker works a five-day week, this will mean 28 days' annual leave. Bank holidays taken by the worker count to satisfy the entitlement to annual leave: *Campbell and South Construction Group Ltd v Greenwood* [2001] IRLR 588 (EAT).

Who is entitled to the statutory right?

15.04 The right to paid holiday extends to all workers, and is not confined to employees. The definition of 'worker' (see 9.15) is to be found in reg 2 of the WTR 1998:

> 'worker' means an individual who has entered into or works under (or, where the employment has ceased, worked under)—
> (a) a contract of employment; or
> (b) any other contract, whether express or implied and (if it is express) whether oral or in writing, whereby the individual undertakes to do or perform personally any work or services for another party to the contract whose status is not by virtue of the contract that of a client or customer of any profession or business undertaking carried on by the individual;
> and any reference to a worker's contract shall be construed accordingly.

How is the length of paid holiday entitlement determined?

15.05 The first issue is to determine when the leave year starts. The rules for ascertaining the start of the leave year are set out in reg 13(3) of the WTR 1998:

> 13 (3) A worker's leave year, for the purposes of this regulation, begins—
>   (a) on such day during the calendar year as may be provided for in a relevant agreement; or
>   (b) where there are no provisions of the relevant agreement which apply—
>   (i) if the worker's employment began on or before 1 October 1998, on that date and each subsequent anniversary of that date; or
>   (ii) if the worker's employment begins after 1 October 1998, on the date on which that employment begins and each subsequent anniversary of that date.

15.06 The entitlement to annual leave within each leave year is set out in reg 13, as supplemented by reg 13A:

> 13 (1) Subject to paragraphs (5) and (7), a worker is entitled to four weeks' annual leave in each leave year.
>   ...
>   (5) where the date on which a worker's employment begins is later than the date on which (by virtue of the relevant agreement) his first leave year begins, the leave to which he is entitled in that leave year is a proportion of the period applicable under paragraph (1) equal to the proportion of that leave year remaining on the date on which his employment begins.
> 13 A (1) ... A worker is entitled in each leave year to a period of additional leave determined in accordance with paragraph (2).
>   (2) the period of additional leave to which a worker is entitled under paragraph (1) is—
>   ...
>   (e) in any leave year beginning on or after 1 April 2009, 1.6 weeks.

15.07 There are further provisions within reg 13A relating to leave years which commence before 1 April 2009. There is also a provision equivalent to reg 13(5) in reg 13A(5) relating to the additional 1.6 weeks.

15.08 The right to leave, and the holiday pay which accompanies it, accrue from day one. If the worker's contract commences part-way through the leave year, the worker receives a pro rata amount. In the first year of employment, leave accrues at the rate of one-twelfth of that entitlement on the first day of each month. In such a case, fractions of a day will be rounded up to a half day, if they are less than a half day and a whole day, if they are more than a half day (reg 15A of the WTR 1998).

How is the amount of holiday pay calculated?

15.09   Regulation 16 of the WTR 1998 states that:

> 16 (1) A worker is entitled to be paid in respect of any period of annual leave
> to which he is entitled under regulation 13 and regulation 13A at the
> rate of a week's pay in respect of each week of leave.
>
> (2) Sections 221 to 224 of the 1996 Act shall apply for the purpose of
> determining the amount of a week's pay . . .

15.10   See Chapter 10 on Unfair Dismissal for the terms of ss 221 to 224 of the Employment Rights Act 1996 (ERA 1996).

15.11   In *Williams v British Airways plc* [2011] IRLR 948, the CJEU set out the general principle that 'paid annual leave' means that workers must receive their 'normal remuneration'. The Court held that a claimant pilot was entitled during annual leave 'not only to the maintenance of his basic salary, but also, first, to all the components intrinsically linked to the performance of the tasks which he is required to carry out under his contract of employment and in respect of which a monetary amount, included in the calculation of his total remuneration, is provided and, second, to all the elements relating to his personal and professional status as an airline pilot'. Although the case was brought under the special legislation governing working time in civil air transport, the CJEU made it clear that the principles set out were equally applicable to cases under the WTR 1998. This decision seems to be at odds with the decision of the Court of Appeal in *Bamsey v Albon Engineering and Manufacturing* [2004] IRLR 457, according to which compulsory overtime is excluded from the calculation of holiday pay unless it is guaranteed by the employer. In contrast, the Court of Justice in *Williams* included in the definition of remuneration upon which holiday pay should be based the tasks which the worker is 'required to carry out under his contract of employment'. It would appear that the statutory provisions in reg 16 of the WTR 1998 and ss 221 to 224 of the ERA Act 1996 should be interpreted in accordance with the decision of the CJEU in *Williams*. The CJEU further held in *Lock v British Gas* (Case C-539/12) that holiday pay should include the commission which a worker would have earned if working during the period in question.

What notice requirements are there?

15.12   The dates upon which leave is taken are set out in reg 15 of the WTR 1998:

> 15 (1) A worker may take leave to which he is entitled under regulation 13
> and regulation 13 A on such days as he may elect by giving notice to
> his employer in accordance with paragraph (3), subject to any require-
> ment imposed on him by his employer under paragraph (2).

(2) A worker's employer may require the worker—
  (a) to take leave to which the worker is entitled under regulation 13 or regulation 13 A; or
  (b) not to take such leave,
     on particular days, by giving notice to the worker in accordance with paragraph (3).
(3) a notice under paragraph (1) or (2)—
  (a) may relate to all or part of the leave to which a worker is entitled in a leave year;
  (b) shall specify the days on which leave is or (as the case may be) is not to be taken and, where the leave on a particular day is to be in respect of only part of the day, its duration; and
  (c) shall be given to the employer or, as the case may be, the worker before the relevant date.
(4) the relevant date, for the purposes of paragraph (3), is the date—
  (a) in the case of a notice under paragraph (1) or (2) (a), twice as many days in advance of the earliest date specified in the notice as the number of days or part of days to which the notice relates, and
  (b) in the case of a notice under paragraph (2) (b), as many days in advance of the earliest day so specified as the number of days or part days to which the notice relates.
(5) any right or obligation under paragraphs (1) to (4) may be varied or excluded by a relevant agreement.
(6) this regulation does not apply to a worker to whom Schedule 2 applies (workers employed in agriculture) except where, in the case of a worker partly employed in agriculture, a relevant agreement so provides.

15.13   As stated in reg 15(5), the employer and the worker may agree upon a procedure for the taking of leave, and this is frequently the case. The remainder of the regulation constitutes a default procedure, to cover the situation where there is no such agreement. In any event, it is clear that the employer has the right to insist that leave should, or should not, be taken at particular times. So, for example, a schoolteacher will be obliged to take his or her leave during the school holiday, and retail workers are commonly obliged to avoid the pre-Christmas period when arranging their holidays.

Can a worker carry over entitlement to leave?

15.14   A worker must, in accordance with reg 13 of the WTR 1998, take any annual leave which is due within the year in which it accrues. The position is set out in reg 13(9):

13 (9) leave to which a worker is entitled under this regulation may be taken in instalments, but—
  (a) it may only be taken in the leave year in respect of which it is due, and
  (b) it may not be replaced by a payment in lieu except where the worker's employment is terminated.

15.15 With respect to any holiday pay which is owed upon termination, reg 13A applies:

> 13A (6) Leave to which a worker is entitled under this regulation may be taken in instalments, but it may not be replaced by a payment in lieu except where—
> (a) the worker's employment is terminated…

15.16 However, the position with regard to carrying over any entitlement to leave is different where it is carried over because of sick leave (see 15.22).

What entitlement to holiday pay does the worker have upon termination of employment?

15.17 Holiday pay upon termination is calculated in accordance with reg 14 of the WTR 1998:

> 14 (1) This regulation applies where—
> (a) a worker's employment is terminated during the course of his leave year, and
> (b) on the date on which the termination takes effect ('the termination date'), the proportion he has taken of the leave to which he is entitled in the leave year under regulation 13 and regulation 13 A differs from the proportion of the leave year which has expired.
> (2) Where the proportion of leave taken by the worker is less than the proportion of the leave year which has expired, his employer shall make him a payment in lieu of leave in accordance with paragraph (3).
> (3) the payment due under paragraph (2) shall be—
> (a) such sum as may be provided for the purposes of this regulation in a relevant agreement, or
> (b) where there are no provisions of a relevant agreement which apply, a sum equal to the amount that would be due to the worker under regulation 16 in respect of a period of leave determined according to the formula—
>
> $$(A \times B) - C$$
>
> where—
> A is the period of leave to which the worker is entitled under regulation 13 and regulation 13 A;
> B is the proportion of the worker's leave year which expired before the termination date, and
> C is the period of leave taken by the worker between the start of the leave year and the termination date.
> (4) a relevant agreement may provide that, where the proportion of leave taken by the worker exceeds the proportion of the leave year which has expired, he shall compensate his employer, whether by a payment, by undertaking additional work or otherwise.

15.18   Regulation 2 of the WTR 1998 defines 'relevant agreement' as:

> ... a workforce agreement which applies to [a worker], any provision of a collective agreement which forms part of a contract between him and his employer, or any other agreement in writing which is legally enforceable as between the worker and his employer.

15.19   It follows that (in the absence of agreement) the procedure for calculating holiday pay upon termination of employment is as follows:

(1)   determine the worker's leave year (see 15.05);
(2)   determine the annual entitlement to leave (see 15.06 to 15.08);
(3)   determine the proportion of the worker's leave year which expired before the termination date;
(4)   ascertain the period of leave taken by the worker between the start of the leave year and the termination date;
(5)   perform the calculation in reg 14 of the WTR 1998.

This involves taking the amount of annual leave to which the worker was entitled during the proportion of the leave year which had expired, and deducting from it the period of annual leave for which the worker was paid.

15.20   In *NHS Leeds v Larner* [2012] IRLR 825, the Court of Appeal considered the impact of EU law upon the Working Time Regulations, and held that Regulation 14 of the WTR 1998 must be amended so as to add the words 'where a worker's employment is terminated on the termination date he remains entitled to leave in respect of any previous leave year which was carried over under reg 13(9)(a) because of sick leave, the employer shall make him a payment in lieu equal to the sum due under reg 16 for the period of untaken leave'.

What is the effect of sickness upon entitlement to leave?

15.21   In *Stringer v HMRC* [2009] IRLR 214, the ECJ held that workers must not lose their holiday entitlement because they are off sick. Therefore a worker who has exhausted his or her entitlement to sick pay must be allowed their statutory paid annual leave. It would appear that the *Stringer* judgment applies only to the entitlement which workers receive by virtue of the EC Working Time Directive (which lays down annual leave of four weeks for the full-time worker). It does not apply to any additional leave over and above this minimum, such as the increased statutory entitlement under the WTR 1998, or any contractual leave entitlement.

15.22 In *Pereda v Madrid Movilidad SA* [2009] IRLR 959, the European Court of Justice held that, where a worker's period of pre-arranged annual leave coincides with a period of sick leave, the worker must have the option to designate an alternative period as his annual leave. In *ANGED v FAS* [2012] IRLR 779, the CJEU confirmed that a worker who falls sick while on holiday is entitled to claim that the period of sickness does not count as holiday, with the result that he or she will be entitled to additional leave at a later time.

15.23 In *NHS Leeds v Larner* [2012] IRLR 825, the Court of Appeal held that a worker prevented from taking her paid annual leave because she was sick was entitled to carry forward her untaken annual leave to the following leave year. It further held that this right applied irrespective of whether she had made any prior request to carry over that leave. The Court of Appeal considered that reg 13(9)(a) of the WTR 1998, which states that the annual leave due under reg 13 'may only be taken in the leave year in respect of which it is due' must be read subject to the words 'save where the worker was unable or unwilling to take it because he was on sick leave and as a consequence did not exercise his right to annual leave'.

Remedies

15.24 Regulation 17 of the WTR 1998 makes it clear that a worker is entitled to leave under the statutory provisions, or their contract, whichever is the more favourable:

> 17 Where during any period a worker is entitled to a rest period, rest break or annual leave both under a provision of these Regulations and under a separate provision (including a provision of his contract), he may not exercise the two rights separately, but may, in taking a rest period, break or leave during that period, take advantage of whichever right is, in any particular respect, the more favourable.

15.25 Where a claim is brought for holiday pay under the WTR 1998, reg 30 applies:

> 30 (1) A worker may present a complaint to an employment tribunal that his employer—
>   (a) has refused to permit him to exercise any right he has under—
>   (i) ... Regulation 13 or 13 A
>   ...; or
>   (b) has failed to pay him the whole or any part of any amount due to him under regulation 14 (2) or 16 (1).
> (2) subject to Article 30A, an employment tribunal shall not consider a complaint under this regulation unless it is presented—
>   (a) before the end of the period of three months ... beginning with the date on which it is alleged that the exercise of the right should

have been permitted (or in the case of a rest period or leave extending over more than one day, the date on which it should have been permitted to begin) or, as the case may be, the payment should have been made;

(b) within such further period as the Tribunal considers reasonable in the case where it is satisfied that it was not reasonably practicable for the complaint to be presented before the end of that period of three ... months.

(3) where an employment tribunal finds a complaint under paragraph (1) (a) well founded, the tribunal—

(a) shall make a declaration to that effect, and

(b) may make an award of compensation to be paid by the employer to the worker.

(4) The amount of the compensation shall be such as the tribunal considers just and equitable in all the circumstances having regard to—

(a) the employer's default in refusing to permit the worker to exercise his right, and

(b) any loss sustained by the worker which is attributable to the matters complained of.

(5) Where on a complaint under paragraph (1) (b) an employment tribunal finds that an employer has failed to pay a worker in accordance with regulation 14 (2) or 16 (1), it shall order the employer to pay to the worker in amount which it finds to be due to him.

[*In claims brought by members of the armed services, three months is extended to six months.*]

15.26 Alternatively, a claim can be brought under the unlawful deduction from wages provisions of the ERA 1996 (see Chapter 14 on Wages), where the provision in relation to time limits means that time does not begin to run until the last in a series of deductions takes place. Such a course of action was authorized in *HMRC v Stringer* [2009] IRLR 677. In that case, the House of Lords held that payment due for a period of statutory annual leave under the WTR 1998 could be categorized as 'wages' for the purpose of s 27 of the ERA 1996, which defines 'wages' as including 'holiday pay'. Hence a worker who has not been paid for a period of statutory annual leave may make a claim either under the WTR 1998 or under the deduction from wages provisions of the ERA 1996. The latter provision may in certain circumstances lay down a time limit which enables the claim to extend to the arrears of holiday pay over a longer period (see Chapter 14 on Wages).

16 Discrimination

Introduction

16.01   Certain types of discrimination are unlawful. The prohibition upon such discrimination is set out in statute, and not in common law. Most of the relevant statutory provisions are to be found in the Equality Act 2010 (EqA 2010). Our law of discrimination is fundamentally affected by the framework laid down in various Directives of the European Union. The statutory provisions in question have, of course, been the subject of interpretation in appellate decisions in our courts, and these are in turn influenced by decisions of the CJEU.

16.02   The law relating to discrimination is often complicated, and the amounts at stake are often considerable, as there is no limit on the compensation which may be awarded in a discrimination case. In addition, the parties in such a case frequently have a considerable emotional investment in the outcome. As a result, it is usually advisable for a party in a discrimination case to be professionally represented.

16.03   The law on discrimination is covered in detail in **chapter 26** of *Blackstone's Employment Law Practice 2014*.

Protected characteristics

16.04   It is only upon certain grounds that the law prohibits discrimination. These grounds are termed 'protected characteristics', and are set out in s 4 of the EqA 2010, which reads as follows:

> 4   The following characteristics are protected characteristics—
> age;
> disability;
> gender reassignment;
> marriage and civil partnership;
> pregnancy and maternity;
> race;
> religion or belief;
> sex;
> sexual orientation.

16.05   It is worth stressing that discrimination as such is not unlawful. In fact, one would expect the rational employer to discriminate on grounds which are relevant and logical, eg ability, experience, and qualifications. It is only when discrimination is based on one of the protected characteristics that it becomes unlawful.

16. Discrimination

16.06 It should also be pointed out that most of the provisions relating to discrimination have to be applied in an evenhanded manner. By way of illustration, a man can bring a claim for sex discrimination on the ground that he was less favourably treated than a woman, although the motivation behind making sex discrimination unlawful is largely driven by the discrimination faced by women in the workplace. Equally, a white person could bring a claim for race discrimination, and a heterosexual person could claim discrimination on the basis of sexual orientation.

Race

16.07 The protected characteristic of race is defined in s 9 of the EqA 2010 as follows:

> 9 (1) Race includes—
>   (a) colour;
>   (b) nationality;
>   (c) ethnic or national origins.

Sexual orientation

16.08 This is defined in s 12 of the EqA 2010 as follows:

> 12 (1) Sexual orientation means a person's sexual orientation towards—
>   (a) persons of the same sex,
>   (b) persons of the opposite sex, or
>   (c) persons of either sex.

Religion or belief

16.09 Section 10 of the EqA 2010 states that:

> 10 (1) Religion means any religion and a reference to religion includes a reference to a lack of religion.
>   (2) Belief means any religious or philosophical belief and a reference to belief includes a reference to a lack of belief.

Disability

16.10 The law relating to discrimination on grounds of disability is significantly different from that relating to other protected characteristics. As a result, disability discrimination is dealt with at 16.33 to 16.59.

Age

16.11 Again, there are important differences in the way in which the law treats age discrimination, and this is dealt with at 16.60 to 16.63.

Employment

16.12 The law relating to discrimination covers the supply of goods and services as well as employment. However the scope of this Handbook is limited to the employment aspects of the subject.

16.13 It should be emphasized, however, that discrimination in employment covers a wider range than might be thought in other contexts. First, the definition of 'any employment' as far as protection from discrimination is concerned is much broader than that for most other employment rights (see Chapter 9 on Employment Status). Second, applicants for employment are also subject to protection, and may make a claim for discrimination in appropriate circumstances. Third, protection will continue after employment ends, provided that the act of discrimination is connected with the employment relationship.

Liability of the employer

16.14 The employer is liable for acts of discrimination committed by the employee in the course of employment, subject to a defence of 'taking reasonable steps'. This principle is dealt with in s 109 of the EqA 2010 which reads in part as follows:

> 109 (1) Anything done by a person (A) in the course of A's employment must be treated as also done by the employer.
> (2) Anything done by an agent for a principal, with the authority of the principal, must be treated as also done by the principal.
> (3) It does not matter whether that thing is done with the employer's or principal's knowledge or approval.
> (4) In proceedings against A's employer (B) in respect of anything alleged to have been done by A in the course of A's employment it is a defence for B to show that B took all reasonable steps to prevent A—
> (a) from doing that thing, or
> (b) from doing anything of that description.

Prohibited forms of conduct

16.15 The sections which follow deal with discrimination because of race, sex, religion or belief, and sexual orientation. These areas have a number of features in common, so that they can be dealt with together. As mentioned earlier, discrimination because of disability, or because of age, has rather different features, and those subjects are dealt with later, in separate sections.

16.16 To summarize, an act of discrimination can take the following legal forms:

(a) direct discrimination;

(b) indirect discrimination;

(c) victimization;

(d) harassment.

16. Discrimination

Direct discrimination

16.17 In the commentary which follows, only one protected characteristic will be mentioned, but the principle applies to race, sex, religion or belief, and sexual orientation.

16.18 Direct discrimination occurs when one person treats another less favourably than another person (the comparator) is treated on grounds of his race, etc. It is defined in s 13(1) of the EqA 2010:

> 13 (1) A person (A) discriminates against another (B) if, because of a protected characteristic, A treats B less favourably than A treats or would treat others.

> **Example**: Assume that an employee is passed over for promotion, and someone else is promoted. He believes that the reason why he was passed over is because he was Asian. The person who was appointed was white. In any subsequent tribunal hearing, the unsuccessful applicant for promotion will be the claimant, and his comparator will presumably be the person who was appointed. In this instance, there is an actual comparator.

> **Example**: Assume, on the other hand, that the person who claims discrimination is arguing that he has not received promotion after a number of years, and that he would have if he was white. In these circumstances, his case may be: 'if I were white with the same attributes, qualifications and ability, I would have been promoted'. A case argued on this basis will be more difficult to prove than that in the previous example. Nevertheless, the claimant in such a situation is entitled to rely upon a hypothetical comparator, ie a white person with the same relevant characteristics.

16.19 Whether the comparator is actual or hypothetical, the comparison must be of like with like. As it is put in s 23(1) of the EqA 2010:

> 23 (1) On a comparison of cases for the purposes of section 13 . . . or 19 there must be no material difference between the circumstances relating to each case.

16.20 In order to meet the requirements for direct discrimination, there must not only be less favourable treatment, but it must be *because of* race, sex, etc. The reasoning process is set out in **Figure 16.1**. It should be emphasized that the motive of the alleged discriminator is irrelevant. The question which must be asked is: was the less favourable treatment because of the protected characteristic? The fact that the discriminatory act was carried out in order to protect the person discriminated against, eg from racially prejudiced colleagues, is not relevant.

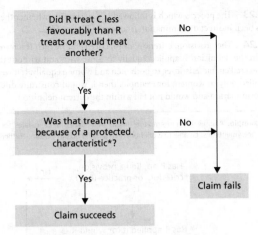

C = Claimant
R = Respondent employer
*Direct Age Discrimination differs - see separate flowchart (figure 16.8).

Figure 16.1 Direct discrimination (s 13 of the EqA 2010)

16.21 A further point to stress is that there is no defence of justification available in the case of direct discrimination (age discrimination is an exception to this rule, and is dealt with at 16.61).

Indirect discrimination

16.22 Indirect discrimination is defined in s 19 of the EqA 2010, which reads as follows:

> 19 (1) A person (A) discriminates against another (B) if A applies to B a provision, criterion or practice which is discriminatory in relation to a relevant protected characteristic of B's.
>
> (2) For the purposes of subsection (1), a provision, criterion or practice is discriminatory in relation to a relevant protected characteristic of B's if—
>
> (a) A applies, or would apply, it to persons with whom B does not share the characteristic,
>
> (b) it puts, or would put, persons with whom B shares the characteristic at a particular disadvantage when compared with persons with whom B does not share it,
>
> (c) it puts, or would put, B at that disadvantage, and
>
> (d) A cannot show it to be a proportionate means of achieving a legitimate aim.

16. Discrimination

16.23 The process which is followed in determining whether there has been indirect discrimination is set out in **Figure 16.2**.

16.24 The provision, criterion, or practice (PCP) which is referred to in the definition is applied equally to those with and without the protected characteristic, eg to both men and women equally. If it were applied only to women, for example, then it would constitute direct discrimination and would not fall within the current definition.

Example: Assume that an employer insists that successful candidates for employment must be able to work from 8.30 am to 4.30 pm. Assume further

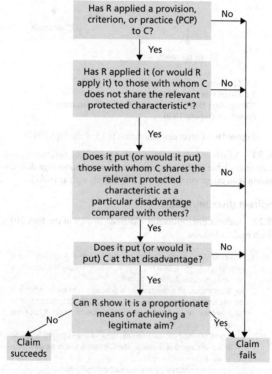

C = Claimant
R = Respondent (employer)
* does not apply to pregnancy and maternity.

Figure 16.2 Indirect discrimination (s 19 of the EqA 2010)

that Amanda applies for a job, and that she has childcare commitments which entail dropping her children off at school after 8.45 am and picking them up no later than 4 pm, as a result she is not appointed. She could make a case that a PCP (working hours from 8.30 am to 4.30 pm) has been applied to her. The employer would apply it equally to a man. It puts women at a particular disadvantage compared with men, because they are more likely to have child-care commitments then men. Further, it has put the woman in question at a disadvantage, because she has not been appointed to the job. On the face of it, this constitutes indirect discrimination. However, there is a defence available to the employer: can it show that its working hours are a proportionate means of achieving a legitimate aim?

16.25 'Proportionate means of achieving a legitimate aim' is often called 'justification' as shorthand. The employer in the example set out at 16.24 may, for instance, put forward a business need for its working hours. It might argue that those are the hours when the business has to deal with its customers. A tribunal would examine whether this did in fact constitute a justification. The business need might well qualify as a legitimate aim. However, there may be alternative means of dealing with the business need, eg by instituting a staff roster. If that were the case, it would be doubtful whether the means adopted were proportionate.

Harassment

16.26 It is unlawful to harass someone if the harassment is related to a protected characteristic. The definition of harassment is set out in s 26 of the EqA 2010:

26 (1) A person (A) harasses another (B) if—
   (a) A engages in unwanted conduct related to a relevant protected characteristic, and
   (b) the conduct has the purpose or effect of—
       (i) violating B's dignity, or
       (ii) creating an intimidating, hostile, degrading, humiliating or offensive environment for B.
(2) A also harasses B if—
   (a) A engages in unwanted conduct of a sexual nature, and
   (b) the conduct has the purpose or effect referred to in subsection (1)(b).
(3) A also harasses B if—
   (a) A or another person engages in unwanted conduct of a sexual nature or that is related to gender reassignment or sex,
   (b) the conduct has the purpose or effect referred to in subsection (1)(b), and
   (c) because of B's rejection of or submission to the conduct, A treats B less favourably than A would treat B if B had not rejected or submitted to the conduct.
(4) In deciding whether conduct has the effect referred to in subsection (1)(b), each of the following must be taken into account—
   (a) the perception of B;

> (b) the other circumstances of the case;
> (c) whether it is reasonable for the conduct to have that effect.

It will be seen that s 26(1) deals with harassment generally, as does s 26(4). Section 26(2) and (3) deal more specifically with sexual harassment.

16.27   Overall, the definition of harassment covers unwanted conduct which intentionally violates the dignity of another. It also covers conduct which is unwanted and intentionally creates an intimidating, hostile, degrading, humiliating, or offensive environment for another. In addition, it prohibits unwanted conduct which has either of these effects, provided that it can reasonably be considered as having the effect in question. In considering what is reasonable, all the circumstances have to be considered, including the perception of the alleged victim.

16.28   The subsections which deal with sexual harassment cover unwanted conduct of a 'sexual nature'. This would, for example, cover sexual advances. In addition, s 26(3)(c) specifically protects those less favourably treated because they submit to, or reject, conduct of a sexual nature.

16.29   The issues which arise in a claim for harassment are set out in **Figure 16.3**.

Victimization

16.30   In everyday speech, the word 'victimization' is used loosely to indicate that someone is being 'picked on'. The meaning in discrimination law, by contrast, is a precise one. In s 27 of the EqA 2010 'victimisation' is defined as follows:

> 27 (1) A person (A) victimises another person (B) if A subjects B to a detriment because—
>   (a) B does a protected act, or
>   (b) A believes that B has done, or may do, a protected act.
> (2) Each of the following is a protected act—
>   (a) bringing proceedings under this Act;
>   (b) giving evidence or information in connection with proceedings under this Act;
>   (c) doing any other thing for the purposes of or in connection with this Act;
>   (d) making an allegation (whether or not express) that A or another person has contravened this Act.
> (3) Giving false evidence or information, or making a false allegation, is not a protected act if the evidence or information is given, or the allegation is made, in bad faith.

16.31   It follows that victimization means less favourable treatment because of a protected act. In summary, the protected acts are:

(a)   bringing proceedings under the legislation;

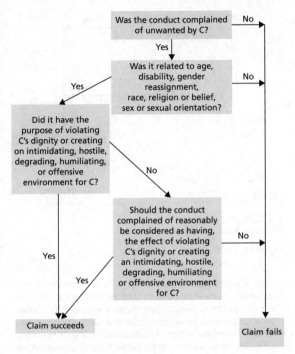

C = Claimant

Figure 16.3 Harassment (s 26 of the EqA 2010)

(b) giving evidence or information in connection with any such proceedings;
(c) otherwise doing anything under or by reference to the legislation;
(d) alleging that anyone has committed an act which contravenes the legislation.

There will be no protection, however, if the act in question was not in good faith.

Example: Assume that an employee believes that he has been discriminated against because of his race, and that this has resulted in suspension over a minor disciplinary matter. During the course of his disciplinary hearing, he alleges that he has been subjected to racial discrimination. In due course, he is disciplined for the offence with which he was charged. On the evidence which is heard during the course

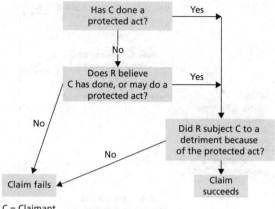

C = Claimant
R = Respondent (employer)

Figure 16.4 Victimization (s 27 of the EqA 2010)

of the disciplinary proceedings, it is clear that the suspension was warranted and there was no racial discrimination. At that point, the employer decides to institute further disciplinary proceedings because the employee made an allegation of racial discrimination which was untrue. Provided that he made the allegation of racial discrimination in good faith, he will have committed a protected act. The employer will be acting unlawfully by victimizing him for making the allegation. The fact that the allegation proved to be untrue will not be a defence for the employer, provided that the employee acted in good faith.

16.32 The issues to be resolved in determining a claim for victimization are set out in **Figure 16.4**.

Disability discrimination

16.33 Disability discrimination is dealt with separately in this chapter because it is subject to a rather different legal framework from the provisions relating to other protected characteristics. It has sometimes been suggested that discrimination law in general aims to ensure a level playing field between different groups, eg men and women, different racial groups, etc. This means, for example, that it is possible for a white person to complain of racial discrimination, alleging less favourable treatment than a black comparator, or for a man to complain of sex discrimination. This is regardless of the fact that the policy behind the law is in part to ensure protection for women and for racial minorities.

16.34 There is a difference, however, when it comes to the way in which disability discrimination operates. It is not possible for someone to claim that he or she was less favourably treated because they were not disabled. The policy appears to be that people who are disabled should be compensated for the resultant disadvantages to which they are subjected. To put it another way, the legislation surrounding disability discrimination does not aim to ensure a level playing field, but rather to tilt the ground to favour disabled people.

16.35 This aim is seen most clearly when it comes to the law relating to reasonable adjustments. The purpose of those provisions is to ensure positive compensatory benefit to disabled people. One of the consequences is that there is no prohibition against 'positive discrimination' towards disabled people, in contrast to the position with regard to the other protected characteristics.

16.36 Another important consequence of the way in which the provisions on disability discrimination operate is that they underline the importance of defining who is disabled, because it is only those who come within the definition who can benefit from the compensatory advantages which that status bestows.

The definition of disability

16.37 Before claiming for any of the forms of disability discrimination, the claimant must establish that he or she is disabled. The basic definition is set out in s 6 of the EqA 2010, which states in part as follows:

> 6 (1) A person (P) has a disability if—
>   (a) P has a physical or mental impairment, and
>   (b) the impairment has a substantial and long-term adverse effect on
>   P's ability to carry out normal day-to-day activities.

16.38 It follows that to ask whether a particular condition is a disability under the 2010 Act is misleading. It poses the wrong question, as the law does not define certain conditions as disabilities, or state that others are not. So it is futile to ask, for example, 'is dyslexia a disability?' The question is rather whether a particular person is disabled as a result, for example, of dyslexia. The answer will depend upon whether the effects to which that person is subjected have a substantial and long-term effect on their normal day-to-day activities.

16.39 When tribunal proceedings for disability discrimination are commenced, the employer will frequently be asked by the claimant and/or the tribunal whether it accepts that the claimant was disabled at the material time. If the employer does not concede this, the question of whether someone is disabled or not is often determined by a preliminary hearing before the main tribunal hearing.

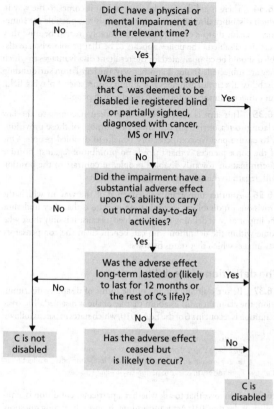

C = Claimant

Figure 16.5 Was the claimant disabled? (Sch 1 to the EqA 2010)

16.40 The issues to be considered in deciding whether someone is disabled are set out in **Figure 16.5**. The various components of the definition are set out in the sections which follow.

'Physical or mental impairment'

16.41 It is clear from the definition that mental as well as physical impairments are covered, eg learning difficulties, dyslexia, depression, etc. They fall potentially within the protection of the legislation, provided that the claimant fulfils the various conditions which are laid down within the definition.

'Long-term adverse effect'

16.42   'Long-term adverse effect' is defined by para 2 of Sch 1 to the EqA 2010 as follows:

> 2   (1)   The effect of an impairment is long-term if—
>   (a)   it has lasted for at least 12 months,
>   (b)   it is likely to last for at least 12 months, or
>   (c)   it is likely to last for the rest of the life of the person affected.
>   (2)   If an impairment ceases to have a substantial adverse effect on a person's ability to carry out normal day-to-day activities, it is to be treated as continuing to have that effect if that effect is likely to recur.
>   (3)   For the purposes of sub-paragraph (2), the likelihood of an effect recurring is to be disregarded in such circumstances as may be prescribed.

'Substantial'

16.43   Section 212 of the EqA 2010 states that 'substantial' means more than minor or trivial. In *Goodwin v The Patent Office* [1999] IRLR 4, the EAT stated that it meant 'more than minor or trivial' rather than 'very large'.

16.44   Although the tribunal is not bound to accept the medical evidence on the question of whether the adverse effect is substantial, it will often wish to have medical evidence to determine the question. In fact, in *Kapadia v London Borough of Lambeth* [2000] IRLR 699 (CA) it was stated that uncontested medical evidence on whether the effect was substantial would normally be conclusive. Where the tribunal rejects medical evidence, it must explain its reasons: *Edwards v Mid Suffolk District Council* [2001] IRLR 190 (EAT).

16.45   Procedural guidance in relation to medical evidence for the employment tribunal was issued in *De Keyser Ltd v Wilson* [2001] IRLR 324 (EAT), the full version of which is set out in **section 6.60** of *Blackstone's Employment Law Practice 2014*. Among the points in the guidance are:

- where the parties intend to rely on medical evidence, the preferred course is that they should instruct a joint expert;
- the parties should agree a joint letter of instruction which specifies in detail the questions to be answered by the expert;
- instructions should avoid partisanship;
- the overriding duty of the expert is to the tribunal.

Normal day-to-day activities

16.46 As stated in the definition, the impairment must have a substantial adverse effect upon the claimant's ability to perform 'normal day-to-day activities'. The focus is upon normal day-to-day activities, rather than the duties which a claimant has to perform at work. Nevertheless, there is often an overlap between the two, and evidence as to the performance of work duties will often be relevant.

16.47 Case law has emphasized that, in determining whether the claimant fulfils this part of the definition, it is necessary to look at the things which he or she cannot do, rather than the things which they can do. In addition, the fact that someone can carry out normal day-to-day activities with difficulty does not exclude the possibility that there has been a substantial adverse effect upon their ability to do so (see *Goodwin* at 16.43).

The categories of disability discrimination

16.48 Within the EqA 2010, disabled persons are given the right to claim for:

(a) direct discrimination;
(b) indirect discrimination;
(c) harassment;
(d) victimization;
(e) failure to make reasonable adjustments;
(f) discrimination arising from disability.

16.49 The first four forms of discrimination listed reflect those which are available for the other protected characteristics, but (e) and (f) are unique to disability discrimination, and each requires some further explanation. In addition, there are certain features about direct discrimination connected with disability which merit further comment.

Direct discrimination

16.50 The issue which particularly affects direct disability discrimination is the selection of a comparator. The comparator can also be a person with a disability, but it must not be the same disability as that which the claimant has. For example, a claimant with dyslexia could use as a comparator someone who is visually impaired. As with the other protected characteristics, the comparator may be either actual or hypothetical.

16.51 In *High Quality Lifestyles Ltd v Watts* [2006] IRLR 850 (EAT), the claimant was HIV-positive. His employers dismissed him from his job as a care worker providing services for people with learning disabilities and autistic disorders. He claimed direct discrimination on grounds of disability, among other causes of action. The tribunal compared his treatment with someone who was in the same position, but was not HIV-positive. The employer appealed, and the EAT held that they should rather have selected a comparator with an attribute (whether caused by medical condition or otherwise) which carried the same risk of causing illness or injury to others.

Discrimination arising from disability

16.52   This form of prohibited conduct is dealt with in s 15 of the EqA 2010, which reads in part as follows:

> 15 (1) A person (A) discriminates against a disabled person (B) if—
>   (a) A treats B unfavourably because of something arising in consequence of B's disability, and
>   (b) A cannot show that the treatment is a proportionate means of achieving a legitimate aim.
> (2) Subsection (1) does not apply if A shows that A did not know, and could not reasonably have been expected to know, that B had the disability.

> **Example**: An employee has been absent from work on a number of occasions during the past two years. The majority of these absences are because of her disability. The employer decides to dismiss her, after going through formal procedures. The employee has been unfavourably treated because of her poor absence record, which arises in large part because of her disability. Assume that the employer knew of the disability and its effects. On the face of it, she has been discriminated against because of something which arises from her disability. The employer will have a defence, however, if it is able to show that the decision to dismiss was 'a proportionate means of achieving a legitimate aim'. The employer might, for example, argue that it was impossible to run the business efficiently with an employee who was absent so frequently, and that her absence meant that her colleagues had to cope with her workload. The tribunal would then have to consider whether these reasons constituted justification, in the sense of proportionate measures to achieve a legitimate aim.

16.53   Section 15(2) makes it clear that a claim will fail if the employer did not know, and could not reasonably be expected to know, that the employee had the disability. As far as the question of reasonable knowledge is concerned, the tribunal would look at the surrounding circumstances to consider whether the employer should have known. Actual knowledge is not required, and it will be enough if the employer should reasonably have known.

16.54   The issues to be considered in determining whether a claim for discrimination arising from disability succeeds are set out in **Figure 16.6**.

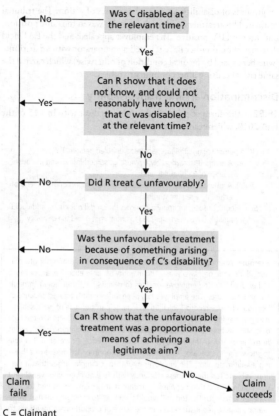

C = Claimant
R = Respondent (employer)

Figure 16.6 Discrimination arising from disability (s 15 of the EqA 2010)

Failure to make reasonable adjustments

16.55   The employer is under a duty in certain circumstances to make reasonable adjustments to alleviate the effects of an employee's disability. Failure to do so constitutes discrimination. This is a significant feature of the law relating to disability discrimination. It involves a degree of 'positive action' to compensate for the effects of features of the work upon the disabled employee. The elements of the duty to make reasonable adjustments are set out in **Figure 16.7**.

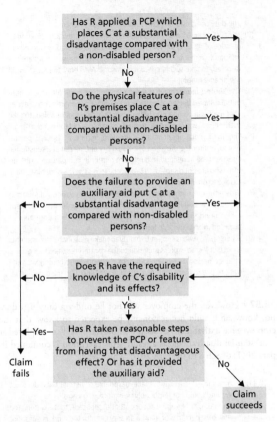

Failure to make reasonable adjustments

Has R applied a PCP which places C at a substantial disadvantage compared with a non-disabled person? — Yes →

No ↓

Do the physical features of R's premises place C at a substantial disadvantage compared with non-disabled persons? — Yes →

No ↓

← No — Does the failure to provide an auxiliary aid put C at a substantial disadvantage compared with non-disabled persons? — Yes →

← No — Does R have the required knowledge of C's disability and its effects?

Yes ↓

← Yes — Has R taken reasonable steps to prevent the PCP or feature from having that disadvantageous effect? Or has it provided the auxiliary aid? — No →

Claim fails

Claim succeeds

C = Claimant
R = Respondent (employer)
PCP = Provision, criterion, or practice

Figure 16.7 Disability: duty to make adjustments (s 20 of the EqA 2010)

16.56 The duty to make reasonable adjustments arises when one of the situations described in s 20 of the EqA 2010 applies:

> 20 (1) Where this Act imposes a duty to make reasonable adjustments on a person, this section, sections 21 and 22 and the applicable Schedule apply; and for those purposes, a person on whom the duty is imposed is referred to as A.

16. Discrimination

> (2) The duty comprises the following three requirements.
>
> (3) The first requirement is a requirement, where a provision, criterion or practice of A's puts a disabled person at a substantial disadvantage in relation to a relevant matter in comparison with persons who are not disabled, to take such steps as it is reasonable to have to take to avoid the disadvantage.
>
> (4) The second requirement is a requirement, where a physical feature puts a disabled person at a substantial disadvantage in relation to a relevant matter in comparison with persons who are not disabled, to take such steps as it is reasonable to have to take to avoid the disadvantage.
>
> (5) The third requirement is a requirement, where a disabled person would, but for the provision of an auxiliary aid, be put at a substantial disadvantage in relation to a relevant matter in comparison with persons who are not disabled, to take such steps as it is reasonable to have to take to provide the auxiliary aid.
>
> (6) Where the first or third requirement relates to the provision of information, the steps which it is reasonable for A to have to take include steps for ensuring that in the circumstances concerned the information is provided in an accessible format.
>
> (7) A person (A) who is subject to a duty to make reasonable adjustments is not (subject to express provision to the contrary) entitled to require a disabled person, in relation to whom A is required to comply with the duty, to pay to any extent A's costs of complying with the duty...

16.57 However, the employer will not be under a duty if it does not know, and could not reasonably be expected to know, that the employee has a disability, or that the employee is likely to be placed at a substantial disadvantage as a result. This exception is contained in para 20(1) of Sch 8 to the EqA 2010, which reads:

> 20 (1) A is not subject to a duty to make reasonable adjustments if A does not know, and could not reasonably be expected to know—
>
> (a) in the case of an applicant or potential applicant, that an interested disabled person is or may be an applicant for the work in question;
>
> (b) ...that an interested disabled person has a disability and is likely to be placed at the disadvantage referred to in the first, second or third requirement.

[*The reference to 'interested disabled person' in 20(1)(b) covers those in employment or within various other categories which are generally entitled to protection from discrimination.*]

16.58 It is not possible to compile an exhaustive list of reasonable adjustments. What is appropriate will depend upon the circumstances, and clearly the crucial requirement is that the adjustment in question should be 'reasonable'. In considering reasonableness, a tribunal would consider, for example:

(1) the effectiveness of the proposed adjustment;
(2) whether it is practicable;
(3) the financial and other costs involved;
(4) the employer's financial and other resources;
(5) any health and safety considerations.

16.59 As to what might constitute a reasonable adjustment, the following are examples:

(1) adjusting the premises;
(2) transferring the disabled person to fill an existing vacancy;
(3) a phased return to work;
(4) training or mentoring;
(5) acquiring or modifying equipment;
(6) providing a reader or interpreter;
(7) altering working hours;
(8) modifying redundancy selection criteria, eg in relation to absence records.

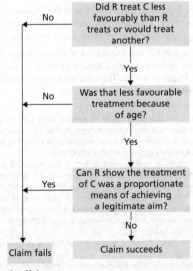

Figure 16.8 Direct age discrimination (s 13 of the EqA 2010)

Age discrimination

16.60   As far as discrimination on grounds of age is concerned, the forms of prohibited conduct are similar to those in relation to sex, race, religion or belief, sexual orientation, etc. As a result, the analysis which appears earlier in this chapter applies in general terms to discrimination because of age. There are, however, some features which are distinct. The elements of age discrimination are set out in **Figure 16.8**.

16.61   The main difference is that direct discrimination because of age can be legally justified, whereas direct discrimination because of the other protected characteristics cannot. In order to justify direct age discrimination, the employer has to establish that it takes place for a legitimate aim and that the means adopted are proportionate. This is based upon s 13(2) of the EqA 2010, which reads:

> 13(2) If the protected characteristic is age, A does not discriminate against B if A can show A's treatment of B to be a proportionate means of achieving a legitimate aim.

16.62   The Equal Treatment Directive of the European Union permits Member States to justify differences of treatment because of age, whether they constitute direct or indirect discrimination (see Art 6).

16.63   One other distinctive feature of discrimination because of age should be mentioned. That is the exception in relation to benefits based upon length of service. This is set out in para 10 of Sch 9 to the EqA 2010 which reads:

> 10 (1) It is not an age contravention for a person (A) to put a person (B) at a disadvantage when compared with another (C), in relation to the provision of a benefit, facility or service in so far as the disadvantage is because B has a shorter period of service than C.
>
> (2) If B's period of service exceeds 5 years, A may rely on sub-paragraph (1) only if A reasonably believes that doing so fulfils a business need.
>
> (3) A person's period of service is whichever of the following A chooses—
>   (a) the period for which the person has been working for A at or above a level (assessed by reference to the demands made on the person) that A reasonably regards as appropriate for the purposes of this paragraph, or
>   (b) the period for which the person has been working for A at any level.
>
> ... For the purposes of this paragraph, the reference to a benefit, facility or service does not include a reference to a benefit, facility or service which may be provided only by virtue of a person's ceasing to work.

The burden of proof

16.64 In a discrimination case, the burden of proof is initially upon the claimant. However, once the claimant has established facts from which the tribunal could conclude that discrimination has occurred, the burden shifts to the employer. It must then provide an explanation which is non-discriminatory. If it fails to do so, the claimant will succeed. This is set out in s 136 of EqA 2010, which reads in part as follows:

> 136 ...(2) If there are facts from which the court [or employment tribunal] could decide, in the absence of any other explanation, that a person (A) contravened the provision concerned, the court [or employment tribunal] must hold that the contravention occurred.
>
> (3) But subsection (2) does not apply if A shows that A did not contravene the provision....

16.65 The following three categories of discrimination are not covered by the EqA 2010, and the rules which cover their status do not reflect those which attach to the various protected characteristics. Nevertheless, in each case there is a measure of protection from discrimination.

Part-time workers

16.66 Part-time workers are covered by the Part-Time Workers (Prevention of Less Favourable Treatment) Regulations 2000. The central principle is that a part-time worker must not be treated less favourably than a comparable full-time worker. The pro rata principle applies, as one would expect, eg a part-time worker working three days a week would normally expect to be paid 60 per cent of the earnings of a full-time worker who works a five-day week. The core right is contained within reg 5, which reads in part:

> 5. (1) A part-time worker has the right not to be treated by his employer less favourably than the employer treats a comparable full-time worker—
>
>   (a) as regards the terms of his contract; or
>
>   (b) by being subjected to any other detriment by any act, or deliberate failure to act, of his employer.
>
> (2) The right conferred by paragraph (1) applies only if—
>
>   (a) the treatment is on the ground that the worker is a part-time worker, and
>
>   (b) the treatment is not justified on objective grounds.
>
> (3) In determining whether a part-time worker has been treated less favourably than a comparable full-time worker the pro rata principle shall be applied unless it is inappropriate....

Fixed-term employees

16.67   The Fixed-Term Employees (Prevention of Less Favourable Treatment) Regulations 2002 provide protection for those who are employed on a fixed-term contract. The pivotal rights are contained within regs 3 and 4, which read:

3. (1) A fixed-term employee has the right not to be treated by his employer less favourably than the employer treats a comparable permanent employee—
   (a) as regards the terms of his contract; or
   (b) by being subjected to any other detriment by any act, or deliberate failure to act, of his employer.

   (2) Subject to paragraphs (3) and (4), the right conferred by paragraph (1) includes in particular the right of the fixed-term employee in question not to be treated less favourably than the employer treats a comparable permanent employee in relation to—
   (a) any period of service qualification relating to any particular condition of service,
   (b) the opportunity to receive training, or
   (c) the opportunity to secure any permanent position in the establishment.

   (3) The right conferred by paragraph (1) applies only if—
   (a) the treatment is on the ground that the employee is a fixed-term employee, and
   (b) the treatment is not justified on objective grounds.

   (4) Paragraph (3)(b) is subject to regulation 4.

   (5) In determining whether a fixed-term employee has been treated less favourably than a comparable permanent employee, the pro rata principle shall be applied unless it is inappropriate.

   (6) In order to ensure that an employee is able to exercise the right conferred by paragraph (1) as described in paragraph (2)(c) the employee has the right to be informed by his employer of available vacancies in the establishment.

   (7) For the purposes of paragraph (6) an employee is 'informed by his employer' only if the vacancy is contained in an advertisement which the employee has a reasonable opportunity of reading in the course of his employment or the employee is given reasonable notification of the vacancy in some other way.

4. (1) Where a fixed-term employee is treated by his employer less favourably than the employer treats a comparable permanent employee as regards any term of his contract, the treatment in question shall be regarded for the purposes of regulation 3(3)(b) as justified on objective grounds if the terms of the fixed-term employee's contract of employment, taken as a whole, are at least as favourable as the terms of the comparable permanent employee's contract of employment.

   (2) Paragraph (1) is without prejudice to the generality of regulation 3(3)(b).

16.68   In addition, reg 8 of the 2002 Regulations specifies that an employee who has been continuously employed under a fixed-term contract for four years or more will automatically become a permanent employee. The rights contained within regs 3 and 8 are subject to a defence by the employer of objective justification.

Trade union membership

16.69   A series of provisions prohibits an employer from treating a trade union member less favourably than a non-member, or vice versa. In addition, trade union members are protected, within certain limits, from detriment or dismissal because of their activities. The subject is a complex one which is not dealt with here, but the relevant statutory provisions are to be found within Part III of the Trade Union and Labour Relations (Consolidation) Act 1992.

17 Equal Pay

Introduction

17.01 The law relating to equal pay is complex, and because of the complications which surround it (both legal and procedural) a considerable degree of expertise is required to pursue a case to trial. The law and procedure is set out in some detail in **chapter 27** of *Blackstone's Employment Law Practice 2014*. This chapter gives a short summary of the relevant rules.

17.02 Sections 64 to 80 of the Equality Act 2010 (EqA 2010) set out the law in relation to equal pay. This is a particular form of sex discrimination which deals not only with 'pay' in the usual sense, but also with all terms and conditions of employment, eg bonuses, length of service increments, sick pay, holiday pay, and overtime.

17.03 The relevant provisions cover all those who come within the broad definition of being 'in employment' applicable to discrimination law (see Chapter 9 on Employment Status), and to office holders.

17.04 As the equal pay provisions apply to claims in relation to terms and conditions, generally any claim for discrimination on grounds of sex in respect of such terms should be brought as an equal pay claim. With respect to other allegations of sex discrimination, however, the other provisions of the EqA 2010 are applicable. This general rule is subject to an exception, set out in s 71 of the 2010 Act (see 17.20).

17.05 In the explanation which follows, it is assumed that the claimant is a woman and the comparator is a man. However, the legislation allows a man to bring a claim for equal pay, using a woman as a comparator. It is worth stressing that the law relating to equal pay deals only with inequality between the sexes, and an allegation, for example, that black workers are paid less than white workers, or that workers are paid less because of their disability, must be dealt with under the provisions relating to race discrimination, disability discrimination, etc contained within the EqA 2010.

17.06 In an equal pay claim, a real comparator is essential, and a hypothetical comparator is not permitted.

17.07 The foundation of the law relating to equal pay is that everyone's contract of employment is deemed to include an equality clause, wherever a woman and a man in the same employment are employed on:

(1) like work;
(2) work rated as equivalent under a job evaluation scheme; or
(3) work of equal value.

17.08 This means that if the claimant has a term in her contract which is less favourable than a term of a similar kind in the contract of her comparator, her term will be altered so that it is no less favourable than his. However, the equality clause will not operate if the employer is able to justify the difference on the basis of a genuine material factor, which must not be the difference of sex. If the comparator's contract contains a term which is favourable to him, and the claimant does not have such a term in her contract, then her contract will be deemed to include that term, once again subject to the material factor defence.

Like work

17.09 In order to be classified as 'like work', the work in question must be broadly similar, and any differences must not be of practical importance. The tribunal will have regard to the practical reality of the work undertaken, rather than the wording of a particular job description; although a job description may constitute important evidence.

Work rated as equivalent

17.10 Work will be rated as equivalent where a job evaluation study gives the work an equal value in relation to the demands made upon the worker. Where such a study has been completed, and the work of the claimant and her comparator has been awarded the same grade, she may claim equivalence with the comparator. The job of each worker covered by the study should be valued in terms of demands made under various objective criteria. For example:

(1) mental ability;
(2) emotional demands;
(3) numeracy;
(4) literacy;
(5) manual dexterity;
(6) responsibility.

17.11 A job evaluation study can be challenged if it is 'sex specific' in that it sets different values for men than it sets for women. In such a case, the task of the tribunal is to consider what the study would have shown if it had not been tainted by discrimination.

Work of equal value

17.12   Where the claimant is not employed to undertake like work with her comparator, and has not been rated as equivalent, an alternative route is to show that she is employed on work which is of equal value in terms of the demands placed upon her and her comparator. Such a claim is not available where there has been a job evaluation study which has determined that the work of the claimant and her comparator are not of equal value (unless the study in question is 'sex specific').

17.13   A claimant can claim equal pay with a comparator where she is employed to undertake work of greater value than the work undertaken by the comparator.

Comparators

17.14   A claimant may compare herself with a comparator who is employed by the same employer or an associated employer:

(1) at the same establishment; or
(2) at different establishments where common terms of employment apply, either generally or in relation to the claimant and her comparator.

17.15   If the claimant is an office holder, rather than an employee, she may compare herself with a comparator who is an office holder, where the person responsible for paying the claimant is also responsible for paying the comparator.

The material factor defence

17.16   The material factor defence is set out in s 69 of the EqA 2010. It provides that the equality clause has no effect as between the terms of the woman's contract and the terms of the men's contract, where it is shown that the disparity is:

(a) because of a material factor; and
(b) that material factor is not directly discriminatory; and
(c) that material factor is not indirectly discriminatory.

17.17   The case law establishes that, in order to succeed in a material factor defence, an employer must show that:

(a) it is not a pretence or sham;
(b) it explains the differential;
(c) it is a relevant and significant difference between the case of the claimant and that of the comparator;
(d) it is not the difference in sex itself.

17.18 The following are among the factors which employers frequently put forward in order to establish the defence:

(1) market forces;
(2) collective agreements;
(3) preserving the salary of employees by 'red circling';
(4) reasons personal to the comparator, eg a particular ability or skill;
(5) incremental pay scales.

17.19 This list is not, of course, exhaustive. Further, any factor is likely to be examined to establish whether it is caught by points (a) to (d) set out in 17.17, eg whether it is tainted by historic discrimination.

Section 71 of the Equality Act 2010

17.20 According to s 71 of the EqA 2010, where a term or condition of employment relates to pay, but the sex equality clause has no effect, a claim for sex discrimination can be pursued under ss 13 and/or 14 of the 2010 Act. This provision is likely to come into play where a comparator cannot be identified, and a hypothetical comparator is necessary, or because a material factor defence was successful. In such a case, a complaint about unequal contractual terms which relate to pay can be pursued as a sex discrimination complaint, and a hypothetical comparator can be relied upon.

Procedure

17.21 An equal pay claim starts in the usual way, but the procedure which applies thereafter will vary depending upon whether the claim is based on 'like work' or 'work rated as equivalent' or 'equal value'. The first two categories are dealt with under the ordinary tribunal rules, but equal value claims are subject to a special procedure, which is detailed in **sections 27.61** to **27.74** of *Blackstone's Employment Law Practice 2014*.

17.22 As far as a claim in the tribunal is concerned, there is a strict time limit. The claim must be brought within six months of the end of the contract in respect of which the equality clause has been breached, and there is no discretion to extend that period. However, it is also possible for a claim to be pursued in the county court when the tribunal time limit has expired. Where this route is taken, the normal time limit for claims for breach of contract applies, ie six years (five years in Scotland): *Birmingham City Council v Abdulla* [2013] IRLR 38 (SC).

Remedies

17.23 The remedies available to a successful claimant are the same as those in a claim for breach of contract. They will normally involve a claim for damages for breach of contract. A declaration may also be applied for. As a result of the successful claim, an equality clause will be inserted into the claimant's contract. Where this has the effect of altering a term relating to wages as defined in s 27(1) of the Employment Rights Act 1996, a claim may be brought for recovery or non-payment of wages.

17.24 Compensation is limited to financial loss. It cannot be recovered for injury to feelings or aggravated damages.

18 **Family Friendly Rights**

Introduction

18.01　Employment law recognizes a number of rights which attach to maternity, paternity, or to the family in a general way. Generically, these rights are often styled 'family friendly'. They include:

(1) maternity rights;
(2) paternity rights;
(3) parental rights;
(4) leave to care for dependants;
(5) flexible working.

This chapter deals with each of those sets of rights in turn.

Maternity rights

18.02　There are a number of statutory provisions conferring maternity rights. The most important for present purposes are those set out in the Maternity and Parental Leave etc Regulations 1999, SI 1999/3312.

18.03　A pregnant employee is entitled to take 26 weeks of ordinary maternity leave (OML), and 26 weeks of additional maternity leave (AML).

18.04　The rights in question are dependent upon employee status, but the pregnant employee does not have to have worked for the employer for any length of time. Maternity leave is a 'day one right'.

18.05　The employee must inform the employer of the planned start date of leave no later than 14 weeks before the expected week of childbirth (EWC). The notice must cover the fact that she is pregnant, the date of EWC (with a medical certificate, but only if required by the employer), and state the date when she intends to start her OML. The start date can be at any time after 11 weeks before the EWC. There is then a requirement on the employer to serve a counter-notice not later than four weeks after the employee's notice stating her expected date of return. In serving the counter-notice, it should be assumed that the employee will take AML after OML.

18.06　During the OML and AML, the woman is entitled to all her usual contractual rights, with the exception of pay.

18.07　On return from OML, she is entitled to return to the job that she had before her absence, on terms and conditions no less favourable than would have applied had she not been absent. It follows that any seniority and pension rights must be recognized just as if she had continued working. If there has been a salary increase during her absence, she is entitled to that.

18.08 The position with regard to return to work after AML is slightly different. She is entitled to return to her old job or, if it is not reasonably practicable, to another job which is both suitable and appropriate for her. The relevant statutory provision is reg 18 of the Maternity and Parental Leave etc Regulations 1999.

18.09 Prior to the birth of the child the woman is entitled to paid time off for any ante-natal appointments which she has been advised to attend.

18.10 The employer is obliged to carry out a risk assessment with respect to the work which she does, and if the employee has to be suspended for reasons of health and safety as a result, she is entitled to be offered any suitable alternative employment which is available, on terms and conditions no less favourable than those applicable to her usual job. If there is no such work available, then she is entitled to be paid on her usual basis while she is suspended (see ss 66 and 67 of the Employment Rights Act 1996 (ERA 1996)).

18.11 The period taken as maternity leave must include two weeks of compulsory maternity leave immediately after the date when the child is born (s 72 of the ERA 1996).

Maternity pay

18.12 The pregnant employee is entitled to a maximum of 39 weeks' statutory maternity pay (SMP). For the first six weeks of maternity leave, she is entitled to 90 per cent of her average weekly earnings. For the remaining 33 weeks, she is entitled to the lesser of 90 per cent of average weekly earnings or £138.18 (this latter figure was effective from 6 April 2014, and is updated annually).

18.13 There may be more generous rights with regard to leave or pay under her contract. As is the case with statutory employment rights generally, the woman is entitled to the better of the statutory and contractual rights.

Paternity leave

18.14 There are two types of paternity leave:

(a) ordinary paternity leave; and
(b) additional paternity leave.

Each has its own conditions of eligibility, and each confers certain rights.

Ordinary paternity leave

18.15 Entitlement to ordinary paternity leave is conferred by the Paternity and Adoption Leave Regulations 2002, SI 2002/2788. In order to be eligible, someone claiming ordinary paternity leave must be:

(1) the father;

(2) the husband or partner of the mother (or adopter); or

(3) the child's adopter.

18.16 He must be taking time off in order to look after the child. In addition, he must be an employee who has worked for the employer continuously for at least 26 weeks by the end of the 15th week before the EWC. He must tell the employer at least 15 weeks before the expected date of the birth, the date when he wants the leave to begin (eg the day of the birth, or the week after the birth). In addition, he must tell the employer whether he wants one or two weeks' leave.

18.17 Provided that the conditions are fulfilled, the entitlement is to either one or two weeks, a week being the same amount of days that he normally works in a week, eg for a part-time worker working only two days a week, a week's leave would be two days. If leave is to be taken, it must be either one week or two weeks and it must be taken in one block. It is paid leave, and the question of pay is dealt with in 18.20.

Additional paternity leave

18.18 The right to additional paternity leave was conferred by the Additional Paternity Leave Regulations 2010, SI 2010/1055, to which reference should be made for details. Once again, paternity leave is available provided that the claimant is taking time off in order to look after the child and fulfils conditions (1), (2), and (3) set out in 18.15.

18.19 The child's mother or adopter must also have qualified for statutory maternity leave or pay, maternity allowance, or statutory adoption leave or pay. Further, the mother must have returned to work and must no longer be in receipt of those benefits. Additionally, in order to receive additional paternity leave, he must:

(a) have worked for the employer continuously for at least 26 weeks by the end of the 15th week before the EWC;

(b) still be employed by the employer in the week before the leave or pay starts;

(c) earn at least £109 a week before tax (the amount is updated annually);

(d)   confirm the start and end dates of his partner's leave; and

(e)   give the employer notice at least eight weeks before he wants the period of leave to begin.

Paternity pay

18.20   The statutory weekly rate for both ordinary paternity pay and additional paternity pay is £138.18 (updated annually) or 90 per cent of average weekly earnings, whichever is the lower.

18.21   During the course of paternity leave, the employee is entitled to protection in respect of accruing contractual rights, such as holiday pay and seniority, in the same way as someone who is on maternity leave. The right to return to work is also similar to that for a woman on maternity leave.

Adoption leave and pay

18.22   Rights for adoptive parents are set out in the Paternity and Adoption Leave Regulations 2002, SI 2002/2788. An employee who has been employed for 26 weeks at the date they are informed they have been matched with a child is entitled to 26 weeks' ordinary adoption leave and 26 weeks' additional adoption leave. The leave can either be taken from the date of placement, or up to 14 days before that date. It cannot start after the date of placement.

18.23   If a couple are adopting jointly, either can take the leave but they cannot split it. The other adopter can take paternity leave, as can the partner of a single person adopting. Such a person must take the leave to care for the child or to support the adopter. The employer is entitled to seek evidence of the right to take adoption leave.

18.24   Notice has to be given to the employer within seven days of being informed of having been matched for adoption. Thereafter the employee can vary the start date upon giving the employer 28 days' notice. Once adoption leave is over, the employee is entitled to return to work on the same basis as a woman on additional maternity leave.

18.25   The rate of pay is the same as for statutory maternity and paternity pay, ie £138.18 (updated annually) or 90 per cent of pay, whichever is the lower.

Parental leave

18.26   The statutory provisions are set out in the Maternity and Parental Leave etc Regulations 1999, SI 1999/3312. Parental leave is unpaid. An employee will qualify for this right if he or she has been continuously employed for not less than a year, and has or expects to have, parental responsibility for a child under the age of five. The leave may only be taken up to the child's fifth birthday, or the fifth anniversary of the adoption. This means that the right ceases at school age, and cannot be used to take time off during the school holidays. In the case of a disabled child, the leave may be taken up to the child's 18th birthday. 'Disabled' in this context means entitled to a Disability Living Allowance.

18.27 The entitlement to leave is for a total period of 13 weeks per child per parent. For the parent of a disabled child, it is 18 weeks per child. The employer can require evidence of the employee's responsibility for the child, its date of birth (or adoption), and/or entitlement to Disability Living Allowance.

18.28 The employee must give at least 21 days' notice of the proposed leave.

Time off for dependants

18.29 This is covered in s 57A of the ERA 1996. An employee can take a reasonable amount of time off during working hours in order to take action in respect of dependants. The purpose of the time off must be:

(a) to provide assistance to a dependant in the event of their illness, childbirth, injury, or assault;

(b) to make arrangements for the provision of care of a dependant who is ill or injured;

(c) in consequence of the death of a dependant;

(d) because of the unexpected disruption or termination of a dependant's care arrangements; or

(e) to deal with an incident which occurs unexpectedly while the employee's child is at school.

18.30 As far as (c) in 18.29 is concerned, the time off must be in order to take necessary action in consequence of the death. It was 'not intended to introduce a right to compassionate leave as a result of bereavement': *Forster v Cartwright Black* [2004] IRLR 781 (EAT).

18.31 In *Qua v John Ford Morrison Solicitors* [2003] IRLR 184, the EAT looked at the definition of 'a reasonable time off'. It held that the correct perspective from which to decide this question was not the needs of the employer's business, but the individual's circumstances. However, if, for example, a child developed an illness from which it would take time to recover, the employee parent should be able to plan for care, and the statutory leave set out in (d) (see 18.29) would not be appropriate. It was stressed that the purpose of the leave is to deal with unforeseen situations.

18.32 A dependant is defined as a spouse (or civil partner), a child, parent, or a person living in the same household (apart from a lodger, boarder, employee, or tenant). It also includes other persons who rely upon the employee to assist when they are ill or injured or assaulted, and anyone who reasonably relies on the employee to make arrangements for the provision of care.

18.33 The employee must tell the employer the reason for the absence as soon as reasonably practicable. He or she should also tell the employer for how long they expect to be absent. The latter requirement is waived if the employee cannot deal with the matter until after he or she has returned to work.

Flexible working

18.34 Employees have the right to ask the employer for a different work pattern in order to care for a young or disabled child, or an adult falling within certain categories. The rights in question are contained within ss 80F to 80I of the ERA 1996. The changing terms and conditions may relate to:

(a) hours of work;

(b) times of work;

(c) place of work, ie the employee's home or the employer's place of business.

18.35 The employee must have 26 weeks' continuous service with the employer. The application for flexible working must be to enable the employee to care for the person with whom they are in a particular relationship. As far as that relationship is concerned, it covers:

(a) a child under the age of six;

(b) a disabled child or young person under the age of 18 provided that the employee is the mother, father, adoptive parent, guardian or foster parent of the child, or the spouse or partner of such a person. In addition, the employee must have, or expect to have, responsibility for the child's upbringing.

18.36 In addition to the right to request flexible working to care for a child, there has been since 2007 such a right to care for an adult who is:

(a) married to, or the partner or civil partner of the employee;

(b) is a near relative of the employee (this covers parents, parents-in-law, sons and daughters-in-law, adult children, siblings, uncles, aunts, grandparents, and step relatives. This right also covers anyone who lives at the same address as the employee). From 30 June 2014, the right to flexible working was further extended—see 18.44.

18.37 The request for flexible working must be in writing and dated. It must state whether a previous application has been made, and when it was made, since the employee must not have made another application in the preceding 12 months. The application should specify what change in working pattern is requested, when it should come into effect, what effect the employee thinks it will have on the employer (if any), and how that effect might be dealt with. It should explain how the employee meets the conditions of eligibility.

18.38 The employer should arrange a meeting with the employee to discuss the application within 28 days, unless it is accepted. At such a meeting, the employee has a right to be accompanied by a work colleague. Within 14 days thereafter, the employer must give the employee written notice of its decision, which must be dated, state the variation agreed, and the date it is to take effect.

18.39 There are certain specified grounds upon which a request may be rejected. These are set out in s 80G(1)(b) of the ERA 1996 as follows:

(i) the burden of extra cost to the business;
(ii) detrimental effect on the ability to meet customer demand;
(iii) inability to organize work among the existing staff;
(iv) inability to find additional staff;
(v) detrimental effect upon quality;
(vi) detrimental effect upon performance;
(vii) insufficiency of work during the periods the employee proposes to work; and
(viii) planned structural changes.

18.40 If the request is rejected, or an alternative arrangement is proposed, the notification sent to the employee must contain the business grounds for refusing the application, with sufficient explanation as to why those grounds apply. It should also set out the right to appeal. There is then a right to appeal within 14 days of the notification, and the employer must arrange an appeal meeting within 14 days of receipt of the notice of appeal. Again the employee has the right to be accompanied by a colleague. The employer must inform the employee of the result of the appeal within 14 days of the meeting.

18.41 Any change to the terms and conditions will constitute a variation in contract. The employee cannot therefore expect to return to the previous position unless the employer is prepared to accept such a return, ie any variation to the previous terms must be by mutual consent.

18.42 If the employer refuses to grant the application for flexible working, the employee can present a claim to the employment tribunal on the grounds that the employer failed to carry out the correct procedure, or that the rejection of the application was on grounds other than those listed in 18.39, or the decision was based upon incorrect facts. In the event that the employee is successful, the tribunal can award up to eight weeks' pay, capped at a maximum of £464 (with effect from 6 April 2014, revised annually).

Protection from dismissal or detriment

18.43 Dismissal for reasons connected with pregnancy, maternity leave, paternity leave, parental leave, adoption leave, dependant care leave, or flexible working is automatically unfair. Detriment for one of these protected reasons will entitle the employee concerned to claim compensation from an employment tribunal (see, for example, ss 47C and 99 of the ERA 1996; regs 19 and 20 of the Maternity and Paternity Leave Regulations 1999; and regs 28 and 29 of the Paternity Additional Leave Regulations 2002).

Extension of the right

18.44 With effect from 30 June 2014, the right to request flexible working was extended from employees who are parents or carers to all employees with 26 or more weeks' service. At the same time, the previous statutory procedure for considering flexible working requests was abolished, allowing employers to consider requests using their existing HR processes. However, employers are under a duty to deal with applications for flexible working 'in a reasonable manner' and to notify the employee of their decision within three months of the employee's application unless a longer period is agreed by the employer and the employee. ACAS has published a statutory Code of Practice to explain what the minimum requirements are in order to consider a request in a reasonable manner. The Code of Practice and further guidance can be found at <http://www.acas.org.uk>.

19 **TUPE**

Introduction

19.01 Employees who are working within an enterprise which is transferred are given certain protections. These are contained within the Transfer of Undertakings (Protection of Employment) Regulations 2006, SI 2006/246 (TUPE). Those regulations are based on the 'Acquired Rights Directive' of the European Union (2001/23/EC).

19.02 The main effects of the TUPE Regulations are, in summary:

(a) The employee's employment will usually be automatically transferred from the transferor (the former owner of the business) to the transferee (the new owner).
(b) The terms and conditions of employment will remain the same (with the exception of any occupational pension).
(c) Any employee who is dismissed as a result of the transfer will be automatically unfairly dismissed (other than in certain limited circumstances).
(d) Trade unions or other employee representatives are entitled to be consulted.

What qualifies as a TUPE transfer?

19.03 The Regulations only apply where there is a 'relevant transfer'. This is defined in reg 3 to include the following two routes:

(a) a transfer of an undertaking to another person where there is a transfer of an economic entity which retains its identity (the 'traditional transfer'); or
(b) a service provision change.

These two routes are dealt with in the following two sections.

The traditional transfer

19.04 The first of the two routes described in 19.03 is set out in reg 3(1)(a):

> 3 (1) These Regulations apply to—
>   (a) a transfer of an undertaking, business or part of an undertaking or business situated immediately before the transfer in the United Kingdom to another person where there is a transfer of an economic entity which retains its identity . . .

19.05 This route is sometimes called 'the traditional transfer', and it stems from the 1981 version of the TUPE Regulations, which preceded the 2006 TUPE Regulations. Useful guidance on the interpretation of the terms involved in determining whether there has been a traditional transfer is contained within the case of *Cheesman v Brewer Contracts Ltd* [2001] IRLR 144. In that case, the EAT stressed that there are two separate questions for the tribunal to consider in deciding whether there had been a relevant transfer. They are:

(1) is there an undertaking, and
(2) has it been transferred?

19.06 With regard to question (1) in 19.05, the EAT indicated that the following factors were important:

(a) Was there a stable economic entity? There would need to be an organized grouping of persons and assets, permitting the exercise of an economic activity with a specific objective.
(b) That entity must be autonomous and structured. However, it need not have significant assets.
(c) Its assets could, in certain sectors, be mainly based upon manpower.
(d) Provided that it was permanently assigned to a common task, an organized grouping of wage-earners could amount to an economic entity.
(e) The identity of an entity could be determined from matters such as the workforce, management staff, and methods and resources upon which operations were based. The EAT stressed that an 'entity' is different from an 'activity'.

19.07 Dealing with question (2) in 19.05, the EAT emphasized the following points:

(a) Had the entity in question retained its identity?
(b) Had it resumed or continued the operation in question?
(c) The following factors should be considered:
  • the type of undertaking;
  • the value, at the time of transfer, of any intangible assets;
  • whether most of its employees went over to the new company;
  • whether its customers were transferred to the new company;
  • the extent of similarity between the activities carried on before the transfer, and those carried on after it took place;
  • any period of suspension of those activities.
(d) the factors set out under (c) should be considered as a whole, and none of them should be viewed in isolation.

Service provision change

19.08 A relevant transfer may also occur as a result of a service provision change. This route is defined in reg 3(1)(b):

> 3 (1) These Regulations apply to—
>
>   ...
>
>   (b) a service provision change, that is a situation in which—
>   (i) activities cease to be carried out by a person ('a client') on his own behalf and are carried out instead by another person on the client's behalf ('a contractor');
>   (ii) activities cease to be carried out by a contractor on a client's behalf (whether or not those activities had previously been carried out by the client on his own behalf) and are carried out instead by another person ('a subsequent contractor') on the client's behalf; or
>   (iii) activities cease to be carried out by a contractor or a subsequent contractor on a client's behalf (whether or not those activities had previously been carried out by the client on his own behalf) and are carried out instead by the client on his own behalf,
>
>   and in which the conditions set out in paragraph (3) are satisfied.
>   (2) In this regulation 'economic entity' means an organised grouping of resources which has the objective of pursuing an economic activity, whether or not that activity is central or ancillary.
>   (2A) References in paragraph 1(b) to activities being carried out instead by another person (including the client) are to activities which are fundamentally the same as the activities carried out by the person who has ceased to carry them out.
>   (3) the conditions referred to in paragraph (1)(b) are that—
>   (a) immediately before the service provision change—
>   (i) there is an organised grouping of employees situated in Great Britain which has as its principal purpose the carrying out of the activities concerned on behalf of the client;
>   (ii) the client intends that the activities will, following the service provision change, be carried out by the transferee other than in connection with a single specific event or task of short term duration; and
>   (iii) the activities concerned do not consist wholly or mainly of the supply of goods for the client's use.

19.09 As a result, a service provision change resulting in a relevant transfer will take place if the appropriate conditions are met in three situations:

(a) contracting out;
(b) contracting back in;
(c) changing from one service provider to another service provider.

19.10 These changes are illustrated in **Figure 19.1**.

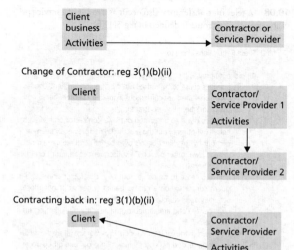

Contracting out: reg 3(1)(b)(i)

Change of Contractor: reg 3(1)(b)(ii)

Contracting back in: reg 3(1)(b)(ii)

Figure 19.1 Service provision changes (reg 3(1)(b) of the TUPE Regs 2006)

19.11 For there to be a service provision change, an 'economic entity' is not required, so long as there is an organized grouping of employees, and the various conditions laid down in reg 3(1)(b) and (3) are met. In addition, provided that the same activities are carried out for the client before and after the service provision change, it is not necessary that they should be carried out in the same way. They must, however, be carried out for the same client: *Hunter v McCarrick* [2012] IRLR 274 and see reg 3(2A).

Public administration exception

19.12 The Regulations do not apply to a transfer of an administrative function between public administrations, or any reorganization of a public administration: reg 3(5). Employees do, however, usually acquire similar rights under the Cabinet Office's Statement of Practice 'Staff Transfers in the Public Sector'.

To which employees does TUPE apply?

19.13 In view of the important consequences of a TUPE transfer, it is crucial to identify which employees are transferred.

19.14 The first point is that the regulations apply only to people who are employed under a contract of employment or apprenticeship or otherwise (reg 2(1)). Second, they must have been employed in the undertaking by the transferor immediately before the transfer. Alternatively, they will be included in the transfer if they would have been so employed if not dismissed in accordance with reg 7(1).

19.15 The provisions within the regulations which determine the employees to whom the transfer applies are contained within reg 4:

> 4 (1) Except where objection is made under paragraph (7), a relevant transfer shall not operate so as to terminate the contract of employment of any person employed by the transferor and assigned to the organised grouping of resources or employees that is subject to the relevant transfer, which would otherwise be terminated by the transfer, but any such contract shall have effect after the transfer as if originally made between the person so employed and the transferee.
>
> ...
>
> (3) any reference in paragraph (1) to a person employed by the transferor and assigned to the organised grouping of resources or employees that is subject to a relevant transfer, is a reference to a person so employed immediately before the transfer, or who would have been so employed if he had not been dismissed in the circumstances described in regulation 7(1), including, where the transfer is effected by a series of two or more transactions, a person so employed and assigned or who would have been so employed and assigned immediately before any of those transactions.

19.16 The references in reg 4(3) to reg 7(1) have the effect of including, in those transferred, any who would have been employed if they had not been dismissed unfairly because of the transfer (see 'Unfair dismissal and transfer' at 19.28).

19.17 In determining whether an employee works in the undertaking or part of the business that is transferred, the following considerations are likely to be important:

- that he or she is regarded as part of the human stock or permanent workforce of that business or part of the business, eg spending all or most of his or her time working in that part of the business;
- that they value their work in that part of the business above their work in other areas;
- that the cost of employing them is charged to that part of the business;
- that their contract of employment specifically assigns them to that part of the business (although this will not be decisive, eg a mobility clause which is not in fact used will be irrelevant: *Securicor Guarding Ltd v Fraser Security Services Ltd* [1996] IRLR 552).

19.18 If the employee has expressly informed either the transferor or the transferee that he or she objects to the transfer, the employee will not transfer. Their employment will be deemed to terminate on the transfer, but it will not be regarded as a dismissal by the transferor: reg 4(7) and (8).

What rights and duties transfer?

19.19 When an undertaking is transferred, any contract of employment of a person employed by the transferor and assigned to the undertaking has effect as if it had been made between the employee in question and the transferee. This means that the transferee takes over all the rights and liabilities under the employment contract. The position is governed by reg 4(1), (2), and (3). The text of reg 4(2) is reproduced here (for the text of reg 4(1) and (3) see 19.15):

> 4 (2) Without prejudice to paragraph (1) but subject to paragraph (6), and regulations 8 and 15(9), on the completion of a relevant transfer—
>
> (a) all the transferor's rights, powers, duties and liabilities under or in connection with any such contract shall be transferred by virtue of this regulation to the transferee; and
>
> (b) any act or omission before the transfer is completed, of or in relation to the transferor in respect of that contract or a person assigned to that organised grouping of resources or employees, shall be deemed to have been an act or omission of or in relation to the transferee.

19.20 Regulation 4(6) makes it clear, however, that criminal liability does not transfer.

19.21 The other major exception to the general rule that rights and liabilities transfer is contained in reg 10, which deals with pensions. It states, in part:

> 10 (1) Regulations 4 and 5 shall not apply—
>
> (a) to so much of a contract of employment or collective agreement as relates to an occupational pension scheme within the meaning of the Pension Schemes Act 1993; or
>
> (b) to any rights, powers, duties or liabilities under or in connection with any such contract or subsisting by virtue of any such agreement and relating to such a scheme or otherwise arising in connection with that person's employment and relating to such a scheme.
>
> (2) for the purposes of paragraphs (1) and (3), any provisions of an occupational pension scheme which do not relate to benefits for old age, invalidity or survivors shall not be treated as being part of the scheme.

19.22 It is only rights under an occupational pension scheme which are excluded in this way. Any contractual provision, such as that the employer will pay 7 per cent of salary into a personal pension scheme, would not be caught by this exception. It would constitute a contractual term, and the transferee would have to honour it.

19.23 There is a further major exception to the general rule that rights and duties transfer, and that relates to insolvency, which is dealt with in the following section.

What happens where the transferor is insolvent?

19.24 Frequently, a TUPE transfer occurs where the transferor is insolvent. In such a case, the usual test is applied in determining whether or not there has been a relevant transfer. If there has been a transfer, however, then the regulations laid down different consequences in relation to the effects of the transfer. The provisions in question apply only from the time when the insolvency proceedings come 'under the supervision of an insolvency practitioner'. From that time, the implications vary according to which of two categories the insolvency proceedings in question fall into.

19.25 Regulation 8(7) deals with the situation where the transferor is subject to relevant insolvency proceedings:

---

8   (1) If at the time of a relevant transfer the transferor is subject to relevant insolvency proceedings paragraphs (2) to (6) apply.

(2) In this regulation 'relevant employee' means an employee of the transferor—

    (a) whose contract of employment transfers to the transferee by virtue of the operation of the Regulations; or

    (b) whose employment with the transferor is terminated before the time of the relevant transfer in the circumstances described in regulation 7(1).

(3) The relevant statutory scheme specified in paragraph (4)(b) (including that sub-paragraph as applied by paragraph 5 of schedule 1) shall apply in the case of the relevant employee irrespective of the fact that the qualifying requirement that the employee's employment has been terminated is not met and that for those purposes the date of the transfer shall be treated as the date of the termination and the transferor shall be treated as the employer.

(4) In this regulation the 'relevant statutory schemes' are—

    (a) Chapter VI of part XI of the 1996 Act; and

    (b) part XII of the 1996 Act.

(5) Regulation 4 shall not operate to transfer liability for the sums payable to the relevant employee under the relevant statutory schemes.

(6) In this regulation 'relevant insolvency proceedings' means insolvency proceedings which have been opened in relation to the

---

> transferor not with a view to the liquidation of the assets of the
> transferor and which are under the supervision of an insolvency
> practitioner.
>
> (7) Regulations 4 and 7 do not apply to any relevant transfer where the
> transferor is the subject of bankruptcy proceedings or any analogous
> insolvency proceedings which have been instituted with a view to the
> liquidation of the assets of the transferor and are under the supervision
> of an insolvency practitioner.

19.26 In summary then, where the terms of reg 8(1) are met, reg
4 and reg 7 do not apply. (Regulation 4 deals with the transfer of
contract of employment and associated liabilities, while reg 7 deals
with automatically unfair dismissal.) In *Key2Law (Surrey) LLP v
D'Antiquis* [2012] IRLR 212, it was held that reg 8(7) does not apply
where the insolvency process is administration, because the primary
object of an administration is to rescue the business.

19.27 Where the terms of reg 8(6) are met, then different provisions will apply. 'Relevant insolvency proceedings' bring reg 8(6) into
play. These are proceedings under the supervision of an insolvency
practitioner, provided that they are 'not with a view to the liquidation
of the assets of the transferor'. In such a case, there are two different
special provisions:

(a) certain specified sums which the transferor is due to pay to
employees will not become a claim on the transferee, but will
instead become a claim upon the National Insurance Fund. The
claims in question are set out in reg 8(4), and include, for example, arrears in pay, statutory redundancy pay, payment in lieu
of notice, holiday pay, and the basic award of compensation for
unfair dismissal.

(b) There is provision to enable worker representatives to agree certain permitted variations under reg 9(1). Such variations are
permitted they are 'designed to safeguard employment oppor-
tunities by ensuring the survival of the undertaking, business
or part of the undertaking or business that is the subject of the
relevant transfer' (reg 9(7)(b)). There are, in addition, various
safeguards with which any variation agreement has to comply
(see reg 9(5)).

Unfair dismissal and transfer

19.28 Where there is a relevant transfer, employees have the
right not to be dismissed because of the transfer, or for a reason
connected with it. A dismissal will be automatically unfair where
the 'sole or principal reason' is the transfer. The position is set out

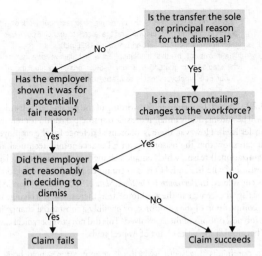

Unfair dismissal and transfer

Is the transfer the sole or principal reason for the dismissal?

No — Has the employer shown it was for a potentially fair reason?

Yes — Is it an ETO entailing changes to the workforce?

Did the employer act reasonably in deciding to dismiss

Yes

Yes

No

No

Claim fails

Claim succeeds

Figure 19.2 TUPE: unfair dismissal (reg 7 of the TUPE Regs 2006)

in **Figure 19.2** on TUPE Unfair Dismissal. The relevant provision is set out in reg 7:

7   (1) Where either before or after a relevant transfer, any employee of the transferor or transferee is dismissed, that employee shall be treated for the purposes of Part 10 of the 1996 Act (unfair dismissal) as unfairly dismissed if the sole or principal reason for the dismissal is the transfer.
    (2) this paragraph applies where the sole or principal reason for the dismissal is a reason connected with the transfer that is an economic, technical or organisational reason entailing changes in the workforce of either the transferor or the transferee before or after a relevant transfer.
    (3) where paragraph (2) applies—
        (a) paragraph (1) does not apply;
        (b) without prejudice to the application of section 98(4) of the 1996 Act (test of fair dismissal), for the purposes of sections 98(1) and 135 of that Act (reason for dismissal), the dismissal is regarded as having been for redundancy where section 98(2)(c) of that Act applies, or in any other case, the dismissal is regarded as having been for a substantial reason of a kind such as to justify the dismissal of an employee holding the position which that employee held.
    (3A) In paragraph (2), the expression 'changes in the workforce' includes a change to the place where employees are employed by the employer

227

> to carry on the business of the employer or to carry out work of a
> particular kind for the employer (and the reference to such a place has
> the same meaning as in section 139 of the 1996 Act).
>
> (4) The provisions of this regulation apply irrespective of whether
> the employee in question is assigned to the organised grouping of
> resources or employees that is, or will be, transferred.

19.29 As will be seen from the wording of the regulation, a dismissal will be automatically unfair if the sole or principal reason for it is the transfer itself. However, there is a potential defence for the employer if it can show that the reason was an ETO (economic, technical, or organizational) reason which entailed changes in the workforce. The question of whether an ETO reason entails changes in the workforce was considered in *Berriman v Delabole Slate* [1985] IRLR 305 (CA). To satisfy the 'change in the workforce' test, there must be a change in the composition of the workforce, or possibly a substantial change in the job descriptions of those involved. This did not cover a typical case of 'harmonization'. The Court of Appeal stated:

> To our minds, the word 'workforce' connotes the whole body
> of employees as an entity: it corresponds to the 'strength' or the
> 'establishment'. Changes in the identity of the individuals who
> make up the workforce do not constitute changes in the workforce
> itself so long as the overall numbers and functions of the employees
> looked at as a whole remain unchanged.

19.30 A change in the location of the workforce includes a change in the location of the business or that part of it in which the employee works (reg 7(3A) see 19.28).

19.31 To be covered by reg 7, the dismissal could be before, at the time of, or after the transfer. The question is: was the transfer the sole or principal reason for the dismissal? In addition, reg 7(4) makes it clear that the enhanced protection against unfair dismissal applies whether or not the employee was assigned to the transferred undertaking. It can even apply where the eventual transferee had not been identified at the time of the dismissal: *Spaceright Europe Ltd v Ballavoine* [2012] IRLR 111. A dismissal which aims to make the undertaking a more attractive purchase for a future transferee is not for an ETO reason: *Spaceright*.

19.32 The statement of the law relating to unfair dismissal and transfer set out earlier applies to cases where the transfer and the dismissal took place on or after 31 January 2014. For dismissals or transfers preceding that date, the test is somewhat wider, and reference should be made to **chapter 29** of *Blackstone's Employment Law Practice 2014*.

Constructive dismissal and transfer

19.33 The usual test for whether an employee has been constructively dismissed is: did the employee resign as a result of a fundamental breach of contract by the employer? (see Chapter 10 on Unfair Dismissal at 10.33). This method of establishing that an employee has been constructively dismissed applies in the case of a transfer. However, it is supplemented by the provisions of reg 4(9):

> 4 (9) Subject to regulation 9, where relevant transfer involves or would involve a substantial change in working conditions to the material detriment of a person whose contract of employment is or would be transferred under paragraph (1), such an employee may treat the contract of employment as having been terminated, and the employee shall be treated for any purpose as having been dismissed by the employer.
>
> (10) No damages shall be payable by an employer as a result of a dismissal falling within paragraph (9) in respect of any failure by the employer to pay wages to an employee in respect of the notice period which the employee has failed to work.
>
> Paragraphs (1), (7), (8) and (9) are without prejudice to any right of an employee arising apart from these regulations to terminate his contract of employment without notice in acceptance of a repudiatory breach of contract by his employer.

19.34 The reference to reg 9 is to the position on certain types of insolvency (see 19.25). Regulation 4(11) preserves the right of the employee to rely upon the traditional path to showing a constructive dismissal.

19.35 In *Tapere v South London and Maudsley NHS Trust* [2009] IRLR 972, questions arose as to what was 'substantial' and what was 'material detriment'. The EAT held that in determining whether the change is 'substantial', the focus should be on the nature of the change, rather than on its degree. It further held that 'material detriment' is to be construed in the same way as 'detriment' in a discrimination case. The tribunal should therefore look at the subjective perception of the employee, and decide whether it is reasonably held.

19.36 In *Abellio v Musse* [2012] IRLR 360, the EAT stated that 'working conditions', as used in reg 4(9), was wider than 'contractual conditions': 'It is capable of relating to contractual conditions; it is capable of relating to physical conditions'. In that case, the EAT held that a geographical change in the bus garage from which the drivers worked was capable of being a change in 'working conditions', and was not excluded from being so by a mobility clause in the contract of the drivers.

Contractual variations and transfer

19.37   Employees who are transferred take with them their existing terms and conditions of employment. Any variation of those terms will usually be invalid if it is due to the transfer. The situation is dealt with in reg 4(4) to (5C) of the Regulations:

> 4   (4)   Subject to regulation 9, any purported variation of a contract of employment that is, or will be, transferred by paragraph (1), is void if the sole or principal reason for the variation is the transfer.
>
>   (5)   Paragraph (4) does not prevent a variation of the contract of employment if—
>
>   (a)   the sole or principal reason for the variation is an economic, technical, or organisational reason entailing changes in the workforce, provided that the employer and employee agree that variation; or
>
>   (b)   the terms of that contract permit the employer to make such a variation.
>
>   (5A)   In paragraph (5), the expression 'changes in the workforce' includes a change to the place where employees are employed by the employer to carry on the business of the employer or to carry out work of a particular kind for the employer (and the reference to such a place has the same meaning as in section 139 of the 1996 Act(1)).
>
>   (5B)   Paragraph (4) does not apply in respect of a variation of the contract of employment in so far as it varies a term or condition incorporated from a collective agreement, provided that—
>
>   (a)   the variation of the contract takes effect on a date more than one year after the date of the transfer; and
>
>   (b)   following that variation, the rights and obligations in the employee's contract, when considered together, are no less favourable to the employee than those which applied immediately before the variation.
>
>   (5C)   Paragraphs (5) and (5B) do not affect any rule of law as to whether a contract of employment is effectively varied.

19.38   The effect of these provisions is to make void any purported variation of contract where the sole or principal reason for varying the contract is the transfer itself. There are three exceptions to this general prohibition:

(1)   cases where reason for the variation is an ETO reason (see 19.29), entailing changes to the workforce;

(2)   cases in which the terms of the transferred contract of employment permit the employer to make the variation;

(3)   cases where the contractual term derives from a collective agreement, the variation takes place a year after the date of the transfer, and the variation considered as a whole is no less favourable than the previous contractual terms.

The position is set out in **Figure 19.3**.

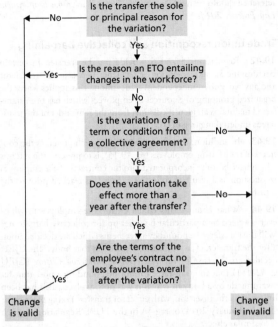

ETO = Economic, technical, or organisational reason

Figure 19.3 TUPE: contractual variation (reg 4 of the TUPE Regs 2006)

19.39 *Power v Regent Security Services Ltd* [2008] IRLR 66 laid down the principle that it is for the employee to decide whether to invoke the rule that a variation in contract which is due to the transfer is void. In other words, the employee is not prevented from taking advantage of terms which fall foul of reg 4(4), but the transferee is so prevented.

19.40 The question of what constitutes an ETO reason entailing changes to the workforce is dealt with in the section on 'Unfair dismissal and transfer' (see 19.29).

19.41 The statement of the law relating to contractual variation set out earlier applies to cases where the transfer and the variation took place on or after 31 January 2014. For variations or transfers preceding that date, the prohibition is somewhat wider, and reference should be made to **chapter 29** of *Blackstone's Employment Law Practice 2014*.

Trade union recognition and collective bargaining

19.42   Regulations 5 and 6 provide for the transfer, in certain circumstances, of recognition agreements between the transferor and any recognized independent trade union. This applies where the organized grouping of resources or employees which has been transferred maintains an identity distinct from the remainder of the transferee's undertaking (reg 6(1)).

19.43   In addition, the effect of reg 4(1), which preserves the contracts of transferring employees (see 19.15), is to preserve those terms which have become incorporated into the contracts of the employees in question as a result of collective agreements reached prior to the transfer.

19.44   What about terms which entitle the employee to whatever is agreed by a particular body set up for collective bargaining? Will the transferee be bound by agreements which are decided upon after the transfer, even if it is not involved in that body? The CJEU decided in the case of *Alemo-Herron v Parkwood Leisure* (CJEU C-426/11) that the transferee cannot be bound by a post-transfer award made by a body in which it was not involved. This has been followed by the insertion, with effect for transfers taking place on or after 31 January 2014, of reg 4A in the TUPE Regulations, which is to similar effect.

Duty to inform and consult

19.45   Both the transferor and the transferee must notify representatives of employees who may be affected by the forthcoming transfer of certain specified information. In addition, if measures may be taken which will affect the employees, they must consult those representatives.

19.46   As to the identity of the representatives, they will be representatives of the trade union where one is recognized. If no union is recognized, information and consultation must take place with representatives who are elected by the employees, either generally or specifically for the purposes of consultation in relation to any TUPE transfer: reg 13(3).

19.47   In the case of micro-businesses with fewer than ten employees, they can inform and consult the individual employees if there are no elected representatives (if the transfer took place on or after 31 July 2014).

19.48 The information which must be given to the representatives is set out in reg 13(2):

> 13 (2) Long enough before a relevant transfer to enable the employer of any affected employees to consult the appropriate representatives of any affected employees, the employer shall inform those representatives of—
>   (a) the fact that the transfer is to take place, the date or proposed date of the transfer and the reasons for it;
>   (b) the legal, economic and social implications of the transfer for any affected employees;
>   (c) the measures which he envisages he will, in connection with the transfer, take in relation to any affected employees or, if he envisages that no measures will be so taken, that fact; and
>   (d) if the employer is the transferor, the measures, in connection with the transfer, which he envisages the transferee will take in relation to any affected employees who will become employees of the transferee after the transfer by virtue of regulation 4 or, if he envisages that no measures will be so taken, that fact.

19.49 Regulation 13(2A) specifies the information which must be given in relation to the numbers and location of agency workers.

19.50 Regulation 13(4) fixes the transferee with a specific duty as follows:

> 13 (4) the transferee shall give the transferor such information at such a time as will enable the transferor to perform the duty imposed on him by virtue of paragraph (2)(d).

19.51 Regulation 13(6) lays down the duty to consult representatives:

> 13 (6) An employer of an affected employee who envisages that he will take measures in relation to an affected employee, in connection with the relevant transfer, shall consult the appropriate representatives of that employee with a view to seeking their agreement to the intended measures.

19.52 Regulation 13(7) gives some further indication of what consultation must involve:

> 13 (7) In the course of those consultations the employer shall—
>   (a) consider any representations made by the appropriate representatives; and
>   (b) reply to those representations and, if he rejects any of those representations, state his reasons.

19.53 The consequences of a failure to inform or consult are dealt with in reg 15. In summary the position is as follows:

(a) If it is not in dispute that the employer dealt with the correct representative, but the claim is about a defect in the process, the proper claimant is the representative rather than an individual employee.

(b) If the claim relates to the election or choice of representatives, any affected employee may claim.

(c) The proper respondent to a claim that the transferor has failed to provide the necessary information is the transferor. If the transferor's case is that the transferee failed to pass information to it, then it must make the transferee a party to the proceedings and rely upon that failure as its defence.

(d) Where the claim succeeds, the tribunal makes a declaration, and orders that compensation should be paid to 'such descriptions of the affected employees as may be specified in the award': reg 15(8)(a).

(e) If an individual employee who falls within the ambit of that award does not receive the appropriate compensation, he or she may present a follow-up claim. The tribunal is then able to award the compensation in question.

(f) As to the compensation, the amount is set out in reg 16(3):

> ...such sum not exceeding 13 weeks' pay for the employee in question as the tribunal considers just and equitable having regard to the seriousness of the failure of the employer to comply with his duty.

(g) The amount of a week's pay is not subject to a statutory limit (contrast the basic award for unfair dismissal or a statutory redundancy payment: *Zaman v Kozee Sleep Products* [2011] IRLR 196).

(h) The primary purpose of the award is punitive, so that it should relate to the degree of fault on the part of the employer. The degree of loss suffered may also be taken into account in considering what is just and equitable: *Todd v Strain* [2011] IRLR 11.

(i) The award of the tribunal may be either against the transferor or the transferee, depending on which party has failed to meet its obligations.

(j) The award will be against the transferee if the default was caused by the failure of the transferee to pass on information.

In any event, the transferee will be jointly and severally liable with regard to any other award made against a transferor, and the tribunal has no discretion to apportion its award between transferor and transferee.

Part C
Remedies

Employee liability information

19.54 Regulation 11(2) sets out information which the transferor must provide to the transferee about those employees assigned to the organized grouping of resources or employees that is the subject of the transfer. The information to be provided is:

(a) the identity and age of the employee;

(b) the statutory particulars of employment;

(c) information about any disciplinary procedure taken against, or grievance procedure taken by, the employee within the previous two years;

(d) information about any actual or pending court or tribunal case within the last two years;

(e) information about any collective agreements.

19.55 This information must be notified to the transferee not less than 28 days before the transfer (reg 11(6)). (For transfers which took place before 1 May 2014, notification must take place not less than 14 days before the transfer.)

19.56 The information must be up to date 14 days before the date on which it is provided (reg 11(3)).

19.57 In the event of a failure to provide the relevant information, the transferee may make a claim to the tribunal within three months of the relevant transfer. The time limit is subject to the usual 'reasonably practicable' extension (see Chapter 6 on Time Limits). The tribunal may make a declaration and award compensation, the minimum amount being £500 per employee.

20 **Remedies for Unfair Dismissal**

Introduction

20.01 If the tribunal decides that the claimant has been unfairly dismissed, it will proceed to determine the remedy. The possible remedies, and the order in which they must be considered, are set out in s 112 of the Employment Rights Act 1996 (ERA 1996):

> 112 (1) This section applies where, on a complaint under section 111, an employment tribunal finds that the grounds of the complaint are well-founded.
>
> (2) The tribunal shall—
>
>   (a) explain to the complainant what orders may be made under section 113 and in what circumstances they may be made, and
>
>   (b) ask him whether he wishes the tribunal to make such an order.
>
> (3) If the complainant expresses such a wish, the tribunal may make an order under section 113.
>
> (4) If no order is made under section 113, the tribunal shall make an award of compensation for unfair dismissal (calculated in accordance with sections 118 to 126 . . .) to be paid by the employer to the employee.
>
> 113 An order under this section may be—
>
>   (a) an order for reinstatement (in accordance with section 114), or
>
>   (b) an order for re-engagement (in accordance with section 115),
>
>   as the tribunal may decide.

20.02 This procedure is mandatory for the tribunal. It must explain reinstatement and re-engagement and ask the claimant whether he or she wishes an order for reinstatement or re-engagement to be made. If that is the claimant's wish, it must consider each of the possibilities. If it is not, it will proceed to consider monetary compensation.

20.03 Reinstatement is defined in s 114(1) of the ERA 1996 as:

> . . . an order that the employer shall treat the complainant in all respects as if he had not been dismissed.

20.04 An order for a re-engagement is, according to s 115(1) of the ERA 1996 an order:

> … on such terms as the tribunal may decide, that the complainant be engaged by the employer, or by a successor of the employer or by an associate employer, in employment comparable to that from which he was dismissed or other suitable employment.

20.05 Broadly speaking, then, reinstatement involves getting the old job back; re-engagement involves getting a similar job with the same or an associated employer.

20.06 The consideration of reinstatement and re-engagement is obligatory: *Pirelli General Cable Works Ltd v Murray* [1979] IRLR 190 (EAT). This is so, even if the claimant has indicated on the claim form that it is compensation which is sought. As a matter of proper procedure, however, it is sensible for the claimant to inform the respondent as far in advance as possible of any changed intentions, so as to avoid the need for an adjournment and an application for costs.

20.07 In reality, the great majority of claimants do not seek reinstatement or re-engagement. Even when they do, the tribunal may decide not to make such an order. As a result, some 99 per cent of successful unfair dismissal claims result in an award of monetary compensation, rather than reinstatement or re-engagement.

20.08 In deciding whether to order reinstatement or re-engagement, the tribunal must take into account:

(a) the wishes of the claimant;

(b) whether such an order is practicable; and

(c) where the complainant contributed to the dismissal, whether it would be just to make an order for reinstatement or re-engagement.

(s 116(1) and (3) of the ERA 1996).

20.09 If the claimant does not wish to be reinstated or re-engaged, the tribunal will proceed to consider compensation, dealing with factors (b) and (c) just listed.

Practicability of re-employment

20.10 In deciding whether reinstatement or re-engagement are practicable, the tribunal must consider whether such an order can be put into effect successfully. In so doing, it must take into account the employment relations realities of the situation: *Coleman v Magnet Joinery Ltd* [1974] IRLR 343 (CA). The tribunal should take into account the impact which such an order will have upon other employees: *Meridian Ltd v Gomersall* [1977] IRLR 425 (EAT). An order for re-employment is unlikely where the employer genuinely believes that the employee is incapable of doing the job, or where there is a fundamental loss of trust between the parties: *Nothman v London Borough of Barnet (No 2)* [1980] IRLR 65 (CA).

20.11 Among the matters to be considered in deciding whether an order for re-employment is practicable is whether it will result in over-staffing or redundancies. However, such an order will not necessarily be considered impracticable merely because the employer has taken on a permanent replacement. This issue is dealt with in s 116 of the ERA 1996:

> 116 (5) Where in any case an employer has engaged a permanent replace-
> ment for a dismissed employee, the tribunal shall not take that fact
> into account in determining, for the purposes of subsection (1)(b) or
> (3)(b), whether it is practicable to comply with an order for reinstate-
> ment or re-engagement.
>
> (6) Subsection (5) does not apply where the employer shows—
> (a) that it was not practicable for him to arrange for the dismissed
> employee's work to be done without engaging a permanent
> replacement, or
> (b) that—
> (i) he engaged the replacement after the lapse of a reasonable
> period, without having heard from the dismissed employee
> that he wished to be reinstated or re-engaged, and
> (ii) when the employer engaged the replacement it was no longer
> reasonable for him to arrange for the dismissed employee's
> work to be done except by a permanent replacement.

Justice and contributory fault

20.12 In addition to considering practicability, the tribunal must take into account the justice of ordering reinstatement or re-engagement where the employee has been found to have contributed to his or her unfair dismissal. If there is blameworthy conduct which has contributed significantly to the dismissal, it is unlikely that such an order will be made, although the tribunal is not entirely excluded from so ordering: *Nairne v Highlands and Islands Fire Brigade* [1989] IRLR 366 (CS).

Compensation

20.13 Where an order for re-employment is made, the tribunal will also need to consider compensation for the period between dismissal and re-employment. This will include any wages or other benefits which the claimant would have expected to receive if they had not been dismissed. From that amount should be deducted any wages received in lieu of notice, any *ex gratia* payment which relates to the dismissal, and any payments received in respect of employment with another employer. This award will be subject to the Recoupment Regulations (see the section entitled 'Recoupment' at 20.75). It is not, however, subject to the statutory cap, which is explained later at 20.67.

Enforcement

20.14 If re-employment has been ordered, and the employer does not comply, the matter will return to the tribunal for a further remedy hearing. At that hearing, the employer will have a second opportunity to raise arguments relating to practicability. However, the onus will then be upon the employer to show that it is impracticable to reinstate or re-engage.

Additional award

20.15 If the employer has failed to carry out the order for reinstatement or re-engagement, and is unable to succeed in showing that it was impracticable to comply, the tribunal is required to make:

- the standard award of compensation for unfair dismissal; and
- an additional award for the failure to carry out the order to re-employ.

20.16 The additional award is a penalty for non-compliance, which is fixed at an amount of not less than 26 weeks' pay, and not more than 52 weeks' pay, subject to the statutory maximum (£464 per week with effect from 1 February 2014, updated annually). As this award is a penalty, the most important factor in determining the amount is the conduct of the employer—the more serious the violation, the higher the award will be.

Compensation

20.17 In the great majority of cases, the tribunal makes no order of reinstatement or engagement, and proceeds to consider financial compensation. This consists of two elements:

(a) the basic award; and
(b) the compensatory award.

Basic award

20.18 The basic award is calculated in accordance with s 119 of the ERA 1996, which lays down that an employee who is unfairly dismissed should receive:

(a) one and a half weeks' pay for each year of employment in which he or she was not below the age of 41;
(b) one week's pay for each year of employment (not within (a)) in which he or she was not below the age of 22; and
(c) half a week's pay for each year of employment not within (a) or (b).

20.19   The weekly pay in question is gross wages, ie before tax, and including allowances and any commission or overtime which is contractual. There is a statutory limit to the weekly pay, which is currently capped at £464 per week (updated annually).

20.20   Generally, there is no minimum basic award. However, there is a statutory minimum award of £5,676 with respect to union-related, health and safety, and whistleblowing dismissals.

Reductions to the basic award

20.21   In certain circumstances, the basic award may be reduced in accordance with s 122 of the ERA 1996. In practice, these are:

(a) where the claimant has unreasonably refused an offer of reinstatement;

(b) where the claimant's conduct before dismissal makes it just and equitable to reduce the basic award; and

(c) where the claimant has received a redundancy payment.

20.22   The basic award cannot be reduced, however, for failure to mitigate, and it is not liable to a reduction under the *Polkey* principle (see 20.57 to 20.62).

Compensatory award—the principles

20.23   Usually, the compensatory award will make up the larger part of the financial award for compensation which the tribunal makes. The principle upon which it is assessed is set out in s 123 of the ERA 1996:

> 123 (1) Subject to the provisions of this section and sections 124, 124A and 126, the amount of the compensatory award shall be such amount as the tribunal considers just and equitable in all the circumstances having regard to the loss sustained by the complainant in consequence of the dismissal in so far as that loss is attributable to action taken by the employer.
>
> (2) The loss referred to in subsection (1) shall be taken to include—
>
> (a) any expenses reasonably incurred by the complainant in consequence of the dismissal, and
>
> (b) subject to subsection (3), loss of any benefit which he might reasonably be expected to have had but for the dismissal.

20.24   The object of the compensatory award is to compensate the employee for financial loss suffered, but not to punish or express disapproval of the actions of the employer. It includes:

(a) immediate loss of earnings—this refers to the period between the date of dismissal and the date of the remedy part of the hearing;

(b) future loss of earnings—this covers the period after the remedy hearing;

(c) loss of statutory rights—this deals with compensation for the loss of the right not to be unfairly dismissed, or to receive a redundancy payment, from a future job in the period before the claimant has acquired sufficient continuous employment; and

(d) expenses incurred as a result of the dismissal, eg postage, telephone, and travel in seeking a new job.

20.25 As to the loss of earnings, compensation can be claimed for pay, but also for the loss of any benefit which can be valued in money terms and which forms part of the employee's remuneration. Examples include:

* wages,
* notice pay,
* bonus or commission,
* holiday pay,
* use of a company car and petrol allowance,
* accommodation provided by the employer,
* childcare costs,
* medical insurance,
* mobile phone and laptop,
* travel concessions,
* membership of a gym or other club,
* stock options.

20.26 Where appropriate, these various categories of remuneration and others can fall to be considered as either immediate or future loss or both.

Injury to feelings

20.27 The compensatory award does not include compensation for injury to health or injury to feelings: *Dunnachie v Kingston-upon-Hull City Council* [2004] IRLR 727 (HL). However, compensation for financial loss may be awarded where the manner of dismissal means that the claimant will be at a disadvantage in future in seeking work, or where psychological injury prevents the claimant from looking for a new job. If the tribunal finds that this was the case, it should take that disadvantage into account in calculating future loss. Hence, it does not constitute an award for injury to feelings as such.

Calculating the loss

20.28 As the aim of the compensatory award is to compensate the claimant, it is net or take-home pay which forms the basis of the calculation. In this respect, the method of calculation differs from that for the basic award. Another difference from the calculation of the basic award relates to bonus and commission. It is not necessary, in calculating the compensatory award, to show that the claimant has a contractual right to the sum claimed. A claim lies for the loss of any benefit which the claimant 'might reasonably be expected to have had but for the dismissal' (s 123(2)(b) of the ERA 1996).

20.29 Normally the calculation of take-home pay is straightforward. Where the claimant's pay has varied from week to week, a common practice for the tribunal is to calculate the average amount earned over the 12 weeks prior to dismissal. However, a different reference period might be put forward by one or other of the parties.

20.30 Notice pay can form part of the claim for loss of earnings. Where the solvency of the employer is in doubt, it is advisable to ask for a separate award for notice pay. If the respondent is in fact insolvent, statutory notice pay is recoverable from the Secretary of State, whereas the compensatory award is not (s 184(1)(b) of the ERA 1996).

20.31 Similarly, where there are doubts about the solvency of the employer, the tribunal should be invited to make an award for holiday pay which is separate from the compensatory award, as, in the event of the insolvency of the employer, up to six weeks' holiday pay is recoverable from the Secretary of State (s 184(1)(c) of the ERA 1996).

Expenses

20.32 A claimant is entitled to claim, as part of the award, the expenses involved in looking for work, eg postage for job applications, telephone calls to seek employment, travel to interviews.

Future loss

20.33 In addition to calculating the *immediate* loss up to the time of the remedy hearing, the tribunal must also calculate the likely *future* loss which the claimant will suffer. Inevitably this involves speculation, both about the prospects which the claimant would have had in remaining in their old job, and in determining their likely earnings in any new job. Although the exercise is speculative, it is clear that the tribunal is not allowed to opt out of the task simply because it is a difficult one: *Scope v Thornett* [2007] IRLR 155 (CA).

20.34 The calculation is based upon the net earnings which the claimant would have received in the old job, less the net earnings which he or she should receive in the new job. There are three main situations to consider:

(a) The claimant has acquired permanent new employment by the time of the remedies hearing, and that employment is at the same or a higher wage than that received in the job which was lost. There will be no award for loss of future earnings.

(b) The claimant is in new employment, but at a lesser wage than that earned in the old job. The Tribunal must decide upon the extent of the shortfall, and its likely duration. Once these figures have been ascertained, the extent of future loss as a result of the lower wage is a matter of simple arithmetic. For example, the tribunal determines that the claimant is being paid £25 a week less, and that it will be 12 months before she reaches her old wage level. It should award £1300 for future loss.

(c) The claimant has been unable to find a job, despite reasonable efforts to do so. The tribunal must then decide when he is likely to get a job, and what the wage is likely to be. In so doing, it will take into account the claimant's characteristics, and the state of the job market locally. It will then take what is inevitably a rough and ready decision as to how long the period of future unemployment will be, and what financial loss will result.

20.35 As far as situations (b) and (c) in 20.34 are concerned, the tribunal will take account of the claimant's efforts to mitigate his loss by seeking alternative employment (see 20.49).

Loss of statutory rights

20.36 The tribunal will usually make an award for the loss of statutory rights. This compensates for the need to re-qualify for statutory protection against unfair dismissal and other statutory rights. This takes the form of a fixed award, nowadays frequently £250 or £300.

Pension loss

20.37 The claimant is entitled to recover compensation for pension loss where this results from the unfair dismissal. This can be a difficult area to quantify. Guidance on how to deal with an award for the loss of pension is given in the booklet *Compensation for Loss of Pension Rights: Employment Tribunals* (pub TSO), which tribunals are encouraged to apply, although they are not bound to do so. Extracts from the booklet are set out in **Appendix 4** of *Blackstone's Employment Law Practice 2014*. Pension provision may be by way of:

(a) a defined contribution (money purchase) scheme; or

(b) a defined benefits (final salary) scheme.

20.38 A defined contribution scheme is one where the scheme defines the contribution made by the employer and any made by the employee. On retirement, the employee receives the pension which can be bought with those contributions, usually by way of an annuity. Calculation of past and future loss in a defined contribution scheme is usually relatively straightforward. It is based on the loss of the employer's contribution up to the date of the hearing (an immediate loss) and (if appropriate) beyond the hearing (future loss).

20.39 The calculation of pension loss in the case of a defined benefits or final salary scheme, however, may be anything but simple. An explanation is outside the scope of this Handbook, and reference should be made to **sections 32.98** to **32.110** of *Blackstone's Employment Law Practice 2014*.

ACAS Code adjustment

20.40 Where an employer has 'unreasonably' failed to comply with the Acas Code of Practice on Disciplinary and Grievance Procedures (2009) (see Appendix 1), the tribunal has a discretion to adjust any awards by up to 25 per cent. This means that if the tribunal feels that an *employer* has unreasonably failed to follow the guidance set out in the Code they can *increase* any award they have made by up to 25 per cent. Conversely, if they feel an *employee* has unreasonably failed to follow the guidance set out in the Code, they can *reduce* any award they have made by up to 25 per cent.

20.41 In practice, increases are made in a significant number of awards for unfair dismissal (as well as other types of claims). It is much less common for a reduction to be made. This flows from the fact that the increase or reduction is to an award which has been made on the basis that the employer is at fault. That means that it is more likely that the employer has acted unreasonably, and that the tribunal will exercise its discretion in favour of the claimant.

Contributory fault

20.42 Where a tribunal finds that the dismissal was to any extent caused or contributed to by a culpable action of the claimant, it should reduce the amount of the compensatory award by such proportion as it considers just and equitable, in accordance with s 123(6) of the ERA 1996:

> 123 (6) Where the tribunal finds that the dismissal was to any extent caused or contributed to by any action of the complainant, it shall reduce the amount of the compensatory award by such proportion as it considers just and equitable having regard to that finding.

20.43 In *Optikinetics v Whooley* [1999] ICR 984 (EAT) the principles in relation to reductions for contributory fault were summarized as follows:

(a) the claimant must have acted in a culpable, blameworthy, or wholly unreasonable manner;

(b) in deciding this point, the tribunal should focus upon the conduct of the claimant, rather than that of the employer;

(c) the conduct must be known to the employer prior to the dismissal and have been the (partial) cause of it;

(d) once blameworthy and contributory conduct is established, the tribunal must reduce the award by the amount which it considers just and equitable. It retains complete discretion, however, over the amount of the reduction, and is entitled to decide that it is too trivial to justify any reduction;

(e) the tribunal may reduce the basic and compensatory awards by different amounts;

(f) the appellate courts will not usually interfere with the tribunal's assessment of a reduction for contributory fault.

20.44 If the tribunal has decided to make a reduction for contributory fault, the question arises as to the size of the reduction. In *Hollier v Plysu Ltd* [1983] IRLR 260, the Court of Appeal endorsed guidance which had been given by the EAT on the correct approach to this task. That guidance suggested that there were four types of case:

(a) where the employee is wholly to blame for the dismissal, compensation could be reduced by 100 per cent;

(b) where the employee is largely to blame, the award could be reduced by 75 per cent;

(c) where both parties are equally to blame, the award could be reduced by 50 per cent;

(d) where the employee is slightly to blame the award could be reduced by 25 per cent.

Credit for payments received

20.45 In assessing the loss which the claimant has suffered, it is necessary to give credit for any payments or other benefits received since dismissal which arise as a result of the dismissal.

20.46 Generally, credit must be given for any payment received from new employment since dismissal, including part-time employment. The employee is not, however, required to give credit for payments received from the new employer during the notice period from the old job: *Langley v Burlo* [2007] IRLR 145 (CA).

20.47   State benefits which are recoverable by the Benefits Agency under the Recoupment Regulations (see the section on 'Recoupment' at 20.75) are not deducted from the compensatory award. The reason is that they form part of the monetary award to which the Recoupment Regulations apply, and therefore the claimant does not in the last resort acquire any benefit from such payments. These include job-seeker's allowance, income support, and income-related employment and support allowance.

20.48   Other state benefits such as industrial disablement benefit, disability living allowance, and incapacity benefits are deductible in full: *Morgans v Alpha Plus Security Ltd* [2005] IRLR 234 (EAT).

Mitigation

20.49   The general principle in determining the loss suffered by the claimant is to take the amount which he or she would have earned in the old job and deduct from that the amount which they actually did earn. The calculation is not quite as simple as that, however. The claimant has an obligation to mitigate loss, which is set out in s 123(4) of the ERA 1996:

> 123 (4) In ascertaining the loss referred to in subsection (1) the tribunal shall apply the same rule concerning the duty of a person to mitigate his loss as applies to damages recoverable under the common law of England and Wales or (as the case may be) Scotland.

20.50   This means that the claimant must make reasonable efforts to seek out alternative employment. At the tribunal hearing, it is open for the employer to argue that the employee has not made such efforts as are reasonable, and, if so, evidence will be heard on the point. From the claimant's point of view, evidence should cover details of vacancies sought, job applications made, advertisements replied to, etc. For its part, the respondent will aim to put forward evidence as to jobs which were in fact available, according to local newspapers, the trade press, the internet, etc.

20.51   In mitigating, the duty of the former employee is to act as a reasonable person, unaffected by the prospect of compensation from the former employer: *Wilding v British Telecommunications plc* [2002] IRLR 524 (CA). The burden of proving a failure to mitigate is on the employer: *Fyfe v Scientific Furnishings Ltd* [1989] IRLR 331 (EAT). In *Savage v Saxena* [1998] IRLR 182, the EAT suggested that the tribunal should ask the following questions in relation to mitigation:

(a) What steps should the claimant have taken to mitigate his or her loss?

(b) On what date would such steps have produced an alternative income?

20.52 Once those questions have been answered, the award should be reduced accordingly. It is worth emphasizing that the employer needs to show not only that the claimant failed to take reasonable steps, but also that such steps would (on the balance of probabilities) have produced a result in the form of income.

20.53 As the duty to mitigate arises only after dismissal. It follows that an offer of re-employment made prior to dismissal is not relevant to the duty to mitigate: *Gillham v Kent County Council* [1986] IRLR 56 (EAT).

20.54 If the tribunal finds that the claimant has failed to mitigate, the compensatory award will be reduced or extinguished from the date when alternative employment should have been found, given reasonable efforts. The date and the amount of reduction will depend upon a finding of fact as to what income would have resulted from such alternative employment. The tribunal should not reduce the award on a percentage basis, as is done in assessing contributory fault, but should make findings of fact as to what should have been earned, and from what date.

20.55 Although the claimant must make reasonable efforts to seek alternative employment, it may not be reasonable to look for, or to take, the first job that comes along. Claimants who have been out of work for some time, however, may be expected to be more flexible in their approach to job seeking, both in terms of the level of pay and the nature of the work which they are looking for. It may also be reasonable for the search which the claimant conducts for alternative employment to become wider geographically as time goes on. In addition, the job search should extend to temporary or part-time work if the outlook for permanent or full-time work is bleak: *Hardwick v Leeds Area Health Authority* [1975] IRLR 319 (EAT).

20.56 Where no suitable alternative employment is available, it may be reasonable to mitigate loss by setting up a business, becoming self-employed, and/or retraining.

Polkey reduction

20.57 In *Polkey v AE Dayton Services Ltd* [1987] IRLR 503 (HL), the position was considered where, in an unfair dismissal case, the employer's failure to follow a fair procedure did not affect the outcome, ie the employee would have been dismissed in any event. The House of Lords made it clear that such a dismissal was still unfair. They went on to decide, however, that in a case where the employee would have been dismissed in any event, this would have consequences for the amount of the compensatory award.

20.58 Lord Bridge stated that, if the tribunal was in doubt about whether the employee would have been dismissed, that doubt: 'can be reflected by reducing the normal amount of compensation by a percentage representing the chance that the employee would still have lost his employment'.

20.59 The employer may therefore show that dismissal would have been likely even if a proper procedure had been followed. Inevitably, this will involve the tribunal in speculation about a hypothetical situation where the unfairness would not have occurred.

20.60 In *Scope v Thornett* [2007] IRLR 155, the Court of Appeal said that the task of an employment tribunal in deciding what was just and equitable:

> ...will almost inevitably involve a consideration of uncertainties. There may be cases in which evidence to the contrary is so sparse that a tribunal should approach the question on the basis that loss of earnings and the employment would have continued indefinitely, but, where there is evidence that it may not have been so, that evidence must be taken into account.

20.61 In *King v Eaton Ltd (No 2)* [1998] IRLR 686, the Court of Session considered whether a *Polkey* reduction could be applied to an error which was not merely procedural, but one of substance. It held that there was no reason why the *Polkey* principle should be limited to procedural errors alone, but recognized that it might be more difficult to envisage what would have happened where the error was one of substance.

20.62 Where the tribunal does find that a case is appropriate for a *Polkey* reduction, it must decide:

(a) when the employer might reasonably have dismissed if it had acted according to a fair procedure; and

(b) what the chances were that it would reasonably have dismissed at that point expressed as a percentage.

Example: Assume that the tribunal finds that the employer would (on the balance of probabilities) have taken a further two weeks to carry out the procedures necessary to act reasonably and fairly. It might then go on to decide that, on carrying out those procedures, there was a 75% chance that the claimant would have been dismissed. The compensatory award would then be calculated on the basis that the claimant would receive two weeks at full pay, followed by a period on a quarter of full pay, which would last until such time as he or she acquired (or ought to have acquired) alternative employment.

Enhanced redundancy payments

20.63 What is the position if the employer pays an enhanced redundancy payment, perhaps as a result of a contractual provision? This is dealt with in s 123(7) of the ERA 1996:

> 123 (7) If the amount of any payment made by the employer to the employee on the ground that the dismissal was by reason of redundancy exceeds the amount of the basic award that would be payable ... that excess goes to reduce the amount of the compensatory award.

20.64 It follows that such a payment should be set off against the compensatory award: *Digital Equipment Ltd v Clements (No 2)* [1998] IRLR 134 (CA). This is only the case, however, where the dismissal is for redundancy.

Ex gratia payments

20.65 An *ex gratia* payment is one which the employer pays without legal obligation to do so. Normally, where such a payment is made with reference to the dismissal, it is taken into account in assessing the loss which must be compensated, and will be deducted from the compensatory award. It will not, however, be deducted if the employee would have received it even if he or she had not been dismissed: *Roadchef Ltd v Hastings* [1988] IRLR 142 (EAT).

Payment in lieu of notice

20.66 Where the employer has paid the claimant a sum in lieu of notice, that falls to be deducted from the compensatory award: *Babcock FATA Ltd v Addison* [1987] IRLR 173 (CA).

Maximum for compensatory award

20.67 The maximum amount for the compensatory award is whichever is the lower of:

(a) £76,574 (with effect from 1 February 2014, revised annually); or
(b) 52 weeks' gross pay (applies where the effective date of termination was on or after 29 July 2013).

20.68 The limit is revised annually. There is no statutory limit to the weekly earnings of the claimant upon which the award is based. The limit applies to the compensatory award taken by itself, excluding the separate amount for the basic award.

20.69 There are certain unfair dismissal cases where the statutory cap on the compensatory award does not apply. In summary these are:

(a) cases where the claimant was dismissed for making a protected disclosure, ie whistleblowing (s 103A of the ERA 1996);

(b) cases where the claimant was dismissed contrary to s 100 of the ERA 1996 (certain specified health and safety reasons); and

(c) selection for redundancy on the grounds of either (a) or (b).

Accelerated payment

20.70　Where an award is made for future loss of earnings and benefits, the claimant may be put in a better position than would have been the case had the payment been received at the times when it fell due. As a result, a reduction should be made for the accelerated receipt of the payment, unless the award for future loss is relatively small: *Les Ambassadeurs Club v Bainda* [1982] IRLR 5 (EAT). For the method of calculating the reduction, reference should be made to **section 32.217** of *Blackstone's Employment Law Practice 2014*.

Order of calculation and deductions

20.71　The order in which the calculation is carried out and deductions are made will affect the overall total of the compensatory award. According to *Digital Equipment Ltd v Clements (No 2)* [1998] IRLR 134 (CA), as read with subsequent statutory provisions, the order should be as follows:

(1) calculate the financial loss which the claimant sustained in consequence of the dismissal;

(2) deduct any payment which the employer made as compensation for the dismissal (eg an *ex gratia* payment), other than an enhanced redundancy payment;

(3) deduct any amount for which the claimant must give credit, including amounts earned during the period of loss, or to take into account the failure to mitigate reasonably;

(4) make any percentage reduction as a result of the operation of the *Polkey* principle;

(5) make any increase or decrease because of an unreasonable failure to follow the ACAS Code of Practice;

(6) make any percentage reduction for the claimant's contributory fault;

(7) deduct any enhanced redundancy payment, to the extent that it exceeds the basic award;

(8) apply the statutory limit to the compensatory award, unless one of the exceptions applies.

Interest

20.72　The award of the employment tribunal will not in itself contain an amount for interest. However, if the award is a monetary one, and the respondent delays paying for more than 14 days after the decision is sent to the parties, interest will accrue from the date when the decision was sent.

20.73 The rate of interest is that which is specified in s 17 of the Judgments Act 1838. This is currently 8 per cent.

20.74 Where there is a review or appeal, interest will still accrue from the date on which the original decision was sent, but it will be on such greater or lesser sum as is appropriate.

Recoupment

20.75 During a period of unemployment, the claimant may well have received jobseeker's allowance, income support, or income-related employment support allowance. If he or she has claimed any of these benefits, then the compensatory award will be subject to the Recoupment Regulations—more formally the Employment Protection (Recoupment of Job Seeker's Allowance and Income Support) Regulations 1996, SI 1996/2349 and the Social Security (Miscellaneous Amendments) (No 5) Regulations 2010, SI 2010/2429.

20.76 The portion of the compensatory award which reflects wages from the date of dismissal to the date of the remedies hearing is known as the 'prescribed element'. The period in question is known as the 'prescribed period'. When it gives its decision, the tribunal must, if the award is subject to recoupment, state the prescribed period and the prescribed element. The respondent must then pay the claimant the award less the prescribed element. The Department for Work and Pensions will then work out, after being notified by the tribunal, the amount received by the claimant in jobseeker's allowance, income support, or income-related employment support allowance during the prescribed period. It must notify the respondent within 21 days of the hearing, or nine days after judgment has been sent to the parties (whichever is sooner), of the amount which it reclaims. The respondent must then pay the amount reclaimed to the Department for Work and Pensions, and the remainder to the claimant.

20.77 The Recoupment Regulations do not apply to the basic award. Nor do they operate in relation to future loss, although the claimant's entitlement to future benefits for the period covered by the award for future loss will be affected.

Example: The claimant is awarded compensation of £7000. The tribunal states that the prescribed element within this award is £3000. The claimant has received income support of £1500. The position is as follows:

(1) the respondent should pay the claimant £4000 (failure to do so within 14 days will mean that interest accrues upon this sum);

---

(2) the respondent should retain the remaining £3000 pending notification from the Benefits Agency;

(3) if the Benefits Agency notifies the respondent that it wishes to recoup the amount of £1500, the respondent must pay that amount to it;

(4) on receipt of that notification, the respondent should send the claimant the remaining £1500;

(5) if the Benefits Agency notifies the respondent that it does not wish to exercise any recoupment, the balance of the prescribed element (the whole £3000) should be sent to the employee.

20.78 The process of recoupment results in an incentive to the parties to settle. If there is a settlement, then the Recoupment Regulations do not apply, since the settlement will not identify any prescribed amount or prescribed period. This means that whatever is settled should be paid in full to the claimant, regardless of the benefits which he or she has received. This is a matter which should be kept in mind by both parties. It opens up the possibility that the claimant may settle for rather less than the likely award from the tribunal, in the knowledge that this would be slightly more than he or she would receive if the tribunal came to a decision which involved recoupment. In the foregoing example, a settlement over £5500 would benefit the claimant, whilst a settlement under £7000 would benefit the respondent. This means that it will be of benefit to both parties if they negotiate a settlement in the band between £5500 and £7000.

Taxation

20.79 Payments made in connection with the termination of employment enjoy a tax-free allowance of £30,000, and fall outside the scope of national insurance deductions. The question of taxation of tribunal awards and settlements is dealt with in detail in **chapter 36** of *Blackstone's Employment Law Practice 2014*. However, the position with regard to the compensatory award for unfair dismissal can be briefly described as follows.

20.80 Where the award is less than £30,000, no tax is payable, provided that there have been no other payments on termination—if there have, these will count towards the £30,000 total.

20.81 Where an award is made for termination of employment in excess of £30,000, it will be subject to tax with respect to the amount over £30,000. That means that the employee will, in due course, receive a tax demand for the excess. In order to ensure that the claimant receives the amount lost as a result of the dismissal, the tribunal has to 'gross up' the amount of the award. It decides the amount which the claimant should receive, and then adds to it the amount of tax which he or she will have to pay on it.

> **Example**: Before taking into account the taxation position, the tribunal decides that the award should be £40,000. The tribunal hears evidence as to the tax position, and decides that the claimant will be a higher rate taxpayer during the current year. That means that the tax on the amount over the threshold will be:
>
> $$£40,000 - £30,000 = £10,000 \times 40\% = £4,000.$$
>
> In order to put her in the position of receiving £40,000 after tax, the tribunal must award £46,666.67. As a result she will receive after taxation:
>
> | | |
> | --- | --- |
> | | £30,000 tax free |
> | (£16,666.67 less tax at 40%) | £10,000 |
> | | Total £40,000 |

Overlapping claims

20.82   An employee may well claim for two or more of the following, based upon the same facts:

(a) unfair dismissal;
(b) wrongful dismissal;
(c) a redundancy payment; and/or
(d) a discriminatory dismissal.

20.83   Assume that the claimant succeeds upon two or more of these claims. The general principle is that where such overlapping claims succeed, there should not be double recovery. For example, if compensation falls to be awarded for unfair dismissal and also for discrimination, the tribunal must offset the compensation awarded under one set of provisions against the other (s 126 of the ERA 1996).

20.84   Where claims for wrongful and unfair dismissal succeed, the claimant may be entitled to payment for the notice period with regard to each of the successful claims. The tribunal will usually make an award for wrongful dismissal consisting of payment for the notice period. If so, the compensatory award for unfair dismissal would exclude the notice period. If, in such a case, the tribunal had decided upon a reduction for contributory conduct and/or in accordance with *Polkey*, those reductions would not apply to the notice period since the principles in question do not operate in relation to wrongful dismissal. The result would therefore be that the claimant would receive full payment for the notice period, and the reductions would operate for the period thereafter.

21 Remedies for Discrimination

Introduction

21.01 This chapter begins by dealing with the remedies for discrimination contrary to the Equality Act 2010 (EqA 2010), and then considers the remedies for contraventions of the Part-Time Workers Regulations and the Fixed Term Employees (Prevention of Unequal Treatment) Regulations.

21.02 Section 124 of the Equality Act 2010 deals with remedies for discrimination contrary to that Act, and reads as follows:

> 124 (1) This section applies if an employment tribunal finds that there has been a contravention of a provision referred to in section 120(1).
>
> (2) The tribunal may—
> > (a) make a declaration as to the rights of the complainant and the respondent in relation to the matters to which the proceedings relate;
> > (b) order the respondent to pay compensation to the complainant;
> > (c) make an appropriate recommendation.
>
> (3) An appropriate recommendation is a recommendation that within a specified period the respondent takes specified steps for the purpose of obviating or reducing the adverse effect of any matter to which the proceedings relate—
> > (a) on the complainant;
> > (b) on any other person.
>
> (4) Subsection (5) applies if the tribunal—
> > (a) finds that a contravention is established by virtue of section 19, but
> > (b) is satisfied that the provision, criterion or practice was not applied with the intention of discriminating against the complainant.
>
> (5) It must not make an order under subsection (2)(b) unless it first considers whether to act under subsection (2)(a) or (c).
>
> (6) The amount of compensation which may be awarded under subsection (2)(b) corresponds to the amount which could be awarded by a county court or the sheriff under section 119.
>
> (7) If a respondent fails, without reasonable excuse, to comply with an appropriate recommendation in so far as it relates to the complainant, the tribunal may—
> > (a) if an order was made under subsection (2)(b), increase the amount of compensation to be paid;
> > (b) if no such order was made, make one.

Declaration

21.03 The declaration which is referred to in s 124 of the EqA 2010 is one which sets out the rights of the parties. In practice, it usually consists of the judgment that an unlawful act of discrimination has been committed by the respondent against the claimant, specifying the legal category of the act in question, eg harassment, direct discrimination, failure to make a reasonable adjustment, etc.

Recommendation

21.04 This remedy is a discretionary one, and is not much used. If made, it will recommend that the respondent takes specified steps within a specified period. Such steps are 'for the purpose of obviating or reducing the adverse effects of any matter to which the proceedings relate:

(a) on the claimant; and/or

(b) on any other person'.

21.05 The case law in relation to recommendations is set out in **sections 33.67** to **33.73** of *Blackstone's Employment Law Practice 2014*.

Compensation

21.06 Where the claimant has succeeded, the tribunal has a discretion as to whether to award compensation, and in practice it almost invariably does so. There is no limit as to the amount of compensation which can be awarded in respect of a successful discrimination claim.

21.07 The measure of compensation is that which can be ordered in the courts on the basis of the principles of the law of tort. This is because the compensation in question is for the statutory tort of discrimination, and the principles involved are different from those applicable to unfair dismissal or breach of contract.

21.08 The tribunal does not have the power to order reinstatement or re-engagement, as it would for a successful unfair dismissal claim. In addition, the Recoupment Regulations (see 20.75) do not apply to awards for discrimination.

Financial loss

21.09 In calculating compensation, the crucial question is: 'What would have happened if the claimant had not been subjected to the discriminatory act?' The principle is that the claimant should be put in the same position as they would have been without any discrimination. Assume, for example, that the claimant was denied promotion for a discriminatory reason. The question for the tribunal would be: 'What position would she have been in if she had not been discriminated against?' This requires a calculation of the chance that the claimant would have been promoted if there had been no discrimination, and also of the financial loss represented in the difference between her earnings with and without the promotion.

21.10   To take another example, assume that the claimant was dismissed for a discriminatory reason. The tribunal should calculate the sum which the claimant would have earned if they had continued in employment, and deduct the amount which they earned (or should have earned) elsewhere. There should also be a deduction in respect of any chance that the claimant would have left that employment in any event. The principles are set out in *Ministry of Defence v Wheeler* [1998] IRLR 23 (CA).

Foreseeability

21.11   In a claim for personal injury at common law, compensation will only be recoverable for injury which is reasonably foreseeable. In *Essa v Laing Ltd* [2004] IRLR 313, the Court of Appeal held that this principle does not apply to discriminatory claims involving harassment. As a result, it was open to a victim of harassment to claim for any loss which flowed from the discriminatory act, even if it was not foreseeable. This was a case of intentional racial abuse, and there is no direct authority on whether the principle that loss need not be reasonably foreseeable applies to discriminatory acts in general.

Mitigation

21.12   The claimant is under a duty to mitigate his or her loss. The principles which apply in a discrimination case are similar to those in relation to unfair dismissal as far as mitigation is concerned, and reference should be made to Chapter 20 on Remedies for Unfair Dismissal (see 20.49). In particular, just as it is for the claimant to prove loss, it is for the respondent to prove any failure to mitigate.

Can there be a reduction under *Polkey*?

21.13   With regard to an award of compensation for unfair dismissal, the tribunal is obliged to consider the question whether the claimant would have been dismissed in any event. This principle arises from the case of *Polkey v AE Dayton* [1987] IRLR 503 (see 20.57 for general principles in the context of unfair dismissal cases). It does not apply directly to discrimination cases, but the tribunal will often have to determine, for example, whether the claimant would have remained in his or her employment but for the discrimination. In *Chagger v Abbey National plc* [2010] IRLR 47, the Court of Appeal made it clear that a tribunal can apply a *Polkey*-type limitation in discrimination cases where it can be shown that the claimant would have lost his or her job in any event for a lawful reason. It is clear that this way of proceeding flows from the principle that the claimant should be placed in the same position that they would have been in had it not been for the discriminatory act. Frequently this will be done by means of a percentage reduction, to reflect the chance that the claimant would not have sustained loss.

ACAS Code adjustment

21.14   The tribunal has a discretion to increase or reduce an award by such amount as is 'just and equitable' up to a maximum of 25 per cent where there is an unreasonable failure to comply with the Acas Code of Practice on Discipline and Grievance: s 207A of the TULR(C)A 1992. The Acas Code of Practice is reproduced in Appendix 1.

State benefits

21.15   Credit should be given for the receipt by the claimant of state benefits in calculating the compensation award. In other words, such benefits should be deducted from the amount of the award insofar as they are paid to the claimant, but not if they are paid to the claimant's household or children: *Vento v Chief Constable of West Yorkshire Police* [2002] IRLR 177 (EAT). The position differs somewhat from that in relation to unfair dismissal, where jobseeker's allowance and income support are not deducted from the calculation for the award, because they will be recovered via the Recoupment Regulations (see 20.75).

Contributory conduct

21.16   It may be that, in principle, a reduction in compensation can be made to an award for discrimination because of contributory negligence on the part of the claimant. This argument is based upon the status of discrimination as a tort: see s 119 of the Equality Act 2010. In practice, however, it is difficult to see how a claimant could properly be said to have contributed to discriminatory conduct, and no examples of such deductions are available.

Accelerated receipt

21.17   Where the tribunal makes an award for future loss of earnings and benefits, a deduction should be made for the accelerated receipt of the payment. In practice, such a reduction need only be made if the award is significant: *Les Ambassadeurs Club v Bainda* [1982] IRLR 5 (EAT). Where the amount in question is substantial, the tribunal has to bear in mind that the claimant has the benefit of receiving it immediately, rather than waiting to receive it in instalments. It should therefore make a deduction for accelerated receipt, upon the basis of the annual yield of the money in question. For details, reference should be made to **section 33.61** of *Blackstone's Employment Law Practice 2014*.

Injury to health, including psychiatric injury

21.18 In a discrimination case, the tribunal has power to award compensation for injury to health if that has been caused by the discriminatory act: *Sheriff v Klyne Tugs (Lowestoft) Ltd* [1999] IRLR 481 (CA). This is a category which is distinct from injury to feelings, which is dealt with later (see 21.23).

21.19 In practice, by far the most common basis upon which compensation is awarded for injury to health in the employment tribunals is psychiatric injury. The tribunal does not have to base such an award upon medical evidence: *HM Prison Service v Salmon* [2001] IRLR 425 (EAT). It is right to say, however, that the tribunal will usually welcome medical evidence both on the psychiatric injury and upon causation, and may well be reluctant to make an award without such evidence.

21.20 In determining the award, reference will frequently be made to the Judicial College *Guidelines for the Assessment of General Damages in Personal Injury Cases* (12th edn, 2013 OUP). The guidelines suggest that the following factors ought to be taken into account:

- the injured person's ability to cope with life and work;
- the effect on his or her relationships;
- the extent of treatment;
- future vulnerability;
- prognosis;
- whether medical help is being sought;
- the nature of the conduct which caused the injury, and its duration.

21.21 Care will have to be taken to ensure that there is no double counting with respect to any claim for psychiatric injury and the separate category of injury to feelings. As far as psychiatric injury itself is concerned, the guidelines lay down four categories of award:

(1) Severe (£40,000–£85,000), where the claimant has serious problems and the prognosis is very poor.
(2) Moderately severe (£14,000–£40,000), where there are significant problems in relation to the factors cited in (1) but where the prognosis is more optimistic.

(3) Moderate (£4300–£14,000), where there has been a significant improvement and the prognosis is good.

(4) Minor (£1125–£4300), where the illness is of limited duration such as temporary anxiety.

21.22   Where there is a pre-existing medical history, or other contributory factors, a reduction should be made to the figures suggested in 21.21.

Injury to feelings

21.23   Compensation for discrimination differs from an award for unfair dismissal in that s 119(4) of the EqA 2010 specifically provides for compensation for injury to feelings to be recoverable. Generally, an unfair dismissal award cannot include compensation for injury to feelings, although this can be awarded for detriment other than dismissal itself in a whistleblowing claim (see Chapter 12 on Whistleblowers and Protected Disclosure).

21.24   A claimant is entitled to recover compensation for injury to feelings caused by an act of discrimination, even if he or she did not know that it was discrimination: *Taylor v XLN Telecom Ltd* [2010] IRLR 499 (EAT).

21.25   The onus is upon the claimant to show that injury to feelings has been suffered as a result of the discriminatory act, but the burden is not a difficult one to discharge, and may sometimes be inferred from the surrounding circumstances. Nevertheless, the evidence of the claimant (at least) will usually be required.

21.26   The principles behind determining the award for injury to feelings were set out in the case of *Armitage v Johnson* [1997] IRLR 162 (EAT) as follows:

(a) The award is compensatory, and not punitive. It should not be inflated by feelings of indignation at the conduct of the respondent.

(b) The award should not be so low that it would diminish respect for the policy of anti-discrimination. Nor should it be too high, since an excessive award might be seen as the way to untaxed riches.

(c) Awards should bear some general similarity to the whole range of awards in personal injury cases (rather than any particular type of award).

(d) Tribunals should remind themselves of the value in everyday life of the sum which they have in mind. They can do this by reference to purchasing power, or to earnings.

(e) Tribunals should have regard to the need to retain public respect for the level of awards made.

21.27   Important guidance on the level of awards was set out in the case of *Vento v Chief Constable of West Yorkshire Police (No 2)* [2003] IRLR 102 (CA). That case set out three bands for compensation for injury to feelings. The figures in question were revised upward in accordance with inflation in the case of *Da'Bell v NSPCC* [2010] IRLR 19 (EAT). The three bands, incorporating the revised figures are:

(a)   a lower band of between £750 and £6000 in less serious cases where the unlawful act is isolated or one-off;

(b)   a middle band of between £6000 and £18,000 for serious cases which do not merit an award in the highest band;

(c)   an upper band of between £18,000 and £30,000 for the most serious cases, eg where there has been a lengthy campaign of harassment.

21.28   In *Voith Turbo Ltd v Stowe* [2005] IRLR 228, the tribunal assessed compensation for injury to feelings in the middle band where the act of racial discrimination was dismissal. The EAT upheld their decision, stating that dismissal on grounds of racial discrimination is a very serious incident, and cannot be described as one-off or isolated.

21.29   If the employer admits that it has acted in breach of the law, that may help to reduce the hurt felt by sparing the claimant from the further hurt of rehearsing the nature of her treatment: *Orlando v Didcot Power Station Sports and Social Club* [1996] IRLR 262 (EAT).

Aggravated damages

21.30   Aggravated damages are awarded in a case where the discriminator has acted in a high-handed, malicious, insulting, or oppressive manner in committing the act of discrimination: *Alexander v Home Office* [1988] IRLR 190 (CA). Full guidance was given by Underhill P in *Metropolitan Commissioner of Police v Shaw* [2012] IRLR 242 (EAT). In that case, it was emphasized that aggravated damages were an aspect of the injury to feelings, rather than a separate head of damages. The tribunal should ask itself: What additional distress was caused by the aggravating features in question? It followed that aggravated damages were compensatory (like the award for injury to feelings as a whole) rather than punitive.

Exemplary damages

21.31   Exemplary damages should be distinguished from aggravated damages. They are punitive in nature. They can only be awarded if compensation is insufficient to punish the wrongdoer, and are available only in the following circumstances:

(a)   where there has been oppressive, arbitrary, or unconstitutional action by agents of the government; or

(b) where the actions of the respondent had been calculated to make a profit exceeding the compensation payable to the claimant.

In practice, an award of exemplary damages is exceedingly rare.

Interest

21.32   The rule for awards in discrimination cases is different from that in unfair dismissal cases. Interest in an unfair dismissal case will only begin to accumulate 14 days after judgment has been sent to the parties. For a discrimination claim, however, the position is that interest is calculated for the period before judgment as follows:

(a) for injury to feelings, interest accrues from the date of the act of discrimination;

(b) for the other elements in compensation, eg financial loss, interest accrues from the date midway between the act of discrimination and the date of judgment.

21.33   The rate of interest is set in the Judgments Act 1838 and is currently at 8 per cent per annum.

Unintentional indirect discrimination

21.34   Compensation can be awarded for indirect discrimination, but there is a limitation. If the 'provision criterion or practice was not applied with the intention of discriminating against the complainant', no award can be made unless the tribunal first considers whether (1) to make a declaration and (2) to make a recommendation under s 124 of the Equality Act 2010. If the employer intended the discrimination to occur, then no such limitation applies. Whether there was an intention or not should be gauged at the point when the provision, criterion, or practice was applied, rather than at the time when it was introduced. The intention to apply it, together with knowledge of its impact upon the claimant, is sufficient to establish intention: *London Underground v Edwards* [1995] IRLR 355 (EAT). Intention can be inferred from knowledge of the consequences: *JH Walker Ltd v Hussain* [1996] IRLR 11 (EAT).

Joint and several awards

21.35   Where more than one discriminator has contributed to the same loss, the tribunal has no power to apportion the award between the discriminators. Each of the respondents should be held jointly and severally liable. This means that, where, for example, the employer is the first respondent and an individual employee is the second respondent, and they have both contributed to the same loss, they will both be liable to the full extent, and it will be up to the claimant as to which one it pursues for enforcement: *London Borough of Hackney v Sivanandan* [2013] IRLR 408 (CA). In that case, the Court of Appeal held that 'split' awards should only be made where the injury caused by different discriminators is 'divisible' and then only where such an award is sought by one of the parties, and a proper legal basis is established.

Taxation

21.36   Awards for non-pecuniary loss, eg injury to feelings, are not taxable. It follows that there is no need to gross up that part of any award. The taxation of awards for discrimination is dealt with in detail in **sections 36.42** to **36.48** of *Blackstone's Employment Law Practice 2014*.

Equal pay remedies

21.37   The right of an employee to equal pay is referred to in the Equality Act 2010 as 'equality of terms'. It takes effect by way of the operation of an equality clause, which is implied into the contract of employment: s 66(1) of the EqA 2010. More detail is to be found in Chapter 17 on Equal Pay.

21.38   The remedies available to the employee are, therefore, those which are available for a breach of contract. This will usually consist of a claim for damages for breach of contract, but either side may apply for a declaration: s 132(2) of the EqA 2010. It is possible that an injunction may also be available, but that remedy is not within the power of the employment tribunal. Where wages which are paid are not in accordance with the equality clause, a claim may be brought for the non-payment of wages.

21.39   A claim for equal pay is a financial claim only, and no compensation is available for non-economic loss such as injury to feelings, aggravated damages, or exemplary damages: *Council of the City of Newcastle upon Tyne v Allan* [2005] IRLR 505 (EAT).

Remedies for part-time workers and fixed-term employees

21.40   Provision is made under the Part-Time Workers Regulations 2000 (PTWR 2000) and the Fixed-Term Employees (Prevention of Less Favourable Treatment) Regulations 2002 (FTER 2002) for compensation where a tribunal finds a complaint presented to it under the respective sets of regulations to be well founded. In such a case, it shall take such of the following steps as it considers just and equitable:

(a)   a declaration as to the rights of the complainant and the employer in relation to the matters to which the complaint relates;

(b) an order to the employer to pay compensation to the complainant;

(c) a recommendation that the employer takes, within a specified period, action appearing to the tribunal to be reasonable, in all the circumstances of the case, for the purpose of obviating or reducing the adverse effect on the complainant of any matter to which the complaint relates.

Steps (a) to (c) are set out in reg 8(7) of the PTWR 2000 and reg 7(7) of the FTER 2002.

21.41 Any compensation should be such as the tribunal considers just and equitable in the circumstances, having regard to (a) any infringement to which the complaint relates, and (b) any loss which is attributable to the infringement, having regard, in the case of an infringement covered by reg 5 of the PTWR 2000, to the pro rata principle, except where it is inappropriate to do so.

21.42 Compensation covers financial loss. However, compensation does not include injury to feelings. Awards may be reduced for contributory conduct. The normal rules on mitigation apply. There is no statutory cap on the amount of compensation that can be awarded.

Appendix 1   **ACAS**

April 2009

Code of Practice 1

Disciplinary and Grievance Procedures

Appendix 1

Foreword

The Acas statutory Code of Practice on discipline and grievance is set out at paras 1 to 45 on the following pages. It provides basic practical guidance to employers, employees and their representatives and sets out principles for handling disciplinary and grievance situations in the workplace. The Code does not apply to dismissals due to redundancy or the non-renewal of fixed-term contracts on their expiry. Guidance on handling redundancies is contained in Acas' advisory booklet on Redundancy handling.

The Code is issued under section 199 of the Trade Union and Labour Relations (Consolidation) Act 1992 and was laid before both Houses of Parliament on 9 December 2008. It comes into effect by order of the Secretary of State on 6 April 2009 and replaces the Code issued in 2004.

A failure to follow the Code does not, in itself, make a person or organisation liable to proceedings. However, employment tribunals will take the Code into account when considering relevant cases. Tribunals will also be able to adjust any awards made in relevant cases by up to 25 per cent for unreasonable failure to comply with any provision of the Code. This means that if the tribunal feels that an employer has unreasonably failed to follow the guidance set out in the Code they can increase any award they have made by up to 25 per cent. Conversely, if they feel an employee has unreasonably failed to follow the guidance set out in the code they can reduce any award they have made by up to 25 per cent.

Employers and employees should always seek to resolve disciplinary and grievance issues in the workplace. Where this is not possible employers and employees should consider using an independent third party to help resolve the problem. The third party need not come from outside the organisation but could be an internal mediator, so long as they are not involved in the disciplinary or grievance issue. In some cases, an external mediator might be appropriate.

Many potential disciplinary or grievance issues can be resolved informally. A quiet word is often all that is required to resolve an issue. However, where an issue cannot be resolved informally then it may be pursued formally. This Code sets out the basic requirements of fairness that will be applicable in most cases; it is intended to provide the standard of reasonable behaviour in most instances.

Appendix 1

Employers would be well advised to keep a written record of any disciplinary or grievances cases they deal with.

Organisations may wish to consider dealing with issues involving bullying, harassment or whistleblowing under a separate procedure.

More comprehensive advice and guidance on dealing with disciplinary and grievance situations is contained in the Acas booklet, 'Discipline and grievances at work: the Acas guide'. The booklet also contains sample disciplinary and grievance procedures. Copies of the guidance can be obtained from Acas.

Unlike the Code employment tribunals are not required to have regard to the Acas guidance booklet. However, it provides more detailed advice and guidance that employers and employees will often find helpful both in general terms and in individual cases.

The Code of Practice

Introduction

1. This Code is designed to help employers, employees and their representatives deal with disciplinary and grievance situations in the workplace.

   • Disciplinary situations include misconduct and/or poor performance. If employers have a separate capability procedure they may prefer to address performance issues under this procedure. If so, however, the basic principles of fairness set out in this Code should still be followed, albeit that they may need to be adapted.

   • Grievances are concerns, problems or complaints that employees raise with their employers.

   The Code does not apply to redundancy dismissals or the non renewal of fixed-term contracts on their expiry.

2. Fairness and transparency are promoted by developing and using rules and procedures for handling disciplinary and grievance situations. These should be set down in writing, be specific and clear. Employees and, where appropriate, their representatives should be involved in the development of rules and procedures. It is also important to help employees and managers understand what the rules and procedures are, where they can be found and how they are to be used.

3. Where some form of formal action is needed, what action is reasonable or justified will depend on all the circumstances of the particular case. Employment tribunals will take the size and resources of an employer into account when deciding on relevant cases and it may sometimes not be practicable for all employers to take all of the steps set out in this Code.

4. That said, whenever a disciplinary or grievance process is being followed it is important to deal with issues fairly. There are a number of elements to this:

   • Employers and employees should raise and deal with issues **promptly** and should not unreasonably delay meetings, decisions or confirmation of those decisions.

   • Employers and employees should act **consistently**.

Appendix 1

- Employers should carry out any necessary **investigations**, to establish the facts of the case.

- Employers should **inform** employees of the basis of the problem and give them an opportunity to **put their case** in response before any decisions are made.

- Employers should allow employees to be **accompanied** at any formal disciplinary or grievance meeting.

- Employers should allow an employee to **appeal** against any formal decision made.

Discipline

Keys to handling disciplinary issues in the workplace

Establish the facts of each case

5. It is important to carry out necessary investigations of potential disciplinary matters without unreasonable delay to establish the facts of the case. In some cases this will require the holding of an investigatory meeting with the employee before proceeding to any disciplinary hearing. In others, the investigatory stage will be the collation of evidence by the employer for use at any disciplinary hearing.

6. In misconduct cases, where practicable, different people should carry out the investigation and disciplinary hearing.

7. If there is an investigatory meeting this should not by itself result in any disciplinary action. Although there is no statutory right for an employee to be accompanied at a formal investigatory meeting, such a right may be allowed under an employer's own procedure.

8. In cases where a period of suspension with pay is considered necessary, this period should be as brief as possible, should be kept under review and it should be made clear that this suspension is not considered a disciplinary action.

Inform the employee of the problem

9. If it is decided that there is a disciplinary case to answer, the employee should be notified of this in writing. This notification should contain sufficient information about the alleged misconduct or poor performance and its possible consequences to enable the employee to prepare to answer the case at a disciplinary meeting. It would normally be appropriate to provide copies of any written evidence, which may include any witness statements, with the notification.

10. The notification should also give details of the time and venue for the disciplinary meeting and advise the employee of their right to be accompanied at the meeting.

Hold a meeting with the employee to discuss the problem

11. The meeting should be held without unreasonable delay whilst allowing the employee reasonable time to prepare their case.

12. Employers and employees (and their companions) should make every effort to attend the meeting. At the meeting the employer should explain the complaint against the employee and go through the evidence that has been gathered. The employee should be allowed to set out their case and answer any allegations that have been made. The employee should also be given a reasonable opportunity to ask questions, present evidence and call relevant witnesses. They should also be given an opportunity to raise points about any information provided by witnesses. Where an employer or employee intends to call relevant witnesses they should give advance notice that they intend to do this.

Allow the employee to be accompanied at the meeting

13. Workers have a statutory right to be accompanied by a companion where the disciplinary meeting could result in:

   • a formal warning being issued; or

   • the taking of some other disciplinary action; or

   • the confirmation of a warning or some other disciplinary action (appeal hearings).

14. The chosen companion may be a fellow worker, a trade union representative, or an official employed by a trade union. A trade union representative who is not an employed official must have been certified by their union as being competent to accompany a worker.

15. To exercise the statutory right to be accompanied workers must make a reasonable request. What is reasonable will depend on the circumstances of each individual case. However, it would not normally be reasonable for workers to insist on being accompanied by a companion whose presence would prejudice the hearing nor would it be reasonable for a worker to ask to be accompanied by a companion from a remote geographical location if someone suitable and willing was available on site.

16. The companion should be allowed to address the hearing to put and sum up the worker's case, respond on behalf of the worker to any views expressed at the meeting and confer with the worker during the hearing. The companion does not, however, have the right to answer questions on the worker's behalf, address the hearing if the worker does not wish it or prevent the employer from explaining their case.

Decide on appropriate action

17. After the meeting decide whether or not disciplinary or any other action is justified and inform the employee accordingly in writing.

18. Where misconduct is confirmed or the employee is found to be performing unsatisfactorily it is usual to give the employee a written warning. A further act of misconduct or failure to improve performance within a set period would normally result in a final written warning.

19. If an employee's first misconduct or unsatisfactory performance is sufficiently serious, it may be appropriate to move directly to a final written warning. This might occur where the employee's actions have had, or are liable to have, a serious or harmful impact on the organisation.

20. A first or final written warning should set out the nature of the misconduct or poor performance and the change in behaviour or improvement in performance required (with timescale). The employee should be told how long the warning will remain current. The employee should be informed of the consequences of further misconduct, or failure to improve performance, within the set period following a final warning. For instance that it may result in dismissal or some other contractual penalty such as demotion or loss of seniority.

21. A decision to dismiss should only be taken by a manager who has the authority to do so. The employee should be informed as soon as possible of the reasons for the dismissal, the date on which the employment contract will end, the appropriate period of notice and their right of appeal.

22. Some acts, termed gross misconduct, are so serious in themselves or have such serious consequences that they may call for dismissal without notice for a first offence. But a fair disciplinary process should always be followed, before dismissing for gross misconduct.

23. Disciplinary rules should give examples of acts which the employer regards as acts of gross misconduct. These may vary according to the nature of the organisation and what it does, but might include things such as theft or fraud, physical violence, gross negligence or serious insubordination.

24. Where an employee is persistently unable or unwilling to attend a disciplinary meeting without good cause the employer should make a decision on the evidence available.

Appendix 1

Provide employees with an opportunity to appeal

25. Where an employee feels that disciplinary action taken against them is wrong or unjust they should appeal against the decision. Appeals should be heard without unreasonable delay and ideally at an agreed time and place. Employees should let employers know the grounds for their appeal in writing.

26. The appeal should be dealt with impartially and wherever possible, by a manager who has not previously been involved in the case.

27. Workers have a statutory right to be accompanied at appeal hearings.

28. Employees should be informed in writing of the results of the appeal hearing as soon as possible.

Special cases

29. Where disciplinary action is being considered against an employee who is a trade union representative the normal disciplinary procedure should be followed. Depending on the circumstances, however, it is advisable to discuss the matter at an early stage with an official employed by the union, after obtaining the employee's agreement.

30. If an employee is charged with, or convicted of a criminal offence this is not normally in itself reason for disciplinary action. Consideration needs to be given to what effect the charge or conviction has on the employee's suitability to do the job and their relationship with their employer, work colleagues and customers.

Grievance

Keys to handling grievances in the workplace
Let the employer know the nature of the grievance

31. If it is not possible to resolve a grievance informally employees should raise the matter formally and without unreasonable delay with a manager who is not the subject of the grievance. This should be done in writing and should set out the nature of the grievance.

Hold a meeting with the employee to discuss the grievance

32. Employers should arrange for a formal meeting to be held without unreasonable delay after a grievance is received.

33. Employers, employees and their companions should make every effort to attend the meeting. Employees should be allowed to explain their grievance and how they think it should be resolved. Consideration should be given to adjourning the meeting for any investigation that may be necessary.

Allow the employee to be accompanied at the meeting

34. Workers have a statutory right to be accompanied by a companion at a grievance meeting which deals with a complaint about a duty owed by the employer to the worker. So this would apply where the complaint is, for example, that the employer is not honouring the worker's contract, or is in breach of legislation.

35. The chosen companion may be a fellow worker, a trade union representative or an official employed by a trade union. A trade union representative who is not an employed official must have been certified by their union as being competent to accompany a worker.

36. To exercise the right to be accompanied a worker must first make a reasonable request. What is reasonable will depend on the circumstances of each individual case. However it would not normally be reasonable for workers to insist on being accompanied by a companion whose presence would prejudice the hearing nor would it be reasonable for a worker to ask to be accompanied by a companion from a remote geographical location if someone suitable and willing was available on site.

37. The companion should be allowed to address the hearing to put and sum up the worker's case, respond on behalf of the worker to any views expressed at the meeting and confer with the worker during the hearing. The companion does not however, have the right to answer questions on the worker's behalf, address the hearing if the worker does not wish it or prevent the employer from explaining their case.

Decide on appropriate action

38. Following the meeting decide on what action, if any, to take. Decisions should be communicated to the employee, in writing, without unreasonable delay and, where appropriate, should set out what action the employer intends to take to resolve the grievance. The employee should be informed that they can appeal if they are not content with the action taken.

Allow the employee to take the grievance further if not resolved

39. Where an employee feels that their grievance has not been satisfactorily resolved they should appeal. They should let their employer know the grounds for their appeal without unreasonable delay and in writing.

40. Appeals should be heard without unreasonable delay and at a time and place which should be notified to the employee in advance.

41. The appeal should be dealt with impartially and wherever possible by a manager who has not previously been involved in the case.

42. Workers have a statutory right to be accompanied at any such appeal hearing.

43. The outcome of the appeal should be communicated to the employee in writing without unreasonable delay.

Overlapping grievance and disciplinary cases

44. Where an employee raises a grievance during a disciplinary process the disciplinary process may be temporarily suspended in order to deal with the grievance. Where the grievance and disciplinary cases are related it may be appropriate to deal with both issues concurrently.

Collective grievances

45. The provisions of this code do not apply to grievances raised on behalf of two or more employees by a representative of a recognised trade union or other appropriate workplace representative. These grievances should be handled in accordance with the organisation's collective grievance process.

<http://www.acas.org.uk>

Helpline

08457 47 47 47

08456 06 16 00
helpline for Minicom use

08456 00 34 44
For questions on managing equality in the workplace

08457 38 37 36
Acas customer service team for details of training and services in your area

08702 42 90 90
for ordering Acas publications

Ref: CP01
04/09

July 2013

Code of Practice 4

Settlement Agreements

*(under section 111A of the
Employment Rights Act 1996)*

TSO@Blackwell and other Accredited Agents

Published with the permission of Acas on behalf of Her Majesty's Stationery Office.

Foreword

The Acas statutory Code of Practice set out in paragraphs 1 to 24 on the following pages is designed to help employers, employees and their representatives understand the implications of section 111A of the Employment Rights Act (ERA) 1996 for the negotiation of settlement agreements (formerly known as compromise agreements) before the termination of employment. In particular, it explains aspects of the confidentiality provisions associated with negotiations that take place to reach such agreements. The Code does not cover all aspects of settlement agreements. Further guidance on settlement agreements can be found in the Acas booklet 'Settlement Agreements: A Guide' which also offers more detailed guidance on the confidentiality provisions set out in section 111A.

The Code is issued under section 199 of the Trade Union and Labour Relations (Consolidation) Act 1992 and comes into effect by order of the Secretary of State on 29 July 2013. Failure to follow the Code does not, in itself, make a person or organisation liable to proceedings, nor will it lead to an adjustment in any compensation award made by an employment tribunal. However, employment tribunals will take the Code into account when considering relevant cases.

The discussions that take place in order to reach a settlement agreement in relation to an existing employment dispute can be, and often are, undertaken on a 'without prejudice' basis. This means that any statements made during a 'without prejudice' meeting or discussion cannot be used in a court or tribunal as evidence. This 'without prejudice' confidentiality does not, however, apply where there is no existing dispute between the parties. Section 111A of the ERA 1996 has therefore been introduced to allow greater flexibility in the use of confidential discussions as a means of ending the employment relationship. Section 111A, which will run alongside the 'without prejudice' principle, provides that even where no employment dispute exists, the parties may still offer and discuss a settlement agreement in the knowledge that their conversations cannot be used in any subsequent unfair dismissal claim. It is the confidentiality aspect of section 111A that is the specific focus of this Code.

Throughout this Code the word 'should' is used to indicate what Acas considers to be good employment practice, rather than legal requirements. The word 'must' is used to indicate where something is a legal requirement.

The Code of Practice

Introduction

1. This Code is designed to help employers, employees and their representatives understand the law relating to the negotiation of settlement agreements as set out in section 111A of the Employment Rights Act (ERA) 1996. In particular it gives guidance on the confidentiality provisions associated with negotiations about settlement agreements and on what constitutes improper behaviour when such negotiations are taking place.

2. Settlement agreements are only one way of handling potentially difficult employment situations. Problems in the workplace are best resolved in open conversations, including, where appropriate, through the use of performance management, or informal and formal disciplinary or grievance procedures.

What are settlement agreements?

3. Settlement agreements are legally binding contracts which can be used to end the employment relationship on agreed terms. Their main feature is that they waive an individual's right to make a claim to a court or employment tribunal on the matters that are specifically covered in the agreement. Settlement agreements may be proposed prior to undertaking any other formal process. They usually include some form of payment to the employee by the employer and may also include a reference.

4. For a settlement agreement to be legally valid the following conditions must be met:

   (a) The agreement must be in writing;

   (b) The agreement must relate to a particular complaint or proceedings[1];

   (c) The employee must have received advice from a relevant independent adviser[2] on the terms and effect of the proposed

---

[1] Simply saying that the agreement is in 'full and final settlement of all claims' will not be sufficient to contract out of employment tribunal claims. To be legally binding for these purposes, a settlement agreement has to specifically state the claims that it is intended to cover.

[2] The independent adviser can be a qualified lawyer; a certified and authorised official, employee or member of an independent trade union; or a certified and authorised advice centre worker.

> agreement and its effect on the employee's ability to pursue that complaint or proceedings before an employment tribunal;

(d) The independent adviser must have a current contract of insurance or professional indemnity insurance covering the risk of a claim by the employee in respect of loss arising from that advice;

(e) The agreement must identify the adviser;

(f) The agreement must state that the applicable statutory conditions regulating the settlement agreement have been satisfied.

5. Settlement agreements are voluntary. Parties do not have to agree them or enter into discussions about them if they do not wish to do so. Equally the parties do not have to accept the terms initially proposed to them. There can be a process of negotiation during which both sides make proposals and counter proposals until an agreement is reached, or both parties recognise that no agreement is possible.

Settlement agreement discussions and section 111A of the ERA 1996

6. Section 111A of the ERA 1996 provides that offers to end the employment relationship on agreed terms (i.e. under a settlement agreement) can be made on a confidential basis which means that they cannot be used as evidence in an unfair dismissal claim to an employment tribunal. Under section 111A, such pre-termination negotiations can be treated as confidential even where there is no current employment dispute or where one or more of the parties is unaware that there is an employment problem. Section 111A can also apply to offers of a settlement agreement against the background of an existing dispute, although in such cases the 'without prejudice' principle can also apply.

7. There are, however, some exceptions to the application of section 111A. Claims that relate to an automatically unfair reason for dismissal such as whistleblowing, union membership or asserting a statutory right are not covered by the confidentiality provisions set out in section 111A. Neither are claims made on grounds other than unfair dismissal, such as claims of discrimination, harassment, victimisation or other behaviour prohibited by the Equalities Act 2010, or claims relating to breach of contract or wrongful dismissal. Throughout this Code there are a number of references to unfair dismissal. These references should be read in general as subject to the exceptions set out in this paragraph.

8. The confidentiality provisions of section 111A are, additionally, subject to there being no improper behaviour. Guidance on what constitutes improper behaviour is contained in paragraphs 17 and 18 of this Code. Where there is improper behaviour, anything said or done in pre-termination negotiations will only be inadmissible as evidence in claims to an employment tribunal to the extent that the tribunal considers it just. In some circumstances, for instance where unlawful discrimination occurs during a settlement discussion, this may itself form the basis of a claim to an employment tribunal.

9. Where there has been some improper behaviour for these purposes this does not mean that an employer will necessarily lose any subsequent unfair dismissal claim that is brought to an employment tribunal. Equally, the fact that an employer has <u>not</u> engaged in some improper behaviour does not mean that they will necessarily win any subsequent unfair dismissal claim brought against them.

10. Where the parties sign a valid settlement agreement, the employee will be unable to bring an employment tribunal claim about any type of claim which is listed in the agreement. Where a settlement agreement is not agreed, an employee <u>may</u> bring a subsequent claim to an employment tribunal but where this claim relates to an allegation of unfair dismissal the confidentiality provisions of section 111A of the ERA 1996 will apply.

Reaching a settlement agreement

11. Settlement agreements can be proposed by both employers and employees although they will normally be proposed by the employer. A settlement agreement proposal can be made at any stage of an employment relationship. How the proposal is made can vary depending on the circumstances. It may be helpful if any reasons for the proposal are given when the proposal is made. Whilst the initial proposal may be oral, one of the requirements for a settlement agreement to become legally binding is that the agreement must ultimately be put in writing (see paragraph 4).

12. Parties should be given a reasonable period of time to consider the proposed settlement agreement. What constitutes a reasonable period of time will depend on the circumstances of the case. As a general rule, a minimum period of 10 calendar days should be allowed to consider the proposed formal written terms of a settlement agreement and to receive independent advice, unless the parties agree otherwise.

13. The parties may find it helpful to discuss proposals face-to-face and any such meeting should be at an agreed time and place. Whilst not a legal requirement, employers should allow employees to be accompanied at the meeting by a work colleague, trade union official or trade union representative. Allowing the individual to be accompanied is good practice and may help to progress settlement discussions.

14. Where a proposed settlement agreement based on the termination of the employment is accepted, the employee's employment can be terminated either with the required contractual notice or from the date specified in the agreement. The details of any payments due to the employee and their timing should be included in the agreement.

Improper behaviour

15. If a settlement agreement is being discussed as a means of settling an existing employment dispute, the negotiations between the parties can be carried out on a 'without prejudice' basis. 'Without prejudice' is a common law principle (i.e. non statutory) which prevents statements (written or oral), made in a genuine attempt to settle an existing dispute, from being put before a court or tribunal as evidence. This protection does not, however, apply where there has been fraud, undue influence or some other 'unambiguous impropriety' such as perjury or blackmail.

16. Section 111A of the ERA 1996 offers similar protection to the 'without prejudice' principle in that it provides that any offer made of a settlement agreement, or discussions held about it, cannot be used as evidence in any subsequent employment tribunal claim of unfair dismissal. Unlike 'without prejudice', however, it can apply where there is no existing employment dispute. The protection in section 111A will not apply where there is some improper behaviour in relation to the settlement agreement discussions or offer.

17. What constitutes improper behaviour is ultimately for a tribunal to decide on the facts and circumstances of each case. Improper behaviour will, however, include (but not be limited to) behaviour that would be regarded as 'unambiguous impropriety' under the 'without prejudice' principle.

18. The following list provides some examples of improper behaviour. The list is not exhaustive:

    (a) All forms of harassment, bullying and intimidation, including through the use of offensive words or aggressive behaviour;

(b) Physical assault or the threat of physical assault and other criminal behaviour;

(c) All forms of victimisation;

(d) Discrimination because of age, sex, race, disability, sexual orientation, religion or belief, transgender, pregnancy and maternity and marriage or civil partnership;

(e) Putting undue pressure on a party. For instance:

   (i) Not giving the reasonable time for consideration set out in paragraph 12 of this Code;

   (ii) An employer saying before any form of disciplinary process has begun that if a settlement proposal is rejected then the employee will be dismissed;

   (iii) An employee threatening to undermine an organisation's public reputation if the organisation does not sign the agreement, unless the provisions of the Public Interest Disclosure Act 1998 apply.

19. The examples set out in paragraph 18 above are not intended to prevent, for instance, a party setting out in a neutral manner the reasons that have led to the proposed settlement agreement, or factually stating the likely alternatives if an agreement is not reached, including the possibility of starting a disciplinary process if relevant. These examples are not intended to be exhaustive.

20. In situations where there is no existing dispute between the parties, the 'without prejudice' principle cannot apply but section 111A can apply. In these circumstances the offer of, and discussions about, a settlement agreement will not be admissible in a tribunal (in an unfair dismissal case) so long as there has been no improper behaviour. Where an employment tribunal finds that there has been improper behaviour in such a case, any offer of a settlement agreement, or discussions relating to it, will only be inadmissible if, and in so far as, the employment tribunal considers it just.

21. Where there is an existing dispute between the parties, offers of a settlement agreement, and discussions about such an agreement, may be covered by both the 'without prejudice' principle and section 111A. The 'without prejudice' principle will apply unless there has been some 'unambiguous impropriety'. As the test of 'unambiguous impropriety' is a narrower test than that of improper behaviour, this means that pretermination negotiations that take place in the context of an existing dispute will not be

admissible in a subsequent unfair dismissal claim unless there has been some 'unambiguous impropriety'.

22. In court or tribunal proceedings other than unfair dismissal claims, such as discrimination claims, section 111A does not apply. In these cases, the 'without prejudice' principle can apply where there is an existing dispute at the time of the settlement offer and discussions, meaning that these will not be admissible in evidence unless there has been some 'unambiguous impropriety'.

What if a settlement agreement cannot be agreed?

23. If a settlement agreement is rejected and the parties still wish to resolve the dispute or problem that led to the offer being made then some other form of resolution should be sought. Depending on the nature of the dispute or problem, resolution might be sought through a performance management, disciplinary or grievance process, whichever is appropriate. The parties cannot rely on the offer of a settlement agreement or any discussions about the agreement as being part of this process.

24. It is important that employers follow a fair process, as well as the other principles set out in the Acas discipline and grievance Code of Practice, because, if the employee is subsequently dismissed, failure to do so could constitute grounds for a claim of unfair dismissal.

Acas Helpline 08457 47 47 47

08457 47 47 47
Helpline text relay service

08702 42 90 90
Acas publications orderline

To view a full list of Acas publications go to <http://www.acas.org.
uk/publications>

08457 38 37 36
Acas Customer Services Team who can provide details of services and
training in your area or visit <http://www.acas.org.uk/training>

08456 00 34 44
for questions on managing equality in the workplace <http://www.
acas.org.uk>

PRESIDENTIAL GUIDANCE ON CASE MANAGEMENT

The following extracts from 'Presidential Guidance—General Case Management' are reproduced by kind permission of Judge Brian Doyle, President of Employment Tribunals (England and Wales). Reference can be made to the complete document on:

<http://www.justice.gov.uk/downloads/tribunals/employment/rules-legislation/presidential-guidance-general-case-management.pdf>

DISCLOSURE OF DOCUMENTS AND PREPARING BUNDLES

1 to 5 (omitted).

What is disclosure of documents?

6. Disclosure is the process of showing the other party (or parties) all the documents you have which are relevant to the issues the Tribunal has to decide. Although it is a formal process (governed by the Civil Procedure Rules), it is not hostile but requires co-operation in order to ensure that the case is ready for hearing.

7. Relevant documents may include documents which record events in the employment history, for example a letter of appointment, statement of particulars or contract of employment; notes of a significant meeting such as a disciplinary interview, a resignation or dismissal letter or even electronic and social media documents. The claimant may have documents to disclose which relate to looking for and finding alternative work.

8. Any relevant document in your possession (or which you have the power to obtain) which is or may be relevant to the issues must be disclosed. This includes documents which may harm your case as well as those which may help it. To conceal or withhold a relevant document is a serious matter.

9. A party is usually not required to give a copy of a 'privileged' document, for example something created in connection with the preparation of a party's Tribunal case (such as notes of interviews with witnesses); correspondence between a party and their lawyers; correspondence between parties marked 'without prejudice' or part of discussions initiated on a 'without prejudice' basis with a view to settlement of the matters in issue or records of exchanges with ACAS.

How and when does disclosure take place?

10. The process should start and be completed as soon as possible. A formal order for disclosure of documents usually states the <u>latest</u> date by which the process must be completed.

11. In most cases, the respondent (usually the employer) has most or all of the relevant documents. This often makes it sensible for the respondent to take the lead in disclosure. Each party prepares a list of all relevant documents they hold and sends it as soon as possible to the other party.

12. Sometimes the parties meet and inspect each other's documents. More commonly they agree to exchange photocopies of their documents in the case, which should be 'clean' copies.

How is the hearing bundle produced?

13. They then co-operate to agree the documents to go in the bundle, which should contain only documents to be mentioned in witness statements or cross-examined upon at the hearing and which are relevant to the issues in the proceedings. If there is a dispute about what documents to include, the disputed documents should be put in a separate section or folder and this should be referred to the Tribunal at the start of the hearing.

14. One party—often the respondent, because it is more likely to have the necessary resources—then prepares the documents in a proper order (usually chronological), numbers each page ('pagination') and makes sufficient sets of photocopies which are stapled together, tagged or put into a ring binder.

15. Each party should have at least one copy and the Tribunal will need 5 copies for a full Tribunal panel or 3 copies if the Employment Judge is to sit alone (one copy for the witness table, one for each member of the Tribunal and one to be shown to the public, where appropriate). The Tribunal's copies must be brought to the hearing and should not be sent to the Tribunal in advance, unless requested.

Are the documents confidential?

16. All documents and witness statements exchanged in the case are to be used only for the hearing. Unless the Tribunal orders otherwise, they must <u>only</u> be shown to a party and that party's adviser/representative or a witness (insofar as is necessary). The documents must not be used for any purpose other than the conduct of the case.

17. Since it is a public hearing, the Tribunal will enable persons present at the hearing to view documents referred to in evidence before it (unless it orders otherwise).

. . .

DISABILITY

1 to 10 (omitted).

Evidence [of disability]

11.1 A claimant may be able to provide much of the information required without medical reports. A claimant may be able to describe their impairment and its effects on their ability to carry out normal day to day activities.

11.2 Sometimes medical evidence may be required. For instance, where there is a dispute about whether the claimant has a particular disability or where an impairment is under effective control by medication or treatment.

11.3 The question then to be answered is what effects the impairment would have if the medication was withdrawn. Once more, a claimant may be able to describe the effects themselves but respondents frequently call for some medical evidence in support.

11.4 Claimants must expect to have to agree to the disclosure of relevant medical records or occupational health records.

11.5 Few people would be happy to disclose all of their records or for disclosure to be given to too many people. Employment Judges are well used to such difficulties and will limit documents to be disclosed and the people to whom disclosure should be made. It can be remembered as well that in proceedings disclosure in general is for use only in the proceedings and not for sharing with outsiders.

11.6 Even after a claimant's description of their impairment and disclosure of documents respondents may dispute that they are disabled. If that happens the intervention of an Employment Judge may be necessary. Possibilities include: –

11.6.1 That the claimant has to agree to undergo medical examination by a doctor or specialist chosen and paid for by the respondent.

11.6.2 The claimant agrees to provide further medical evidence at their own expense.

11.6.3 The claimant and respondent may agree to get a report jointly. That would involve sharing the decision as to who to appoint, the instructions to be given and the cost of any report. This may be [the] most effective course but neither party may in the end be bound by the findings of the report even if they agree to this course of action.

11.6.4 It can be expensive to obtain medical evidence. Limited financial assistance may be available but whether it is granted is a matter which only a member of the administrative staff of the Tribunal can decide. Any application for such assistance should be made to the manager of the relevant regional office.

11.6.5 Care should be taken to decide whether a medical report is necessary at all. For instance if a claimant has epilepsy which is well controlled by medication then medical evidence may be unnecessary for a Tribunal to consider what effect would follow if the medication was not taken.

11.6.6 Claimants must remember that they have the burden of proving that they are disabled. They may be satisfied that they can do this, perhaps with the assistance of the records of the General Practitioner and their own evidence.

...

COSTS

1. The basic principle is that employment tribunals do not order one party to pay the costs which the other party has incurred in bringing or defending a claim. However, there are a number of important exceptions to the basic principle as explained below.

What are costs?

2. 'Costs' means some or all of the fees, charges, payments or expenses incurred by a party in connection with the tribunal case. It includes Tribunal fees (since these are not part of any remedy awarded) and the expenses incurred by a party or witness in attending a hearing.

What orders for payment of costs can be made?

3. There are three different types of payment orders: costs orders; preparation time orders (sometimes referred to as PTOs); wasted costs orders. These specific terms have the following meanings.

4. A costs order generally means that a party is ordered to pay some or all of the costs paid by the other party to its legal representatives (barristers and solicitors) or to its lay representative. No more than the hourly rate of a preparation time order, see paragraph 17 below, can be claimed for a lay representative. Separately, costs orders can be made for a party's Tribunal fees and expenses reasonably and proportionately incurred by a party or witness in attending a hearing.

5. Preparation time orders are for payment in respect of the amount of time spent working on the case by a non-represented party, including its employees or advisers, but not the time spent at any final hearing.

6. Wasted costs orders are for payment of costs incurred by a party as a result of any improper, unreasonable or negligent act or failure to act by a representative or for costs incurred after such act where it would be unreasonable to expect the party to bear them. They require payment by a representative to any party, including the party represented by the payer.

Appendix 3

When may orders for costs and preparation time be made?

7. Apart from costs orders for Tribunal fees and the attendance of witnesses or parties at hearings, a party cannot have both a costs order and a preparation time order made in its favour in the same proceedings. So it is often sensible for a Tribunal in the course of the proceedings (for example, at a preliminary hearing) to decide only that an order for payment will be made, but to leave to the end of the case the decision about which type of order and for how much.

8. Orders for payment of costs or for preparation time may be made on application by a party, a witness (in respect of their expenses) or on the Tribunal's initiative, up to 28 days after the end of the case. If judgment on the claims is given at a hearing, it will usually be sensible to make any application for costs or PTOs then, in order to avoid delay and the additional cost of getting everyone back for another hearing. The circumstances when payment orders may be made are as follows.

9. If an employer in unfair dismissal proceedings requires an adjournment to obtain evidence about the possibility of re-employment, the tribunal must order the employer to pay the costs of the adjournment provided:

   – the claimant notified the desire to be re-employed at least seven days before the hearing;
   – the employer cannot prove a special reason why it should not pay.

10. A party may be ordered to pay costs or preparation time to the other party, without any particular fault or blame being shown, where:

   – the paying party has breached an order or practice direction; or
   – an adjournment or postponement is granted at the request of or due to the conduct of the paying party; or
   – the receiving party had paid a Tribunal fee for a claim and has wholly or partly won the claim.

11. A party may be ordered to pay costs in the form of the expenses incurred or to be incurred by a witness attending a hearing, without any particular fault or blame being shown. The order may be in favour of or against the party who called the witness. It may be made on the application of a party, the witness or at the Tribunal's own initiative and may be payable to a party or to the witness.

12. A party may be ordered to pay costs or preparation time to the other party where the Tribunal considers that:

    – a party has acted vexatiously, abusively, disruptively or otherwise unreasonably in bringing or defending the proceedings or in its conduct of the proceedings; or
    – the claim or response had no reasonable prospect of success.

13. The circumstances described at paragraph 11 require a tribunal to consider first whether the criteria for an order are met. Each case will turn on its own facts, but examples from decided cases are that it could be unreasonable where a party has based the claim or defence on something which is untrue (sometimes called 'a lie'). That is not the same as something which they have simply failed to prove, nor does it mean something they reasonably misunderstood. Abusive or disruptive conduct would include insulting the other party or its representative or sending numerous unnecessary e-mails. If the criteria are met, the Tribunal is at the threshold for making an order and will decide whether it is appropriate to order payment. It will consider any information it has about the means of the party from whom payment is sought, the extent of any abusive or unreasonable conduct and any factors which seem to indicate that the party which is out-of-pocket should be reimbursed. For example, some times it becomes clear that a party never intended to defend on the merits (that is, for example, whether the claimant was unfairly dismissed), but pretended that it was doing so until the last minute, causing the claimant to use his lawyer more, before conceding what was really always obvious.

When may a wasted costs order be made?

14. A Tribunal may consider making a wasted costs order of its own initiative or on the application of any party, provided the circumstances described at paragraph 6 above are established. This is a very rare event. When it happens, usually a party will seek costs from the other party and, in the alternative, wasted costs from that party's representative. The representative from whom payment is sought is entitled to notice and so is the party—because they may need separate representation at this costs hearing.

Amount of costs, preparation time and wasted costs orders

15. Broadly speaking, costs orders are for up to the amount of legal fees and related expenses reasonably incurred, based on factors like the significance of the case, the complexity of the facts and

the experience of the lawyers who conducted the litigation for the receiving party.

16. In addition to costs for witness expenses and Tribunal fees, the Tribunal may order any party to pay costs:

   – up to £20,000, by forming a broad-brush assessment of the amounts involved, working from a schedule of legal costs or, more frequently and in respect of lower amounts, just, for example, the fee for the barrister at the hearing;
   – calculated by a detailed assessment in the County Court or by an Employment Judge, up to an unlimited amount;
   – in any amount agreed between the parties.

17. Preparation time orders are calculated at the rate of £33 per hour (until April 2014, when the rate increases by £1 as every April) for every hour which the receiving party reasonably and proportionately spent preparing for litigation. This requires the Tribunal to bear in mind matters such as the complexity of the proceedings, the number of witnesses and extent of documents.

18. Wasted costs orders are calculated like costs orders, amount wasted by the blameworthy (as at paragraph 6) conduct of the representative.

19. When considering the amount of an order, information about a person's ability to pay may be considered, but the Tribunal may make a substantial order even where a person has no means of payment. Examples of relevant information are: the person's earnings, savings, other sources of income, debts, bills and necessary monthly outgoings.

TIMETABLING

1. The overriding objective means that each case should have its fair share of available time, but no more, otherwise other cases would be unjustly delayed. Also, each party must have a fair share of the time allowed for the hearing of their case.

What is timetabling?

2. Each party has a duty to conduct the case so that wherever possible the tribunal can complete the case within the time allowed. Failing to do that may mean a delay of many weeks, and also that other cases waiting to be heard might be delayed. To avoid the risk of this happening the tribunal sometimes divides up the total time allowed for a hearing into smaller blocks of time to be allowed for each part of the hearing. This is called 'timetabling'. It is necessary in particularly long or complicated hearings, or sometimes where a party has no experience of conducting hearings.

How and when is timetabling done?

3. Judges estimate the amount of time to be allowed for a hearing based on all the information they have when the hearing is listed. In straightforward cases that might be when the claim first comes in, or when the response arrives; in complex cases it is often done at a preliminary hearing.

4. For very short cases it is rare for a formal timetable to be issued, although for a hearing of one day it might be helpful for the judge and parties to agree at the beginning of the hearing roughly how long they expect each of the various stages to take. For longer or complex hearings a timetable is often decided in consultation with the parties at a preliminary hearing, or at the start of the hearing itself.

5. Fairness does not always mean that the hearing time must be divided equally between the parties or each witness. For example the party giving evidence first, (in unfair dismissal cases usually the employer, but in discrimination cases often the employee) will often have to explain the relevance of the documents referred to, which requires time. Also, some witnesses might have to give evidence about many separate incidents, whereas others just one short conversation. If an interpreter is required, extra time has to be allowed. The tribunal will take these things into account when estimating how long the evidence of each witness should take.

6. The tribunal will set the timetable using its own experience, but the Judge will often ask for the parties views on how long each stage of the hearing might take.

7. (omitted).

8. If a party believes that the time estimate for the whole or any part of the hearing is wrong, the tribunal will expect them to say so as soon as possible. Waiting till the day before the hearing or the start of it, to ask for extra time, is not helpful. It can save time to try to agree a more accurate estimate and then to ask the tribunal to change the timetable.

What can a party do to assist the Tribunal to keep to the timetable?

9. It is helpful for each party to make a list, for their own use, of the questions to be asked about each of the issues in the case. It is also useful to decide which of the questions are the most important, so that if time is running out the really important questions can be asked, even if others have to be abandoned.

10. Being able to find and quote the page number of the relevant documents in the bundle can save a lot of time. Asking questions using words the witness will understand, so that less time is wasted having to explain what is being asked, also saves time. A series of short precise questions is generally better than one long complicated one. They take less time to ask and answer, and are easier for the tribunal to understand and for everyone to take a note of.

11. There is nothing to be gained by asking the same question several times, or 'arguing' with the witness. That will just waste the time allowed. The purpose of asking questions is not to try to make the witness agree with the questioner, but to show the tribunal which side's evidence is more likely to be accurate. If necessary the tribunal can be reminded in submissions at the end of the case that, for example, the witness would not answer a question, or gave an answer which was not believable, or which was not consistent with a document in the bundle etc. An explanation of why your evidence is more reliable can be given at that stage.

What if the time allowed is exceeded?

12. The parties must try to conclude their questioning of each witness, and their submissions, within the time limit allocated. Usually the judge will, when time is nearly up, remind a party of how long they have left. If a party does not finish in time, they run the risk that the tribunal may stop their questioning of that witness, which

is sometimes called 'guillotining' the evidence. This is not a step tribunals like to take, but sometimes it is necessary, especially if one side takes so long that they might prevent the other side from having a fair opportunity to ask their own questions. If later witnesses take less time than expected, it might be possible to 're-call' the witness who did not have enough time.

…

JUDICIAL MEDIATION

EXPLANATORY NOTE TO THE PARTIES

1. Alternative Dispute Resolution is a priority for the Government. Judicial mediation is seen as one of the possible ways to achieve this. The Employment Tribunals operate a scheme in all regions in England and Wales.

2. Judicial mediation involves bringing the parties in a case together for a mediation preliminary hearing. The judicial mediation is conducted by a trained Employment Judge, who remains neutral and tries to assist the parties to resolve their dispute. The Employment Judge will help to identify issues in dispute, but will not make a decision about the case, nor give an opinion on the merits of the case. The role of the Employment Judge as mediator is to help the parties find ways to resolve their dispute by mutual agreement. Resolution is not limited to the remedies available at a hearing.

3. Whilst judicial mediation is part of the process of resolving employment disputes, it is an alternative to a Tribunal hearing, but not an alternative to ACAS conciliation. ACAS and the judiciary of the Employment Tribunals work collaboratively in relation to judicial mediation. The statutory duty placed on ACAS is not compromised by the process, and ACAS and the judiciary remain independent of each other at all times.

4. There are no restrictions on the jurisdictions that will be considered for judicial mediation, although it is unlikely that equal pay claims will normally be suitable for this process.

5. An important factor in assessing suitability is whether there is an ongoing employment relationship.

6. Whilst cases suitable for judicial mediation are identified in a number of different ways, identification is usually by an Employment Judge at a preliminary hearing for case management purposes. At that preliminary hearing, suitability for judicial mediation is considered, the parties advised of the possibility of an offer of judicial mediation, their interest (or otherwise) noted, and normal case management orders and directions made.

7. If the parties agree to consider an offer of judicial mediation, the file will be passed to the Regional Employment Judge, who will apply agreed criteria and determine whether the case qualifies for an offer of judicial mediation. An offer of judicial mediation is normally made at a telephone preliminary hearing with the parties when timetables for the mediation will be set, a stay or variation

of the existing case management orders made if necessary, and the dates for the judicial mediation agreed. Agreement will also be reached on the issues for the judicial mediation (which may be wider than those determinable by a Tribunal at a hearing), who will attend the mediation (which must include people empowered to make decisions), and any requirements of the parties for the conduct of the mediation.

8. It is not possible to offer judicial mediation in all cases because of resource constraints and suitability of the issues to mediation. Parties are notified if an offer cannot be made.

9. Provided that the offer of judicial mediation is accepted by all parties, the matter proceeds to a one or two day mediation.

10. The judicial mediation will be carried out by an experienced Employment Judge trained in mediation. A facilitative mediation technique is adopted and applied.

11. The judicial mediation is held in private and in circumstances which are entirely confidential with appropriate facilities made available. The contents or the events at a judicial mediation may not be referred to at any subsequent hearing. The Employment Judge mediating will play no further role in the case should it proceed to a hearing.

12. The judiciary of the Employment Tribunals may, on occasions, and with the prior consent of the parties, contact ACAS to reactivate conciliation, either during, or at the end, of the judicial mediation. This contact is usually by telephone conference call with the parties and an appropriate ACAS officer.

13. If there are any matters of concern or any explanation required then please write to the Regional Employment Judge for clarification.

AGENDA FOR CASE MANAGEMENT AT PRELIMINARY HEARING

Rules 29–40 and 53–56 Employment Tribunals Rules of Procedure 2013

You may be assisted by reading Presidential Guidance—General Case Management

It may help the efficient management of the case if you complete this agenda, as far as it applies, and send it to every other party and the Tribunal to arrive at least 7 days before the preliminary hearing ('ph'). A completed agreed agenda is particularly helpful.

1. Parties

1.1	Are the names of the parties correct? Is the respondent a legal entity? If not, what is the correct name?	
1.2	Should any person be joined or dismissed as a respondent? If yes, why?	

2. The claim and response

2.1	What complaints (claims) are brought? This should be just the complaint title or head (eg unfair dismissal). If any are withdrawn, say so.	
2.2	Is there any application to amend the claim or response? If yes, write out what you want it to say. Any amendment should be resolved at the ph, not later.	
2.3	Has any necessary additional information been requested? If not, set out a limited, focussed request and explain why the information is necessary. If requested, can the relevant information be provided for the ph? If so, please do.	

3. Remedy

3.1	If successful, what remedy does the claimant seek? This means eg compensation or re-instatement (where that is possible) etc.	

3.2	What is the financial value of the monetary parts of the remedy? All parties are encouraged to be realistic.	
3.3	Has a schedule of loss been prepared? If so, please provide a copy.	
3.4	Has the claimant started new work? If yes, when?	

4. The issues

4.1	What are the issues or questions for the Tribunal to decide? It is usually sensible to set this out under the title of the complaint/s.	
4.2	Are there any preliminary issues which should be decided before the final hearing? If yes, what preliminary issues? Can they be added to this preliminary hearing? If not, why not?	

5. Preliminary hearings

5.1	Is a further preliminary hearing needed for case management? NB This should be exceptional. If so, for what agenda items? For how long? On what date?	
5.2	Is a further substantive preliminary hearing required to decide any of the issues at 4.1? If so, for which issues? How long is needed? Possible date/s?	

6. Documents and expert evidence

6.1	Have lists of documents been exchanged? If not, date/s for exchange of lists	
6.2	Have copy documents been exchanged? If not, date/s or exchange of copies: • for any further preliminary hearing • for the final hearing	
6.3	Who will be responsible for preparing • index of documents? • the hearing bundles? Date for completion of this task and sending a copy to the other parties?	

6.4	Is this a case in which medical evidence is required?	
	Why?	
	Dates for	
	• disclosure of medical records	
	• agreeing any joint expert	
	• agreeing any joint instructions	
	• instructing any joint expert	
	• any medical examination	
	• producing any report	
	• asking questions of any expert	
	• making any concessions	

7. Witnesses

7.1	How many witnesses will each party call?	
	Who are those witnesses?	
	Why are they needed?	
7.2	Should witness statements be:	
	– exchanged on the same date?	
	– provided sequentially?	
	Dates for exchange:	
	• for further preliminary hearing	
	• for the final hearing	

8. The hearing(s)

8.1	Time estimate for final hearing, with intended timetable.	
	Is a separate hearing necessary for remedy? If yes, why?	
8.2	Dates to avoid (with reasons) or to list.	
	Any dates pre-listed by the Tribunal?	

9. Other preparation

9.1	Should there be admissions and/or agreed facts?	
	If yes, by what date/s?	
9.2	Should there be a cast list?	
	From whom and when?	
9.3	Should there be a chronology?	
	From whom and when?	

9.4	Are there special requirements for any hearing? (eg interpreter, hearing loop, evidence by video, hearing partly in private under rule 50) If yes, give reasons.	

10. Judicial mediation

10.1	Is this a case that might be suitable for judicial mediation?	
10.2	Are the parties interested in the possibility of judicial mediation?	
10.3	JUDICIAL USE ONLY	Judge to consider whether judicial mediation criteria are met; if so, discuss with the parties; record/direct their responses. Refer to REJ, if appropriate

11. Any other matters

Appendix 4

SCHEDULE OF LOSS FOR UNFAIR DISMISSAL

Basic Award (max £464 pw from 6.4.14) £
Less (a) contributory conduct £

    (b) redundancy award/payment £

(A) NET BASIC AWARD £

Compensatory Award (total max £76,574 from 6.4.14, limited to one year's wages)
Prescribed Element (loss of wages to date of assessment)
Net average take home pay of £ ____ per week from ____
to ____ (____weeks) £
And shortfall of £____ per week from ____ to ____
(____weeks) £
Less
(a) Wages or payment in lieu of notice £
(b) Earnings in alternative employment £
(c) Benefits other than jobseekers allowance/
income support/income-related employment
support allowance £
Interim Total £
(d) 'Polkey' reduction (%) £
Increase or decrease for breach of ACAS Code (%) £
Less contributory fault (%) £

(B) PRESCRIBED ELEMENT TOTAL £
Non-prescribed element (other losses)
(a) future loss of wages from ____ to ____ (____weeks)
at £____ per week £
(b) loss of other employment benefits eg car, health
insurance £
(c) loss of statutory industrial rights £
(d) loss of pension rights £
(e) Expenses incurred in seeking employment £
Interim Total £
Less
Any relevant payment by respondent (except excess
of any redundancy payment) £
'Polkey' reduction (%) £

Increase or reduction for breach of the ACAS Code (up to 25%)	£
Award for failure to provide written particulars (2 or 4 weeks' pay)	£
Less contributory fault (%)	£
Less excess of redundancy payment over basic award	£
(C) NON-PRESCRIBED ELEMENT TOTAL	£
PRELIMINARY TOTAL OF COMPENSATORY AWARD (B) + (C)	£
Gross up for taxation purposes	
Apply the statutory cap	
FINAL TOTAL OF COMPENSATORY AWARD	£
GRAND TOTAL OF AWARD FOR UNFAIR DISMISSAL (A) + (B) + (C)	£

RECOUPMENT

(a) Grand Total	£
(b) Prescribed Element	£
(c) Period of Prescribed Element from __ to __	
(d) Excess of Grand Total over Prescribed Element	£

The above schedule outlines a simplified process, eg it does not deal with any additional award, nor does it deal in detail with the calculations for grossing up for taxation purposes. It should, however, provide the basis for calculating the great majority of unfair dismissal awards, making use of Chapter 20 on Remedies for Unfair Dismissal.

Index

Index

Index

Index

Index

Index

Index